Performance-Based Management Systems

Effective Implementation and Maintenance

PUBLIC ADMINISTRATION AND PUBLIC POLICY

A Comprehensive Publication Program

EDITOR-IN-CHIEF

EVAN M. BERMAN

Distinguished University Professor
J. William Fulbright Distinguished Scholar
National Chengchi University
Taipei, Taiwan

Founding Editor

JACK RABIN

Available Electronically

Principles and Practices of Public Administration, edited by
Jack Rabin, Robert F. Munzenrider, and Sherrie M. Bartell

PublicADMINISTRATION*netBASE*

Performance-Based Management Systems

Effective Implementation and Maintenance

Patria de Lancer Julnes

CRC Press
Taylor & Francis Group
Boca Raton   London   New York

CRC Press is an imprint of the
Taylor & Francis Group, an **informa** business

CRC Press
Taylor & Francis Group
6000 Broken Sound Parkway NW, Suite 300
Boca Raton, FL 33487-2742

© 2009 by Taylor & Francis Group, LLC
CRC Press is an imprint of Taylor & Francis Group, an Informa business

Library of Congress Cataloging-in-Publication Data

Julnes, Patria de Lancer.
 Performance-based management systems : effective implementation and maintenance / Patria de Lancer Julnes.
   p. cm. -- (Public administration and public policy ; 151)
   Includes bibliographical references and index.
   ISBN 978-1-4200-5427-9
   1. Public administration--United States--Evaluation. 2. Administrative agencies--United States--Management. 3. Nonprofit organizations--United States--Evaluation. 4. Organizational effectiveness. 5. Performance--Management. I. Title. II. Series.

JK468.P75J85 2008
352.6'6--dc22   2008023003

Visit the Taylor & Francis Web site at
http://www.taylorandfrancis.com

and the CRC Press Web site at
http://www.crcpress.com

DEDICATION

To George

Contents

PART III: LETTING PRACTICE INFORM THEORY

7 Interpreting Survey Findings

ACKNOWLEDGMENTS

A project of this magnitude and scope is never the work of only one person. It requires the support of many individuals. Such is the case here, and I mention some of those individuals below. I am indebted to them and many others for sharing their knowledge and giving me opportunities over the years to gain valuable experience and achieve intellectual growth.

I'm deeply indebted to Marc Holzer, of Rutgers University-Newark, for the inspiration to promote government performance and the countless learning and growth opportunities he has provided me. Marc was also instrumental in the preparation of the article "Promoting the Utilization of Performance Measures in Public Organizations: An Empirical Study of Factors Affecting Adoption and Implementation" which appeared in Public Administration Review 61(6) pp 693 – 708, winner of the William E. Mosher and Frederick C. Mosher Award for best article written by an academician for the issue year 2001 and the 2001 Joseph Wholey Distinguished Scholarship Award of the American Society for Public Administration's Center for Accountability and Performance. The article was based on the theoretical grounding and survey data used in this book; to Jay Fountain, of the Government Accounting Standards Board, for helping me build a foundation from which my research has sprung; to Cheryle Broom, from King County, Seattle, and Martha Marshall, Management Consultant, whose work I admire and have learned from over the years; and to the late Marcia Whicker, whose tenacity and brilliance inspired me.

I've also benefited from the consulting and collaborating opportunities I've had. They provided me with practical knowledge, which has influenced my thinking and given me a level of depth and wisdom that I could not have obtained otherwise.

Very special appreciation goes to all the public servants who participated in the studies that I report here and those who in one way or another contributed examples and other information to help me complete this book. I could not have done this without them. Also to the editorial team at Auerbach, Taylor & Francis, especially Raymond O'Connell, Jessica Valiki, and Eva Neumann, for all their help and patience.

Finally, I must thank my husband, George Julnes, who has graciously and patiently spent many hours going over multiple drafts of this manuscript. In the process, we had many stimulating discussions. I'm grateful to him beyond what words can convey.

Prologue

The main goals of this book are to support efforts to build and sustain performance-based management (PBM) systems in public organizations and to develop context-sensitive theory to inform such efforts. This involves helping students and practitioners learn about the challenges of prior performance management efforts and gain the knowledge necessary to guide more effective implementation and continuity of PBM systems. A core component of these systems is performance measurement. Although much has been written about the positive influence and, in some cases, negative influence of performance measurement, there is little empirical understanding about its use.

Much of the current problem stems from a lack of integration of theory, evidence, and practical implications in this field. Without an empirically based body of theory to guide research, much of what we know about performance measurement in the public sector is based on anecdotal information. This resulting information is inadequate to guide practice in part because it does not provide a clear picture of the contributions performance measurement is making to the management of public and nonprofit organizations.

Furthermore, a lack of understanding of what it takes to effectively implement and sustain a performance-based management system may be responsible for the apparent failure of organizations to use performance measurement information to guide decision making in the public sector. Thus, this book will address these issues by focusing on two specific questions: (1) Why isn't performance measurement information used more widely and effectively in the public sector? (2) How can we improve implementation of performance measurement? To address these questions, I use here a triangulated methodology that allows me to develop robust theory about the utilization of performance measurement that can be used to guide practice.

To that end, this book is structured around three broad themes. Focusing on performance measurement as a key element of PBM, the first theme, covered in Part I, is making the case for performance measurement and performance management. This part sets the context for the needs addressed by this book. It discusses the place and contributions of performance measurement in PBM, the rich legacy behind performance measurement, limitations of performance measurement, some lessons learned about performance measurement, and competing explanations of the factors that limit effective use. Part II focuses on the second theme: building theory in support of practice through a mixed methods approach. This part is built around a stream of research that reconciles the conflicting explanations about the apparent lack of use of performance measurement information. This reconciliation supports a conceptual synthesis that offers new insights for developing a context-sensitive model of the utilization of performance measurement that can inform practice. The third theme, covered in Part III, letting practice inform theory, develops these insights into a pragmatic model of performance-based management. It provides a more realistic explanation of the contributions of performance measurement and gives advice derived from current practice. The book ends with a concluding chapter in Part IV, "Summary and Final Recommendations for Theory and Practice." The chapter highlights the rationale, methods, and findings of the survey study and follow-up interviews that served as the foundation for this book. In addition, it provides final insights into how to move practice and theory forward.

It should be noted that an underlying assumption made here is that performance measurement systems are complex innovations, and that the factors influencing effective implementation are complex as well, but also fairly understandable when considered carefully. As such, the utilization of performance measurement should not be approached as a monolithic concept. Like any policy innovation, there are stages to the utilization of performance measurement, and at the different stages diverse issues that affect this policy process emerge. Specifically, the issues driving the utilization of performance measurement are largely rationally driven (e.g., by resources, technical know-how) when the measurement is being planned at the beginning of the effort, but are more politically driven (e.g., due to external stakeholders) during the later implementation. Therefore, to understand the utilization of performance measurement, we need to go beyond the rational/technocratic ideals and borrow from extant literature on public policy implementation, organizational politics and culture, and knowledge utilization. Achieving a more thorough understanding of the mechanisms that affect the utilization of performance measurement leads to the development of context-sensitive strategies to promote such systems in public organizations.

Consequently, the book will help practitioners understand what it takes to effectively implement policies that have potential impacts on their organizations and the employees, and in particular, it will guide them as they attempt to respond to the calls for performance-based management. It will also help those in academia to analyze critically the theories of implementation of public policies in general, in part by providing a model of the process of theory integration. Students involved in graduate research in this area will benefit from the practical understanding that this book will offer on how to build effective research frameworks based on an ongoing program of research. Furthermore, they will learn how to utilize the available data analysis techniques to build theory and inform practice.

Part I

MAKING THE CASE FOR PERFORMACE MEASUREMENT AND PERFORMANCE-BASED MANAGEMENT

Chapter 1

Introduction

Public and nonprofit organizations have been long confronted with the twin pressures of increasing demands for services and decreasing resources. At the same time, they are facing an increasingly complex global, legal, and competitive environment that requires organizations to adopt effective strategies for achieving organizational goals and demonstrating results. For the public sector this emphasis on demonstrating results has been associated with skepticism by and discontent of the American public with how their tax dollars are being spent. For the nonprofit sector the pressure is coming from donors and funding agencies, who want to know if funds are being spent in the most efficient and effective manner.

Paradoxically, as expectations for performance-based management are growing in the public and nonprofit sectors, there still remains little appreciation and acknowledgment in practice of these and other challenges managers face in implementing performance-based management (PBM) systems. Current research continues to show a gap between developing performance measurement systems and actually using the information (Poister and Streib, 2005; Melkers and Willoughby, 2005; Behn, 2003; Wang, 2000; Joyce, 1997). Assessing this gap is complicated by the lack of agreement as to what constitutes use. For example, does the simple fact that performance measurement information is discussed during the budget allocation process constitute use? Are there different types of use?

In this book I will explain these challenges, the meaning of using performance measurement information, and suggest strategies to improve performance measurement, and hence support performance-based management. To be sure, anything that constitutes change from how the organization is used to doing things will have its setbacks. However, as stated by Heinrich (2002), the "setbacks confronted in implementing outcomes-based performance management in government should not discourage efforts to improve government performance."

3

Responding to Multiple Demands

Although there are a variety of responses to each of the pressures mentioned above, performance-based management holds promise as a strategy for responding to these multiple demands. As defined by Wholey (1999), PBM refers to the "purposeful use of resources and information to achieve and demonstrate measurable progress toward agency and program goals." As a concept, PBM enjoys broad acceptance. However, as will be discussed in this book, in practice it raises many questions that need to be addressed to fulfill its promise.

What makes PBM an ideal approach to meet the multiple demands outlined above is that it has two intimately related components: (1) performance measurement and (2) strategic planning. Performance measurement is the regular and careful monitoring of program activities, implementation, and outcomes. A quality performance measurement system produces timely, reliable, and relevant information on indicators that are linked to specific programs and goals and objectives. Strategic planning, a systematic management process that includes identifying an agreed upon mission, developing goals and objectives that are linked to the mission, and formulating strategies for achieving goals and objectives, provides the direction and the basis for measuring. Therefore, performance-based management should be seen as a system where performance measurement and strategic planning support and complement each other. This book focuses on the performance measurement component of performance-based management.

Performance measurement seeks to answer the following questions: "What are we doing?" and, to some extent, "How well are we doing it?" Managers can then use this information to improve the quality, efficiency, and effectiveness of programs delivered. Kopcynski and Lombardo (1999) argue that performance measurement can help to enlist support and build trust, identify performance targets, and build a culture of accountability. Behn (2003) adds that the information can be used "to evaluate, control, budget, motivate, promote, celebrate, learn, and improve."

Inherent in some of these roles is that performance measurement can serve as a tool for improving the communication between government and citizens. Performance indicators provide a common language for effective communication between service providers and stakeholders (Dusenbury et al., 2000). Furthermore, the process of developing performance measures provides the opportunity for government and other service providers to engage citizens and stakeholders in deliberation about programs, their implementation, and expected outcomes. Ultimately, the goal of performance-based management is to improve performance and increase satisfaction among citizens and other stakeholders with the services they receive.

Figure 1.1 is a graphical representation of performance-based management. The figure suggests several assumptions that are necessary for implementing performance-based management in an organization. It presumes:

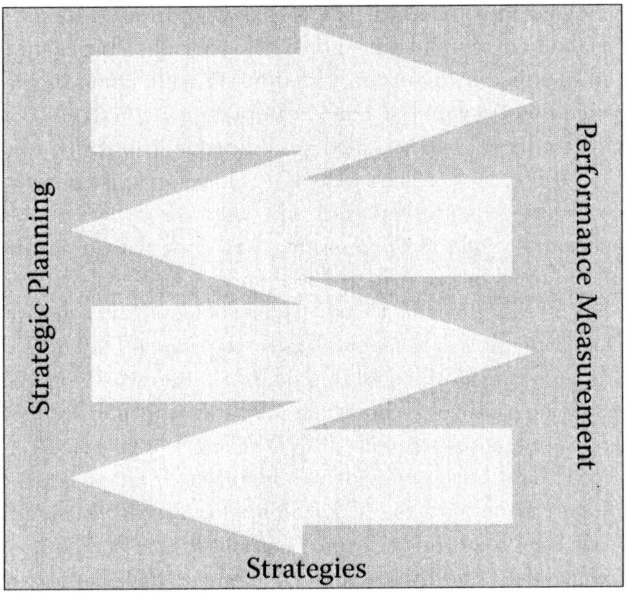

Figure 1.1 Performance-based management.

1. There is agreement on what the goals and objectives of the programs are (Wholey, 1999).
2. There is agreement on the strategies for achieving goals.
3. The appropriate indicators of performance—what and how we are doing—have been developed.
4. The mission, goals, objectives, and measures or indicators are aligned.
5. A quality measurement system is in place.
6. Organizational learning will lead to the refinement of strategies, goals, and objectives.
7. The organization is willing to take risks.

For reasons that will be explained ahead, turning these presumptions into fact tends to be a struggle for many organizations.

Furthermore, some of the assumptions made above are likely to evoke criticism. An implicit assumption of the performance-based management framework is that actions lead to results. That is, our expectation is that the activities of the agency in question will lead to some desired outcome. According to some critics, performance measurement is an inadequate tool for claiming program results (Greene, 1999; Ryan, 2002). Critics contend that information collected on a regular basis cannot be used to show cause and effect, and only rigorously conducted program evaluations can be used for this purpose. That is, some claim that performance measurement information (e.g., outcomes, outputs, inputs) does not answer why we are getting the outcome being observed. It does not tell us why we have or have not made progress toward stated goals. This critique has some merit. However, as will be explained later, there are ways to overcome the limitations of performance measurement so that managers can have confidence in their performance-based management system.

Performance-Based Management among Recent Alternatives

One way to clarify PBM is to relate it to other approaches familiar to the reader. Three recent developments are briefly addressed.

The Balanced Scorecard

At this point, some may be wondering if the model proposed above (Figure 1.1) has anything to do with the increasingly popular balanced scorecard approach developed by Kaplan and Norton (1992) based on the private sector's experience. The answer is yes. The model can be viewed as an encompassing approach that incorporates the balanced scorecard. PBM systems recognize the necessary linkage between the organization's internal processes and internal and external environment in order to deliver quality services. PBM is a systematic approach that relies to a large extent on information.

Also, as shown in the model depicted in Figure 1.1, like the balanced scorecard, PBM is a continuous process that involves setting strategic performance goals and objectives, measuring performance, collecting, analyzing, and reporting data, and using the information to inform decisions aimed at improving performance. Thus performance measurement is central to both the balanced scorecard approach and performance-based management. In addition to PBM encompassing elements included in the balanced scorecard system, there are other major differences. The PBM framework presented here is grounded in the more complex environment of public and nonprofit organizations. The framework also makes finer distinctions about the use of performance measurement information. These grounding and distinctions provide a richer context for understanding the results of performance improvement systems. They also offer a greater array of strategies to choose from when promoting organization innovations such as performance measurement systems and balanced scorecard systems. Therefore, the topics and strategies discussed here will be useful to organizations that are looking to implement a balanced scorecard system.

Benchmarking

In the context of performance measurement, the term *benchmarking* refers to comparing performance against a standard. Without being able to make such comparisons, argues Ammons (2001), the whole exercise of performance measurement becomes futile. There are several ways in which such comparisons can be made. These, suggest Ammons, include comparing current performance marks with those from earlier periods, other units in the organizations, peer organizations, preestablished targets, or existing standards, as well as reporting year-to-year comparisons of performance indicators.

As can be deduced, performance measurement is a critical component of benchmarking because the measures become the vehicle for comparison. The information allows putting the organization in context, helping to identify deviations from expected performance, and, in the cases when the comparisons are with others, to identify best practices. But what is done with the information is also the domain of performance-based management. For, as suggested by Ammons (2001), the identification of gaps may suggest additional analysis of processes and adoption of practices to improve the agency's performance.

Performance-Based Budgeting

Efforts to include performance information into the budget process and deliberation are often termed *performance-based budgeting* (though we may also find terms such as *results-based budgeting, results budgeting,* or *outcome budgeting,* referring to these efforts). The idea behind performance-based budgeting is that it can help to improve the allocation of resources by focusing the dialogue on program outcomes and results rather than on program inputs and outputs (de Lancer Julnes and Holzer, 2008).

As described by Barnett and Atteberry (2007), unlike other approaches to budgeting, this is an interactive and inclusive approach that begins with a set of results that matter to citizens and encourages creativity in achieving those results. Performance measurement is at the core of this approach. Performance-based budgeting requires a quality measurement system that can help monitor results to determine what was achieved. This information is important in budget deliberations as it can help identify the opportunities to make better use of resources and accomplish agency goals (U.S. General Accounting Office, 2001).

Down to the Core: Performance Measurement

Regardless of what agencies call their performance management system, the bottom-line assumption is that managers and other decision makers need adequate information. To respond to current demands for getting and showing results, whether in the public, nonprofit, or private sectors, administrators need evidence. As shown in the three examples above, performance measurement is a tool that can provide the needed evidence. But in order for any performance management system to be successful, we must recognize that it is a complex and long-term process that must be supported by a commitment to develop performance measures, actually use them, and continuously refine them.

Indeed, this need for continuous effort, which by design results in delayed pay-offs, is one of the main obstacles to success for performance-based management systems. As we find with any policy for change, there are two sides to the continuity coin. On the other side of this coin is the need for stability. As discovered by one practitioner at the federal level, after the initial identification and selection of new measures, there is a very difficult and lengthy process of implementation. This implementation process can involve altering data systems, changing reporting requirements, and compelling managers to use the performance data to manage. Therefore, while this process requires stability and determination, it also requires learning and making adjustments as needed. The process requires that the performance measurement system itself be flexible enough to adjust to changes, yet be stable enough to provide usable information over time (Grizzle, 1982). For example, there may be a change in the value system of the organization, sometimes prompted by the measures themselves, which may lead to changes in the perception of what is important to measure. The system must be responsive to this need. At the same time, it should still be able to provide consistent information that can be used to compare performance from one year to the next.

Box 1.1 illustrates the different types of measures that a typical PBM system should include. In the rest of this chapter I discuss why managers should be interested in performance measurement, and how performance measurement can contribute to informing and improving management. I also discuss the perceived limitations of performance measurement and ways to overcome those limitations.

Performance Measurement Is Here to Stay

During a recent interview, a local government employee told me that performance measurement is a fad. Although some may think this way, the systematic measurement of performance to promote better government has a long legacy in the United States. The focus of early performance measurement efforts was to improve efficiency, obtaining more outputs for the inputs in a shorter period of time— managerial efficiency. This focus later evolved to also include effectiveness—then defined in terms of the effect of service delivery. Financial concerns have also been a driving force in performance improvement efforts, and more recently, though by no means new, accountability for results has taken center stage.

The following is a brief review of the historical context of performance measurement. The purpose is to show that although it has taken many forms, and although the incentives may have varied, performance measurement has been at the core of American management practice for a long time, and the goal has always been to achieve good government performance.

BOX 1.1. TYPES OF MEASURES IN A PERFORMANCE-BASED MANAGEMENT SYSTEM

- **Inputs**: refer to the amount of resources used. It may include dollar amounts, and number of employees.
- **Outputs**: refer to product or services delivered. Examples include number of senior citizens receiving the flu vaccine; miles of paved road; tons of garbage collected; number of women receiving prenatal care; number of students trained; and number of calls answered.
- **Outcomes**: refer to results or consequences of program activity. This type of performance measure reflects a change in condition, behavior, or attitude in the target population as a result of the program. Outcome is further divided into:
  - Intermediate outcome: this is not an end in itself but it is expected to lead to a desired result. An example would be the number of people not getting the flu after receiving the flu vaccine.
  - End outcome: the desired end result. Examples of this include the percent decrease in the number of flu-related visits to the doctor and the percent decrease in job absenteeism due to flu-related illnesses.
- **Processes** (or the throughputs): refer to the performance of activities prior to the service or product being delivered. They measure the steps taken to produce the outputs. Indicators of process measures might include the waiting period between getting the appointment for the flu shot and actually getting the flu shot; the amount of time it takes between a water main break and getting it repaired; number of training materials prepared; or number of hours of training provided.
- **Efficiency**: refers to the ratio of the amount of input to the amount of output or outcome. An example would be dollar amounts spent per vaccine unit delivered.
- **Quality**: refers to the extent to which a service was delivered correctly. Although it can represent the level of accuracy or timeliness in the delivery of service, it is also typically reported in terms of customer's satisfaction with the service received. Examples include the frequency of complaints about street dirtiness after the sweeper has gone by and the percent of patients who experience a great level of discomfort during and after the flu shot due to the way in which the vaccine is administered by clinic's personnel.
- **Explanatory information**: although not a type of performance measure, it is highly recommended that this information be included in performance reports. The information can help clarify the reasons for the observed outputs and outcomes with explanations ranging from information about internal organizational factors that may affect performance to changes in the population served leading to changes in expected performance.

From Efficiency Expectations to Performance-Based Accountability

The first recognized efforts of systematic and sustained performance measurement have been attributed to New York City, where in 1906 the Bureau of City Betterment, renamed the Bureau of Municipal Research the following year, was created (Williams, 2003). The Bureau of Municipal Research engaged in the collection of data for use in budget allocation decisions, reporting, and productivity improvement strategies. The data collected included accounting data, workload, outputs, outcomes, and social indicators. Thus began a movement to replace assessment of government performance based on common sense with more systematic and more precise assessment.

In these earlier attempts, the term *productivity* was used interchangeably with the term *performance*. Economists used the term *productivity* to describe the link between resources and products. In that efficiency was the main concern (Nyhan and Marlowe, 1995; de Lancer Julnes, 2003), the focus was on developing procedures and measurement techniques to identify and increase the productivity of workers through managerial controls. Thus, argue Kaplan and Norton (1992), consistent with the "industrial age," traditional performance measurement systems identify the actions that workers need to take and then measure to see "whether the employees have in fact taken those actions." Therefore, efficiency, narrowly defined as the ability to produce more output with less input, was the basis of scientific management studies of the early 1900s. In addition, this period marked the beginning of efforts in government to emulate business practices to be efficient. An efficient government was equated with good government.

Indeed, this focus on efficiency, which according to Radin (2002), is built into the traditional approaches to accountability, was also a reaction to the pervasive patronage and corruption in government. As eloquently discussed by Woodrow Wilson in his 1887 essay, efficiency, professionalization, and the separation of politics and administration were seen as necessary for good governance. As a result, the hierarchical Weberian bureaucratic form of organization, with its emphasis on consistency, continuity, predictability, stability, deliberateness, efficiency, equity, and professionalism, became the preferred approach to ensuring accountability in public administration. The characteristics of the hierarchical bureaucratic arrangement were very appealing during the progressive era of the late 1800s and early 1900s, and continue to be today. The tenets of this approach include a belief in scientific inquiry, the view that workers are rational people pursuing purely economic goals, as well as the assumption that there is one best way to organize, and that productivity is best achieved through the division of labor.

Though the focus on measuring and improving efficiency continued during the early part of the twentieth century, two important figures were ahead of their time in emphasizing the need to use performance measurement for results-based accountability. Herbert Simon and Clarence Ridley, through their work in the

International City-County Government Association, were pioneers in this area. They developed techniques for measuring municipal performance and reporting to citizens, all the while emphasizing the need to measure results (R. J. Fischer, 1994; Lee, 2003). Furthermore, the Brookings Institution, in its earlier incarnation as the Institute for Government Research (IGR) in 1916, in bringing science to the study of government, became an advocate for the efficient and effective conduct of government. The idea, again, was that improved efficiency would lead to better outcomes of public services.

Notwithstanding the recognition of the importance of outcomes, the early emphasis on managerial efficiency led to accountability being understood primarily as financial accountability. Performance measurement came to be the tool for addressing accountability as cost control. Such an emphasis on financial measures has limitations, which include promoting behavior that "sacrifices long-term value creation for short-term performance" (Kaplan and Norton, 2000).

As should be evident by now, the early performance improvement efforts had measurement at their core. This continued to be the case between the 1940s and 1970s with the emergence of approaches such as the Planning Programming Budgeting System (PPBS), Management by Objective (MBO), and Zero-Based Budgeting (ZBB). For the most part measurement of performance focused on measuring program processes, outputs, and inputs for auditing purposes. The approaches to measurement of that time can be understood as focusing on processes, inputs, and auditing. According to Romzek (1998), these approaches to measurement can be classified as hierarchical accountability for inputs and legal accountability for process. With hierarchical accountability, the assumption is that its pyramidal shape leads to a high degree of internal control. Conversely, legal accountability is derived from external sources, and it is characterized by a high degree of oversight and monitoring of activities by an external actor.

Given this background, it is easy to understand why for a long time governments have mostly been measuring outputs and inputs, which tell them nothing about the quality and result of their programs and services. But at the local level, as communities started to experience tax payer revolts in the 1970s, most notably in California, where citizens were demanding that city governments demonstrate what citizens were getting for their tax dollars, measurement of service outcomes could no longer be ignored. Nonetheless, interest in measurement at the local level remained low, as only a handful of cities undertook regular measurement of program outcomes. Important examples of these efforts include the cities of Charlotte, North Carolina; Dayton, Ohio; New York; and Phoenix, Arizona (Hatry, 1999).

As this was happening in the public sector, a similar wave started to hit the nonprofit sector. Foundations, which were also involved in delivering public services, began to take steps toward requiring their grantees to systematically measure and document the results of their activities (Newcomer, 2008). This information was expected to be particularly valuable for decision makers, at foundations involved in the process of making decisions about which programs to fund. Since then, significant contributions toward promoting outcome assessment have been made by nonprofit organizations such as the United Way of America. Think tanks have not been remiss in this effort either. In fact, by the late 1960s the Urban Institute had begun to work with state, local, and federal governments in what became known as program evaluation. The early work of the Urban Institute, under the leadership of Joseph Wholey, focused on applying cost-effectiveness and system analysis to state and local governments' programs and services (Hatry, 1999).

During the 1980s the apparent growth of government and the public's increased concern over the rising cost of government continued to spur cost-cutting efforts. As explained by Schein (1996), the public had become cynical about the money spent by public organizations on social services. Fueled by politician's aphorisms, such as Ronald Reagan's famous quote "Government is not the solution to our problem; government is the problem," the demands for cutting government spending and minimizing the role of government increased. As a result, privatization in government was introduced under the guise that the private sector can deliver the same services that government traditionally delivers, but more effectively and at a lower cost.

Along with privatization, state and local governments embraced the private sector's Total Quality Management (TQM) movement. In essence the TQM movement emphasized customer satisfaction through improvement of processes, services, products, and the culture of the organization. TQM replaced the concept of administration with production and provides employees with methods for identifying and improving production processes (Barzelay, 1992). It also replaced efficiency with quality and value, where quality is understood as meeting or exceeding customer requirements, and value is concerned with what results citizens want.

To some, a less appealing characteristic of TQM was the consequence of defining citizens as customers of public services. But this interest in service quality and in satisfying the citizen-customer was viewed by others as an opportunity. For example, Ammons (1995) stated that the interest "may prove to be a major boom to a reintensified focus on performance measurement." When making this statement, Ammons was referring to an apparent lag between the need for performance measurement, as predicated by the management tools in vogue at various times, and the actual measurement of performance and use of the information. Ammons and King (1983) had argued that the measurement of performance was contingent upon local government officials giving importance to productivity improvement efforts. Otherwise, efforts to promote information use as a means of productivity improvement were going to fail. TQM seemed to be the answer.

In 1984, the importance of systematically measuring performance in government was enhanced by the creation of the Governmental Accounting Standards Board (GASB). The following year, GASB adopted a resolution that encouraged state and local governments to experiment with service efforts and accomplishments reporting (Brown and Pyers, 1998). The primary concern of *accomplish-*

ments in GASB's recommendation refers to results or outcomes of program activities.

The GASB recommendations also led to increased efforts by state legislatures to require that state agencies conduct performance measurement (Hatry, 1997). By the 1990s, states were enacting legislation that required some form of performance measurement. The State of Texas developed a performance measurement system that served as an example to other states and even influenced the efforts of the federal government. At the same time, the emphasis on customer and service quality in the private sector continued to make its way into the public sector, gaining momentum in part due to Osborne and Gaebler's book, *Reinventing Government* (Hatry, 2008), which emphasized performance measurement and managing for results and changed the nature of accountability.

The new expectations were that workers would meet customers' needs for quality and value, while customers were expected to clarify their own needs and provide feedback (Barzelay, 1992). Thus, managing for results gained popularity and acceptance as an approach for meeting these new accountability needs, creating and demonstrating value for the citizen-customer. Managing for results requires that organizations align their goals and objectives with their mission. Organizations then develop performance measures and set performance targets. It also requires regular reporting on those measures so that stakeholders can assess the extent to which performance targets are being achieved. The steps in the managing for results process include planning for results (strategic planning), planning program activities, developing meaningful performance measures, budgeting for results, managing work processes, collecting data and using the data to manage, evaluating and responding to results, and reporting results (GASB, http://www.seagov.org/aboutpmg/managing_for_results.shtml). These steps are not expected to occur in a sequential order. Rather, the expectation is that they would be interconnected, allowing for feedback and adjustments.

Furthermore, at the federal level the passage in 1993 of the Government Performance and Results Act (GPRA) "broadened the federal government's efforts to realign the focus of government accountability and performance analysis away from activities and process measures toward results or outcomes" (Heinrich, 2002). This act, embraced by then Vice President Al Gore's National Performance Review initiative, was designed to improve the effectiveness of federal programs and citizen satisfaction through the systematic measurement and reporting of performance.

Although other performance-related legislation followed GPRA in the mid-1990s (e.g., Government Management Reform Act of 1994 and the Information Technology Management Reform Act of 1996), GPRA remains one of the most important and the first-ever government reform effort that requires government agencies to integrate results in the budgeting process (Piotroski and Rosenbloom, 2002). Under GPRA, federal agencies are required to engage in strategic planning, develop a performance plan, which is to be submitted with budget requests, and prepare a performance report that reviews the success of the agency in meeting performance goals. GPRA also requires that agencies include stakeholders in the development of the mission, goals, objectives, and performance targets, and even in the development of appropriate performance measures (Simeone et al., 2005).

As inferred above, part of this new form of accountability is the notion of citizens as important actors in the process of creating value and requires that organizations provide citizens the opportunities to participate in governance. Epstein et al. (2006) have argued that citizens can play a variety of roles, which may lead the community to "take advantage of citizen's talents, skills, and resources." The process of strategic planning and performance measurement, for example, can be used for this purpose. For performance measurement, citizen participation may promote having the appropriate values represented. It may also help to ensure that more meaningful measures of performance, those that matter the most to the people we are trying to serve, be developed. Without the proper guidance from citizens regarding what is important to them, and their understanding of what is feasible to measure, relevant indicators of performance are difficult to develop. Thus, a process of shared deliberation can provide the opportunity for dealing with these issues and help ameliorate future problems of implementation.

Although no one questions the need to be accountable and the importance that accountability has had since the beginning of American public administration (and later in the nonprofit sector), there has been a great deal of debate regarding the meaning of and means for holding people accountable. At its core, accountability means giving accounts for actions taken and being held accountable for those actions. The current emphasis, as articulated in GPRA and in current management practice, is on accountability for results. With this emphasis, the means for someone to show accountability is referred to as performance-based accountability, which "requires the specification of outputs and outcomes in order to measure results and link them to goals that have been set, in accordance with the norms of management practice" (Roberts, 2002). Like other forms of accountability, this one also requires performance measurement.

In conclusion, performance measurement is not a passing fad. Performance measurement is a useful tool for managers, and the basic value of accountability in public service and the evolving emphasis on results will continue to make performance measurement a necessity rather than a luxury. From Harry Hatry's perspective (2008) there are only two conditions under which the interest in performance measurement will decrease. One is that performance measurement becomes part of what governments and nonprofits normally do; the other is a complete disenchantment because of the perception that implementation of performance measurement systems does not provide information that is useful enough to justify their cost. From my perspective, if performance measurement systems are properly developed and implemented, the evidence points to the former outcome rather than the latter.

Beyond Accountability, What Can Performance Measurement Do for Public and Nonprofit Agencies?

A recurrent theme in the discussion presented above is the centrality of performance measurement to accountability efforts. For a long time, accountability has been the main reason organizations have embraced performance measurement. This, says Hatry (1999), "is a great waste." Accountability is but one of the many possible uses of performance measurement information. Indeed, the underlying assumption of this book is that a performance-based management system can make contributions that go beyond merely providing tools for holding employees, managers, and organizations accountable. Proponents of performance measurement have cited many ways in which performance measurement contributes to public and nonprofit management. Those include providing information that can be used to make program improvements, whether that means "to expand, delete, or modify programs" (Hatry, 1996), improve program results/outcomes, or improve planning and budgeting processes (Olsen and Epstein, 1997; Epstein et al., 2006).

As suggested in Figure 1.1, performance measurement can provide the basis for the refinement of goals and objectives, for monitoring results, and for modifying plans to enhance performance. Colwell and Koletar (1984) encouraged organizations to develop systematic performance measurement systems, suggesting that:

- Performance measurement is one of the primary vehicles by which organizations can assess their effectiveness.
- Performance measurement serves as an effective mechanism of feedback on various organizational systems, subsystems, and strategies.
- During times of resource scarcity, performance measurement provides the basis for decisions related to resource allocation.
- Performance measurement information can provide early warnings of significant changes in the internal and external organizational environment.

Furthermore, managers sometimes need quick and frequent feedback about programs and units. Unlike program evaluation, performance measurement is meant to be an ongoing process that provides regular data on performance. Thus, performance measurement information can be readily available to fulfill a manager's day-to-day information requirements.

Others have also argued that performance measurement contributes to organizational learning. As defined by Torres and Preskill (2001), organizational learning is an integrated and continuous process of growth and improvement that uses information to make changes and is aligned with the values, attitudes, and perceptions of the members of the organization.

Thus, a possible example of organizational learning occurs when the performance information is used to make appropriate adjustments to current practices. In effect, argues Halachmi (2002), when performance measurement is used to improve performance, this is a form of learning. When organizations reallocate resources because of the information they have, that too is a form of learning.

However, as will be illustrated in subsequent chapters, even though organizations may learn, learning may not necessarily translate into a visible, concrete action. That is, learning may not always lead to improvement, an instrumental use of performance measures. For one thing, organizational learning does not occur in a vacuum. As a result many scholars have questioned the ability of organizations to learn (e.g., March and Olsen 1975), with some emphasizing on the need to understand the human behavior that limits such learning (Argyris and Schon, 1978), while others argued that the internal and external organizational context may limit an organization's ability to learn as traditionally defined—learning as transformation or change (Weiss, 1998). These arguments have implications for how performance measurement information is used as part of the PBM system depicted in Figure 1.1. Therefore, a related argument made in this book is that use of performance measurement is not the same thing as purpose or managerial goal of performance measurement. The concept of use is broader than purpose; I argue here that different types of use of performance measurement support different purposes.

In addition to using performance measurement information for organizational learning, others have indicated that performance measurement serves other managerial goals. Behn (2003), Hatry (1999), Wholey and Hatry (1992), and others have identified many managerial goals or purposes for conducting performance measurement. These purposes are not necessarily distinct from one another, and in fact build and overlap with each other. A dissenting voice on the issue is Halacmi (2002), who argues that some of these purposes may contradict one another. Below I group these purposes into four broad categories: evaluation and understanding, controlling and oversight, motivating and mobilizing, and program improvement.

The extent to which organizations use performance measures to meet managerial goals indicates the extent to which performance measures have been implemented. Accordingly, for the purposes of this book and the research that it describes, actually using performance measures to meet managerial goals has been categorized as *implementation*. This is accomplished by using performance measures for strategic planning, resource allocation, program management, monitoring and evaluation, reporting to internal management, reporting to elected officials, and reporting to citizens or media. Having developed performance measures is understood here as *adoption*.

As will be discussed in later chapters, for many reasons organizations may not be able to use performance measures in the manner described below. Nonetheless, theory and experience suggest that performance measurement can be an important aspect of governmental and nonprofit management. Because of this, several organizations, including the Governmental Accounting Standards Board (GASB), the National Academy of Public Administration (NAPA), the International City/

County Management Association (ICMA), and the American Society for Public Administration, are encouraging and working with governments to experiment with performance measurement. Encouragement for nonprofit organizations comes from major donors and professional organizations such as the Alliance for Nonprofit Management.

Performance Measures as a Tool for Evaluation and Understanding

Evaluation, argues Behn (2003), is often not explicitly articulated as one of the purposes of performance measurement. However, in that performance measurement information can be used for assessing the extent to which problems intended to be addressed by a particular program or activity are improving or worsening, evaluation, he argues, is the implicit purpose. Likewise, when performance measurement information is reported across municipalities, agencies, or units, it provides managers, citizens, and other stakeholders with an opportunity to assess how the performance of the organization in question stands out in comparison to the performance of the others. Such comparison amounts to evaluation in day-to-day parlance.

Yet a clarification is in order. This form of evaluation, which amounts to evaluating the state of affairs, is not to be confused with evaluating the impact of program/policy. Although the information can lead to an understanding of the state of affairs—How are we doing? How are things going? What are we doing?—it is not enough to make judgments about the causes of the observed outcome. For the most part, evaluating the impact of programs or policy requires program evaluation information, which concerns determining cause and effect. Nonetheless, performance measurement information can serve as the backbone to such in-depth program evaluation. As stated by Hatry (1999), the data collected by a performance measurement system can often be used to substitute "for some of the data the evaluators would otherwise have to collect ... it can [also] shed light on the issues addressed and even lead to the framing of new hypotheses."

Performance Measures as a Tool for Control and Oversight

Some authors contend that promoting performance measurement is but another mechanism for bureaucratic control (Franklin, 2000). Indeed, traditional performance measurement systems have a control bias. As a result, Behn (2003) suggests that even though everyone is for empowering employees, it would be naïve to think that the desire to control employees and organizations no longer exists. Controlling is the reason we continue to have performance standards, which may be set by high-level officials, legislators, or, as in the case of nonprofits, donors and other stakeholders.

Performance contracting also falls under the domain of using performance measurement information to control behavior. As explained by Hatry (1992), if an agency contracts out services or provides grants, it can set performance targets in the agreements, against which actual performance is compared. Rewards for meeting or exceeding targets, and penalties for failing to meet expectations, are often included in the contracts or agreements.

Performance Measures as a Tool for Motivating and Mobilizing

The idea that performance information can help motivate program managers, line staff, as well as donors and other stakeholders of nonprofit agencies is grounded on achievement goal theory. Proponents of this theory, widely used in sport psychology and cognitive psychology, argue that a task orientation, in which individuals focus on self-improvement and task mastery rather than comparing their own performance to that of others, is conducive to positive behaviors (Nicholls, 1984; Nolen, 1988). Thus, performance measurement information can be used to motivate individuals by providing them feedback on progress toward the desired results (Behn, 2003).

However, Hatry (1999) cautions that although feedback may be sufficient motivation for some, others may need additional encouragement, which may or may not include monetary incentives. Therefore, agencies need to provide an achievement climate that sets goals and incorporates different types of incentives for goals achieved. If an incentive scheme other than performance feedback is going to be used, the inevitable subjectivity involved in deciding who should receive what rewards can be offset if the performance measures used to assess achievement are perceived as being objective.

Celebrating accomplishments toward achievement of stated goals and objectives is another way to motivate individuals because it gives them a "sense of individual and collective relevance, and motivate[s] future efforts" (Behn, 2003). Accordingly, Behn suggests that these celebrations should not take place only at the end of a project, but throughout the life of the project as people accomplish different milestones.

Furthermore, performance measurement can be used to promote and communicate an agency's or government's contribution toward achieving the goals and dreams of its stakeholders. Unfortunately, laments Behn (2003), in the public sector this is not done often enough. Public managers often fail to use the information in this manner. Reporting performance can help capture the public's attention (Ammons 1995). Having the public's attention gives agencies an opportunity to show the merits of the programs—quality of programs and policies, justify their existence, and may also serve to encourage more support for performance measurement efforts.

Moreover, using performance measures to communicate with the public may have a positive effect on perceptions of legitimacy and trust. Trust is developed when citizens feel that there is open and honest communication between them and their government or service provider. This, of course, requires sharing information when results are good and when they are not. Finally, telling citizens and donors how efficiently and effectively their tax dollars and funds are being spent may legitimize the programs and thus increase their priority in the decision-making process. As was reported by Kopcynski and Lombardo (1999), communicating performance may help organizations build coalitions and obtain support in future performance improvement efforts.

Performance Measures as a Tool for Improvement

For Behn, improving performance is the real purpose of performance measurement. Everything else that has been mentioned is a means to this end. Hatry (1999) concurs with this but goes a step further when he asserts that above all, the goal of performance measurement is to provide better services in a more efficient manner. Thus, for example, a quality performance measurement can help determine the areas in which processes need to be improved to increase citizens' satisfaction.

As a feedback mechanism, performance measurement information may tell us whether or not improvements in the expected outcomes have occurred. Hence, it allows organizations to determine how well they are doing, if they are complying with performance standards, and how best to allocate resources to meet the performance standards. Managers can use performance measurement to help justify budget requests and make allocation decisions. Performance measurement allows managers to show the benefits of a particular program. In doing so, the program stands a better chance of being funded.

At the same time, when programs are not performing as expected, and provided that the appropriate information on why this is the case is available, managers can decide how to allocate resources in a manner that is conducive to improving performance. It might be possible that in such situations a new service strategy is needed. Note, however, that this statement is made with caution. As stated by Behn, budgets are "crude tools"; therefore, allocation decisions, particularly budget cuts, suggests Perrin (1998), should consider information that is outside the regular scope of the performance measurement system. The decision maker should consider information on the program logic and special circumstances that may have an impact on performance.

Limitations of Performance Measurement

As critical as performance measurement is to any performance management system, one must not lose sight of some important limitations and drawbacks of performance measurement. Although these are not insurmountable, unless they are properly addressed they may render the system useless at best and crippling at worse. As pointed out by Kravchuk and Schack (1996), a system is not good if it does not provide pertinent information to decision makers, and it can hurt an organization if it misrepresents, misleads, or introduces perverse behavioral incentives. It may also hurt the organization when the performance data are misused by stakeholders to lay blame and criticism without any clear understanding of the reasons why the data show what they show.

These concerns resonate with three important criticisms that have been made of performance measurement by program evaluators (e.g., Mark et al., 2000; Ryan, 2002; Greene, 1999). Critics argue that performance measurement:

- Has a tendency to encourage goal displacement
- Can support confidence in causality only in special circumstances
- Is inadequate for properly representing the concept of quality

These criticisms merit serious attention, and the limitations they highlight need to be properly addressed. Here I will discuss these limitations and suggest strategies for addressing them.

While recognizing that performance measurement as a descriptive mode of inquiry can contribute to various evaluation purposes, Mark et al. (2000) also state that *goal displacement* is one of the most potentially damaging uses of performance measurement in decision making. Goal displacement refers to a tendency to purposely redirect behavior to only those areas in which one is being measured to improve the performance ratings in those areas (Mark et al., 2000; Bohte and Meier, 2000). This causes two major problems. First, by directing their attention to the areas in which they are being measured, the individuals or the organization might neglect other activities that may be more desirable and would lead to achieving organizational and societal outcomes. A quintessential example of this is teachers teaching to the test when they are rewarded based on students' performance on those tests. Unless the test captures all that we want students to learn, in the most extreme of cases teaching to the test will limit instruction to only that which will be tested. Second, as argued by Mark et al., over time goal displacement will diminish the value of the measure. What was once a useful indicator of broader learning becomes a measure of a narrow outcome of limited interest.

Quantitative measures, and particularly output measures, appear to have a tendency to lead to goal displacement. Campbell (1975) noted a disturbing relationship between the use of quantitative social indicators and the possibility of them corrupting behavior. He stated that the more those indicators were used, the more likely it was that they will lead to distortions and corruption in the social processes that they were supposed to help monitor. Similarly, Bohte and Meier (2000) have argued that in the public sector, the tendency to measure agency performance in terms of numeric outputs instead of final outcomes, which are more difficult to measure, leads bureaucrats to maximize and even manipulate outputs for fear of negative consequences.

The question, then, is how to avoid goal displacement and its inherent negative impact on the quality of performance measurement. One of the ways suggested by evaluators is that those measuring performance use multiple indicators selected from a broad array of possible indicators (Mark et al., 2000). This will make it difficult for people to change their behavior toward one particular indicator. Although Mark et al. (2001) also suggest that rotating indicators in and out of a performance measurement system can be helpful in curtailing goal displacement, they also point out that this approach has an important drawback—it will make it difficult to track trends and build up a body of knowledge. As suggested by Weiss (1998), in program evaluation, repeated use of measures allows the evaluator to make comparisons of the effectiveness of one program over another. Another suggestion is that organizations use a broader incentive system and that performance indicators be used more as an input for making more informed decisions about who gets rewarded and who gets punished than as the rationale for rewarding for good performance or punishing for poor performance. Finally, Bohte and Meiers (2000) suggest that organizations should use accepted organizational or professional norms that recognize the inherent difficulties of tasks that individuals and organizations are expected to perform.

Establishing causality is another thorny issue for performance measurement. Critics argue that performance measures, and specifically outcome measures collected on an ongoing basis, can only rarely be used to conclude that the program in question has caused the observed results (Sheirer and Newcomer, 2001; Shadish et al., 1991). Performance outcomes in descriptive methods such as performance measurement can only provide levels of outcomes, not whether or not they are the result of the program state Mark et al., (2000). Such causal attributions, argues Weiss (1998b), are better grounded in evaluation studies that have used a randomized experiment.

However, Wholey (1996) and Hatry (1997) have argued that much of the work that public agencies call evaluation is actually performance measurement or "after the fact outcome measurement" (Hatry, 1997). This is a point of concern for evaluators given that program managers have a tendency to draw causal conclusions from these studies (Shadish et al., 1990).

There are possible solutions to this limitation. One of them is for those who work in performance measurement to collaborate with program evaluators in the development of performance measurement systems. For example, managers can have confidence in drawing conclusions of causal linkages between their programs and observed outcome measures if those measures were developed in a manner consistent with program evaluation methods and techniques. Better yet, an already conducted evaluation can serve as the foundation for developing performance measures.

It is also useful to keep in mind that depending on the program in question, decision makers may not need anything more than performance measurement information to attribute outcomes to program activities. This would be the case if there is no other possible explanation for the particular outcome. An example of this is the outcome of a public vaccination program. It has been established that people who get vaccinated against measles do not get measles later in life. If someone has been vaccinated, we can safely attribute her not getting measles to the vaccine. Likewise, in instances when process measures can easily reveal the causes for the observed outcome, causal conclusions are warranted. For instance, in the summer of 2007, when many patrons of local public pools got sick after swimming, an analysis of the water revealed that it was contaminated by a parasite called *Cryptosporidium*, which causes vomiting, diarrhea, and other stomach-related complications. As a result, public pools implemented a ban on children who were still in diapers; they also did more to treat the water and made public announcements asking individuals who may have any signs of the illness to not use the public pools.

The third criticism, that performance measurement is *inadequate for properly representing the concept of quality*, can be understood from the perspective of the qualitative tradition's crisis of representation phase, described by Mark et al. (2000), which questions the ability of any method of inquiry to provide a meaningful representation of any phenomenon. Accordingly, Greene (1999) argues that an important concept such as quality, which attempts to measure human experience, cannot be reduced to a single measure or small set of measures, as those conducting performance measures often attempt to do. Furthermore, because the meaning of program quality varies from individual to individual and we do not have fixed and objective standards for judging quality, performance measurement systems cannot capture the critical dimensions of program quality.

The implication here is that each observer and each person being observed will have a different conception of quality. Although this may be disconcerting for some given the particularistic value judgment that quality may entail, others believe that this is not necessarily problematic. Mark et al. (2000) argue that there is not "a single right framing to bring to a single situation." Clearly this situation calls for a variety of measures and methods for measuring that can complement each other and thus help to better capture the multiple dimensions of different concepts.

This is true for PM as well as program evaluation. Indeed, every limitation highlighted here can also apply to program evaluation or, for that matter, any method that entails evaluating (Perrin, 1998). The difference is that program evaluators have at their disposal a number of tools and techniques to help them address these issues. Some of these tools include data collection and analysis techniques, a traditional emphasis on construct validity, and methods for understanding program theory. Performance measurement information also contributes to making program evaluation stronger because it can provide the needed assortment of information that is often necessary in program evaluation, and thus serve as the backbone of program evaluation.

Therefore, both program evaluators and those involved in performance measurement can benefit from dialogue and collaboration. Such collaboration can help make better performance measurement systems and more useful and timely program evaluations.

Summary

This chapter highlighted the importance of performance measurement and its centrality to performance-based management. Figure 1.1 depicted performance-based management as a system in which performance measurement feeds from and provides feedback for strategic planning so that managers can develop the necessary strategies to achieve and demonstrate progress toward stated goals and objectives.

Although performance measurement is often touted as a tool for accountability, given its centrality in performance-based management, it was argued here that there are many more purposes and uses of performance measurement than accountability. The chapter described those purposes as falling into four broad categories: evaluation and understanding, motivating and mobilizing, control and oversight, and program improvement. Purposes is a concept distinct from the broader concept of use of performance measures. Furthermore, the concept of implementation, or actually using performance measures in specific tasks, was introduced here along with the concept of adoption, which refers to developing performance measures. These concepts form the basis for the discussions that follow in the chapters ahead.

A discussion of the importance of performance measurement would not be complete without discussing its limitations. I discussed three specific limitations and argued that, although serious, they can be overcome. One strategy advanced here is to strengthen performance measurement by borrowing methods and techniques from program evaluation.

Chapter 2

Using Performance Measurement Information

The previous chapter provided support for the premise that performance measurement, with its 100-year legacy in American public management, can be a useful management tool. Why, then, do we need a book like this? This good question has a good answer. The reason we need a book like this, focused on building theory that can help develop and sustain effective performance management systems, is that we find that despite its purported uses and possible contributions to management, performance measurement information appears to be not widely used. And even where used, it is not done to its full potential.

Accordingly, the purpose of this book is to support practical efforts to build, use, and sustain performance management systems. To accomplish this, I will explain the obstacles and challenges involved in performance measurement efforts and will provide guidance on how to overcome them. It is important, however, that explanations and guidance be based not just on anecdotes, but rather, on the best empirical evidence that we can marshal. This chapter constitutes a summary of the theoretical and practical considerations that guided and informed the research that will be presented in subsequent chapters.

Barriers to Performance Measurement

As with any form of organizational change, those wanting to establish performance-based management (PBM) systems are likely to confront obstacles. In a 1982 article, Gloria Grizzle provided a visionary analysis of the issues that governments should pay attention to before developing and implementing a performance measurement system. Grizzle (1982) argued that developing a comprehensive performance measurement system is not "cheap, easy, or quick" for several reasons:

1. Performance is a multidimensional concept, which can include efficiency, effectiveness, quality, equity, fiscal stability, and conformance with government policy and standards.
2. Data collection is expensive. As a result, managers may not be able to include all the dimensions of performance.
3. Who will use the performance information might dictate which performance dimensions to focus on.
4. It is important to consider who the winners and losers will be in the decision to collect information on one dimension and not others.
5. Although goals should play a role in the design of the performance measurement system, given the multiplicity of goals and sometimes inconsistency among them, it is not easy to determine how.
6. Lack of control over program impacts and the time required for the effect to take place makes measuring program results difficult.

Grizzle's discussion should not be construed as an argument against performance measurement. On the contrary, she remained a firm believer of the need for performance measurement and for measuring program outcomes. What she provided was a realistic view of the difficulties that must be surmounted and the dilemmas that must be resolved to have a successful PBM system. As noted by Marshall (1996), it is not uncommon to find those who are not in favor of the effort seizing "any set-back as an opportunity to kill this painful process." It is difficult to predict the level of resistance and the obstacles that will be encountered, but it is clear that the obstacles will come in different forms, including (Ammons, 1992):

■ Environmental barriers: These are factors that distinguish the public sector from the private sector and negatively impact productivity, including, but not limited to, political factors that influence decision making, civil service restrictions, lack of political appeal, and intergovernmental mandating of expenditures.
■ Organizational barriers: These factors include lack of accountability, insufficient analytic skills or analytic staff, union resistance, perverse reward system, inadequate performance evaluation, requirement of large investment up front, and perceived threat to job security.
■ Personal barriers: These have to do with individuals and derive from their attitudes, traits, and behavior. These individual barriers influence the way in which administrators respond to opportunities for performance improvement. They include risk avoidance, conceptual confusion, inadequate control of time/workday, and managerial alibis.

Consistent with Ammons's categories of potential challenges above, in their analysis of early performance measurement experiences at the federal level, Newcomer and Wright (1997) identified four major challenges faced by programs initiating performance measurement. First, there is the need to have the commitment from the top leadership. Federal program managers stated that without top management support, performance measurement efforts are futile.

Second, the time required to create feasible strategic and measurement systems does not match political appointees' short reelection horizons. The need to produce immediate results for an election cycle as short as 24 months creates a disincentive for support of fundamental efforts. Third, identifying stakeholders and soliciting their input represents not only a logistical challenge, but also a political one. Lastly, reported the authors, early performance measurement experiences indicate a general lack of coordination of performance measurement efforts within the larger organization. Typically there is little communication between programs and units housed within the same agency. Recent research findings (see Pandey and Garnett, 2006) support this observation by showing that there exist structural forces in organizations that impede proper communication and coordination of performance.

Case studies of state and local governments experimenting with performance measurement illustrate challenges similar to those described above (a summary of the cases is provided at the end of the chapter in Box 2.1). One of these challenges is getting the needed commitment from elected officials and top leaders. For example, at the local level, one of the lessons learned in Prince William County, Virginia, was that "unless elected officials and the top leadership are sincerely committed, the effort may succumb at the first signs of resistance." At the state level, the Minnesota Department of Labor and Industry concluded that even when the legislature and governor make the decision for state agencies to measure performance, the commitment of an agency's leadership is still essential for this type of change to succeed (Wilkins, 1996).

Consistent with Grizzle's 1982 analysis, another major obstacle reported in the cases of state and local governments was time. For instance, in their effort to develop and use outcome information, the City of Portland, Oregon, learned that it takes time to develop a good performance measurement system (Tracy, 1996). As mentioned earlier, developing a quality performance measurement system is an iterative process that requires considerable investment of time in planning, developing, and refining. Unfortunately, investing time on something for which benefits will not be immediately apparent is not appealing to many, often leading to diminishing interest in and the eventual abandonment of the effort.

The cost of establishing and implementing a performance measures system was also raised as a possible barrier. For example, in discussing Minnesota's government performance report, Jackson (1996) lamented that the reports cost more than anticipated. Nonetheless, although it appears that the reports had little value to the legislators and the public, they seemed to at least have been helpful for internal operations. Furthermore, in another case study (the case of the City of Portland,

Oregon), the author concluded that the bureaucratic and political benefits that accrued justified the cost of performance measurement (Tracy, 1996). And in the case study of Prince William County, Marshall (1996) concluded that a performance measures system is not more costly than previously used approaches.

Others have had to confront related realities as they moved forward with the development of performance measures—the lack of availability of appropriate and timely data and the right data management system. The ICMA Comparative Performance Measurement Consortium Project, a consortium of cities and counties formed to develop comparative performance measures, faced these issues (Coe, 1999). As the project progressed, it became a struggle to get data that could be trusted. Also, the consortium found it difficult to develop the appropriate systems for handling and analyzing disparate and vast amounts of data.

These issues are tightly related to the fact that in public organizations there are often (Kravchuk and Schack, 1996):

- Divergent perspectives wherein different audiences require different information
- Unclear mission and objectives
- Multiple and contradictory organizational, program, and system goals

Because different audiences will likely be interested in different aspects of performance, and given that goals are fuzzy at best, creating great ambiguity, simply deciding what to measure and for which audience could bring the performance effort to a halt. After all, performance measures are supposed to emanate from goals and the objectives developed to operationalize these goals.

All of this makes developing and implementing a performance measurement system a monumental task to undertake and a great accomplishment when agencies succeed. As a result, we find conflicting accounts on the prevalence of performance measurement. While some say that public organizations continue to collect, analyze, and disseminate performance information in unprecedented quantities, others counter, arguing that performance measurement is not prevalent among public organizations (Kravchuck and Schack, 1996; Nyham and Marlowe, 1995). Further, Fountain (1997) has concluded that there is very little knowledge as to the extent of utilization of performance measurement in the United States. In fact, explained Fountain, most of the information available is anecdotal. Current empirical evidence seems to support both views. On the one hand, organizations are developing performance measurement systems. But on the other hand, their rate of use of the information is low.

This discrepancy—an increasing number of public organizations saying that they have some type of performance measurement system, but a lesser number reporting actually using the information—suggests that the actual use of performance measurement information does not automatically follow from its development. On the theoretical side of things, one of the main difficulties with developing and implementing useful performance management systems is that performance measurement is usually viewed as a rational-technocratic activity. The presumption goes something like this:

> *Organizations are goal-oriented. They have clear goals. Clear goals lead to clear and measurable objectives. After developing objectives, organizations will develop value-free measures and indicators of performance that will be used to assess whether stated goals are being achieved. Based on this information management will make the appropriate decisions*

Thus, this not only assumes that the setting of goals and objectives and subsequent development of performance measures is rational, but also that once organizations measure performance this is immediately followed by the use of the information in a concrete manner.

The accounts provided here thus far show that the place of performance measurement in the political world is not often directly acknowledged. This is particularly evident when legal requirements are imposed on organizations to develop performance measurement systems. The belief is that organizations will comply and make use of the performance information as mandated by the law. One of the criticisms of the GPRA suggested by Radin (1998) is that it presents the process of measurement, the performance information, and the use of information as being rational and objective. Indeed, Section 2(b)[6] of the Act states that it will improve "congressional decision-making by providing more objective information on achieving statutory objectives and on the relative effectiveness and efficiency of Federal programs and spending" (GPRA, 1993). With this kind of mindset as background, performance measurement becomes the domain of "experts" who, in general, view it mainly from a scientific management perspective. This mentality, argues Radin (2000), severely undermines our understanding of the political issues that complicate the implementation of GPRA.

Take as an example the GPRA requirement that performance measurements be aligned with program goals, which are supposed to be the reason why the programs were authorized and funded in the first place. According to the rational model, the first step should be to identify the goals on which to base the performance measures and against which performance will be compared. However, this is not as clean-cut as the rational model of decision-making presumes. As discussed earlier, the characteristics of organizational goals in public organizations make this a more subjective exercise than one is led to believe by the rational model.

But of course, the ideals of the rational model are consistent with the legacy of performance improvement of the beginning of the 1900s, which focused on obtaining efficiency by depoliticizing administration through professionalism (Wilson, 1968; Henry, 1975; Critchlow, 1985). Thus, the technocratic approach to administration that evolved can be understood as part of the political-administration separation, which, until recently, has been a basic tenet of administration. The poor record of utilization of performance measurement, however, makes it clear that even though performance measurement is perceived as a rational activity, its adoption and implementation cannot be explained in such terms.

Indeed, given that performance measurement has winners and losers because of the decisions that must be made about which performance dimensions to collect information on, and also given the fact that the goals on which performance measurement systems are based may be inconsistent, ambiguous, or even nonexistent, and therefore subject to interpretation, it is not possible to separate the design and development of such systems from politics (Grizzle, 1982). Furthermore, Grizzle contended that it is not possible to keep the information from being used in the political process. The political process may include deciding who to hold accountable for program performance, how to distribute rewards, and comparing performance across units or agencies.

To summarize, the barriers to adopting and implementing performance measurement systems fall into two broad categories: practical issues and political issues. Practical issues include the cost of data collection, available personnel, analytical skills, and the ability to attract and sustain participation from stakeholders. The political issues can be internal, related to employees and decision makers, or external, related to the political process. These issues suggest that to advance performance measurement in support of performance-based management, we need to define performance measurement in different terms. Therefore here we will not conceive of performance measurement as a purely rational activity. Rather, we will see it in terms of knowledge production and innovation. Such a conceptualization will allow us to make use of the practical lessons that have been learned by public organizations that have experimented with performance measurement. This will also allow us to consider the political context and to make use of advances that have been made in related fields to gain a broader understanding of the use of performance measurement information in public organizations. This understanding is essential in developing strategies that can help us adopt, implement, and sustain effective and successful PBM systems.

Performance Measurement as Knowledge and Innovation

Performance Measurement as Knowledge Creation

Performance measurement is geared to the production of knowledge that can be used by an organization's inside and outside stakeholders to make decisions. Although not often discussed in such terms, the utilization of performance measures is an issue that should be examined from a knowledge utilization framework. Yet, examining the utilization of performance measures with a model of inquiry from the field of knowledge utilization would be problematic. Wingens (1990) has argued that the field remains underdeveloped, with no adequate theory proven to have power based on empirical testing. As a result, stated Rich (1991), one of the creators of the field of knowledge utilization, as a field of study knowledge utilization was in a state of crisis. According to the author, the field faced four major issues: a crisis of legitimacy, a lacuna in theory building, proper measurement of the phenomena being explored, and stalled development in posing challenging questions. Following suit, as he introduced his argument for examining the nature of knowledge use from the postmodern critical theorist perspective, Watkins (1994) said the field was in a "state of conceptual disarray that has led to problems in the dissemination and use of knowledge."

Central to this apparent state of crisis is the fact that studies on utilization of technical knowledge have often proceeded under the two-communities metaphor. This model explains utilization (and lack of) in terms of differences of perceptions and behavior (culture) between the producers of the knowledge (social scientists) and the intended users (decision makers or policy makers). Thus, for example, one of the most common assumptions of this model that when information comes from internal sources, it is more likely to get used because decision makers trust it and think that it will support the organization's goals (Oh and Rich, 1996; Caplan et al., 1979; Nelson et al., 1987).

Alas, this explanation does not help us understand the lack of utilization of performance measurement information. Performance measurement is, in general, an internal activity conducted by members of the organization. However, evidence suggests that even when organizations decide to adopt performance measures, other issues or obstacles seem to come up that affect implementation. This suggests a differentiation between what can be called the *adoption* of knowledge and the *implementation* of knowledge, a distinction rarely addressed by the field of knowledge utilization. Such lack of differentiation in what constitutes knowledge use has led others to argue that the field is too crude in its definition of knowledge utilization (Landry et al., 2001). In a study of utilization of performance measurement such shortsighted vision could lead us to draw the erroneous conclusion that reasons for adoption are the same as the reasons for implementation, or that implementation unconditionally follows adoption.

Another problem of the field of knowledge utilization, which relates to reliance on the cultural differentiation emphasized by the two-communities metaphor, is that contextual factors have been neglected, making the field too fragmented. This neglect has been acknowledged by knowledge utilization scholars, who have advocated the development of an integrated model of inquiry (Huberman, 1987, 1989, 1994; Wingens, 1990). While this would address the problem of fragmentation of the field, there is a need to go beyond integration of factors. We need to conduct more rigorous studies that allow for causal mechanisms affecting utilization to emerge.

Here I address these issues by using a mixed methods approach that relies on theories from various fields of study to build and further refine an elaborated model of utilization of performance measurement information. Central to this model is the conception of knowledge use advanced by Stehr (1992). In his study of utilization of social science knowledge, Stehr differentiated knowledge as practical knowledge and action knowledge. Practical knowledge is that which gives the capacity to act; action knowledge is knowledge converted into action. For our purposes, I've made a parallel distinction between adoption and implementation of performance measures. I've defined adoption as capacity for action, and implementation of performance measures as knowledge converted into action. In the model presented in this book, the capacity for action is measured as the development of efficiency, output, and outcome measures. The implementation, or knowledge converted into action, refers to using performance measures for strategic planning, resource allocation, program management, monitoring, evaluation, and reporting to internal management, elected officials, and citizens or the media.

Thus, although by itself the field of knowledge utilization is not able to provide sufficient guidance to achieve an understanding of why performance measures are not more widely used, it is a useful starting point. The reason for this is that as discussed above, and as will be shown in the following chapters, there are some key assumptions that hold promise in advancing our understanding of performance measurement. In addition, the criticisms cited above clearly encourage researchers to be more creative in their methodological approaches and to pay attention to theories and experiences outside their usual range of focus. This is the approach taken here.

Performance Measurement as Innovation

As discussed earlier, organizations attempting to adopt and implement performance measures are likely to face a number of practical and political issues. Based on the record of utilization of performance measures, one could speculate that those barriers operate differently on adoption and implementation. As pointed out earlier in the field of knowledge utilization these contextual factors are disregarded by the two-communities metaphor because of its culturalistic focus. Absent this contextual focus on the field of knowledge utilization, alternative models of inquiry must be explored.

The main objective of the emphasis on performance measures is a desire to manage for results. This is part of the Total Quality Management (TQM) movement embraced by many organizations in the United States (Kamensky, 1995). This emphasis on managing for results, however, is, more importantly, a reaction from public organizations to regain the confidence from citizens and other stakeholders that they can create value. Managing for results is an innovation and as such requires organizational change.

Organizational innovation has been defined as "the adoption of change which is new to the organization and to the relevant environment" (Knight, 1967). Change, in turn, has been defined as "planned or unplanned response of an organization to pressures" (Dalziel and Schoonover, 1988). Such a change in the organization produces conflicts that are often resolved by internal political processes, including the formation of interest groups and coalitions, bargaining, and side payments (Harvey and Mills, 1970; Pfeffer, 1981, 1983; Fischer, 1986). Therefore, one could argue that the political model of organizational theory, which directs attention to the political processes that are activated by the efforts to introduce change (Fischer, 1986), can be used to pursue answers to one of the central questions of this book: Why are performance measures not more widely utilized? After answering that question, we can proceed with recommendations for solving the issues involved.

In addition to internal political factors, there are external political factors that provide a context for change in public organizations. Although these factors often take the shape of legal or administrative requirements, the underlying factors often include clashing interests and pressures. The experiences that some public organizations have had with performance measurement suggest that, in general, these legal and administrative requirements are the results of public officials' reactions to public pressures. Thus, their response is a political strategy. Traditional organizational theory, however, discusses change within the realm of managerial goals as presented by the rational/technocratic model. From a technocratic or rational point of view, the adoption and implementation of performance measures are purely technical issues. That is, as long as the organization has the capacity to produce and process the knowledge, knowledge utilization will occur.

In the rational model, as criticized by Howard and Schneider (1994), the adoption of innovation depends on whether certain conditions, such as experts in charge, managerial control, systematic standardization, and work fragmentation (basic principles of scientific management), are present. This perspective neglects the role of context and powerful groups within organizations, leading to myths about the rational nature of problem-solving processes in organizations (Pettigrew et al., 1992).

Furthermore, many scholars have argued that cultural aspects of organizations have an impact on their acceptance of change. Culture refers to the dominating beliefs or ideologies prevalent in organizations that can shape and reflect organizational power relationships (Pettigrew et al., 1992). Pettigrew et al. held that a "central concept linking political and cultural analyses essential to the understanding of continuity and change is legitimacy." Thus, based on cultural views, different groups will use different mechanisms to justify their ideas, creating a conflict that is often resolved by attaining power or influence in the organization (Fischer, 1986). Accordingly, this perspective can be useful in examining the reasons why performance measurement information appears to not be more widely used. It can also point us in the direction of appropriate strategies for dealing with these important issues.

Toward an Elaborated Model

The discussion above suggests that a model that combines rational, political, and cultural elements would have real power in explaining organizational change. And more specifically in the field of knowledge utilization, critics have advocated the development of an integrated model that can help explain why knowledge is or is not used.

Furthermore, Klein and Speer Sorra (1996) have implied that the paucity of innovation implementation studies is due to a choice of methodology (mainly single-case study). This methodology only focuses on describing parts of the implementation process, lacking the ability to capture in an integrated model the "multidetermined, multilevel phenomenon of innovation implementation."

Thus, the focus here is on developing an elaborated model that integrates factors that have been eloquently addressed in different fields of study, but that due to a perception that they contradict each other, have not been properly reconciled. This reconciliation is possible here in light of the conceptualization of the adoption and implementation of performance measures as knowledge and innovation. More importantly, by stressing the importance of separating the adoption of knowledge from its implementation, it is possible to tease out the relationships and different influences that are part of the process of utilization.

With this in mind, I address the need for an integrated model of inquiry in the field of knowledge utilization. I provide some light on the discussion about the appropriate theoretical framework for examining the problem of the apparent lack of utilization of performance measures in the public sector. One of the goals is to provide practitioners with information that can help them address the factors that may inhibit the introduction of performance measures or any other type of innovation in their organizations.

This is accomplished using a mixed methods approach to inquiry that combines quantitative and qualitative methodologies to develop an elaborated model of utilization. The approach entailed collecting data by means of a survey mailed to a cross-sectional sample of state and local governments across the nation, using pattern matching for the interpretation of regression analyses of data collected by means of the survey, and supplementing these data with an analysis of published cases on state and local governments experimenting with performance measures, as well as comments from survey respondents. Moreover, to further examine the dynamics suggested by the survey data, telephone interviews were conducted with a group of state and local government employees that were part of the original sample surveyed.

It should be noted that looking at the impact of decisions or actions based on information obtained from performance measurement systems is not the concern of this book. The concern here is understanding the processes that lead to utilization.

Lessons That Must Be Learned

Given the above discussion, it is argued that the question of why performance measurement systems are not more widely utilized by public entities cannot be effectively answered by focusing only on one set of factors developed within a particular model of inquiry. The answer can be sought, however, by combining these different theories and assessing their impact on, and relationships with, other factors as they relate to both the adoption and implementation of performance measures.

Perhaps more importantly for some, support for this argument is found in the lessons learned by some state, local, and federal government agencies that have experimented with performance measurement (see Box 2.1). In the mid-1990s the American Society for Public Administration's (ASPA) Government Accountability and Accomplishment Task Force coordinated the efforts of several local, state, and federal agencies to prepare case studies on their experiences with performance measures. Both practitioners and scholars collaborated in preparing these cases, which are based on interviews with those involved in the process of adoption and implementation of performance measurement systems.

These cases were reviewed and are summarized in Box 2.1 to provide a qualitative perspective for the quantitative perspective that was followed in the analysis of the mailed survey described in the chapters ahead. The experiences of the state and local government agencies helped to elaborate the hypotheses described in the next chapter and provided substantive meaning to the findings of the mailed survey. From a theoretical perspective, rigorously examining these experiences can contribute to the development of theories and principles that can better help to inform practice. Such examination would allow us to discover behavioral patterns, organizational structures, and dynamics that can be used to suggest strategies for effective implementation of performance-based management.

On the practical side, the experiences highlighted in Box 2.1 also represent a wake-up call for all. They are a testament of what Gloria Grizzle was warning us about back in 1982. They clearly highlight the issues and concerns that must be addressed as organizations endeavor to develop, implement, and sustain performance-based management systems geared toward responding to modern management demands. These lessons are by no means conclusive or exhaustive. They are, however, a good reflection of current practice.

BOX 2.1: SUMMARY AND LESSONS LEARNED OF CASE STUDIES OF GOVERNMENT EXPERIMENTING WITH PERFORMANCE MEASURES

Case 1. Outcome Budgeting: Catawba County, NC

Author: Berry and Ikerd, 1996

In 1992, fiscal pressures generated an interest in changing the way budgets were prepared. In response to these pressures, in 1993 six county departments volunteered to pilot a new budget process that focused on outcomes to be achieved, gave budgetary authority to department heads, and allowed departments to retain all unexpected funds at year end.

Lessons Learned

1. Use of outcomes by line staff as motivation has only worked when the staff was involved in creating the outcome measures and felt that the measures were a meaningful reflection of their work.
2. Lack of benchmarks is a major concern because it limits the ability to compare results to what was accomplished in the past.
3. There is danger in setting goals too high.
4. Developing outcomes helps the organization focus on the core mission of each service.

Case 2. Development and Use of Performance Indicators in the City of Coral Springs, Florida

Author: Schwabe, 1996

Performance measures were adopted to regain the confidence of city residents. This lack of confidence was the result of negative attention by the media due to political infighting among the five city commissions and the failure of highly visible projects in the late 1980s.

Lessons Learned

1. It is critical to develop only those indicators that address the strategic priorities and departmental results. Otherwise, an overburden of irrelevant data collection and reporting process will occur.
2. Performance measures information should be available to all decision makers at all levels in the organization. Therefore, it is essential to have a systematic process of data collection, analysis, and reporting.
3. Training is very important because performance measurement is often an uncharted territory for most elected and appointed officials.
4. There should be a balance between perception-based and operational/financial indicators.
5. Elected officials must be kept involved in developing and using indicators. This is particularly important for those who need to measure progress in meeting strategic priorities.

6. It is important to communicate performance measurement results to all audiences so that they can be informed as to the progress in meeting strategic and departmental objectives. This can be accomplished by using the media and preparing and disseminating reports.

Case 3. Development and Use of Outcome Measures: Long Beach Police Department, Long Beach, CA

Author: Bryant, 1996

Performance measures were adopted as a result of growing dissatisfaction with services provided. The dissatisfaction was such that the city council considered eliminating the department and contracting out the service. One of the major challenges facing the department was a continuously decreasing staffing level while population increased. Without a doubt, this contributed to the department's inability to meet service demands.

Lessons Learned

1. Performance measures should be part of a larger effort. It cannot be something done in isolation; rather, it should be part of systematic changes.
2. Measure what is important to customers.
3. Try to measure results or outcomes from different angles. One single measure will not be enough to capture the effects of services provided.
4. Broad-based participation is needed. The most successful measures are those developed by individuals responsible for doing the work.

Case 4. Development and Use of Outcome Information: Portland, Oregon

Author: Tracy, 1996

Performance measures were developed to experiment with the GASB's service efforts and accomplishments (SEA) and to respond to the city auditor's agenda for improvement of accountability, efficiency, and effectiveness of Portland government. Prior to the new effort, efficiency and effectiveness indicators were rarely reported. The emphasis was on spending (input) and workload statistics, and there were no performance standards or objectives to guide monitoring and evaluating.

Lessons Learned

1. The success of a performance measurement system is heavily dependent on a clear definition of purpose.
2. Performance measures should not be used to reward managers when goals are achieved, nor to punish when performance comes up short—managers will sabotage measurement systems that unfairly hold them responsible for outcomes they only partially control.
3. Performance measures should be used to determine the degree to which goals are being achieved.
4. It takes time to develop a good system that is useful to managers and elected officials and is accepted by the organization.

5. The acceptance of performance results will depend on whether the data from performance measurement systems are viewed as accurate, valid, and credible.
6. Building on existing data and performance systems may help save time and maintain morale.
7. It is important that the information be useful to managers and officials so that performance measurement can endure.
8. Bureaucratic and political benefits from the reporting of information outweigh the costs.

Case 5. Development and Use of Outcome Information in Government, Prince William County, Virginia

Author: Marshall, 1996

Performance measures were adopted in response to citizens' demands for accountability. Prior to adopting a strategic plan, the use of performance measures was limited to workload indicators and not linked to resource allocation or used to provide accountability for results (i.e., reporting to citizens and decision makers).

Lessons Learned

1. An emphasis on accountability can be threatening for managers. Managing for results (i.e., using performance measures) represents a culture change. Consequently, there will be denial, disbelief, and the resistance that accompanies change.
2. The commitment of elected officials and top leadership is necessary for success, or the effort will not succeed.
3. Measures should be linked to real decision making so that benefits can be visible. This will help avoid some resistance.
4. Management and staff should be involved in developing those measures.
5. Developing and implementing a performance measurement system is not more costly than previously used approaches.
6. Managing for results is political because of the resources, time, and commitment necessary to develop the system. As a result, managing for results must be of strategic importance to the organization.

Case 6. Ramsey County, Minnesota: Performance Contracting at the County Level (Community Human Services Department)

Author: Skaff, 1996

There were two key factors that led to the adoption of performance measures. One of these factors was negative media attention because of alleged mistreatment of clients under the care of the county and inefficiencies in service delivery. The other factor was that because of changes in regulations that gave greater discretion to community-level programs, the department needed a reliable way to ensure service effectiveness and accountability.

Lessons Learned

1. One must recognize that the purposes a program is supposed to meet often are not realized.
2. Performance evaluation efforts should be linked to broader goals.
3. When the use of performance measures is not linked to funding decisions, there is more cooperation and support from outside providers and internal programs.

Case 7. The Council on Human Investment: Performance Governance in Iowa
Authors: Weidner and Noss-Reavely, 1996

Performance measures were developed in response to general complaints that government does not involve citizens in decisions, and there is no way for them to know where their tax dollars are going and with what results.

Lessons Learned

1. The process of developing performance measures is iterative. Managers must realize that the system has to be flexible enough to allow for mid-course corrections.
2. Citizen participation with state government is an important change strategy.
3. Long-term sustainability of the effort depends on citizens' involvement. They can create accountability among policy makers.
4. Commitment to developing a credible system is as essential as the involvement of the research community.
5. Ongoing training and support of agencies is necessary.
6. All departments should be involved in the effort.
7. Success is enhanced by the support and participation of the governor and legislature.
8. An overall vision and sufficient staff are needed to develop and maintain a successful system.
9. It is important to have resources to carry out the effort.

Case 8. Lessons Learned from Minnesota's Government Performance Report
Author: Jackson, 1996

In 1993 the Minnesota legislature asked the state's major executive agencies to publish annual performance reports to help citizens and legislators assess agencies' effectiveness. Since then, other agencies have been included and the requirement has been changed to biennial reporting.

Lessons Learned

1. Although reports may cost more than anticipated, and appear to have little value to legislators and the public, they benefit internal operations.

2. Mandated performance reports are no quick fix for the ailments of government. That requires a change in thinking, discipline, and courage.
3. Make performance reports a regular legal requirement with the cooperation of the executive branch.
4. Legislators should not pass these laws without conducting hearings and teaming up the legislative and executive planning commissions with agency heads. Without this collaboration, it is difficult to build support for the concept.
5. In spite of initial difficulties, laws are helpful in compelling follow-through.
6. Provide performance measurement training as well as technical support, especially in developing objectives and collecting data. This would help many program managers (who are responsible for writing the bulk of performance reports), who are technical experts in their own area but have little knowledge of statistics, measurement, research methods, etc.
7. Allow time for performance reports to evolve.

Case 9. Performance Measurement; A Work in Progress: Minnesota's Department of Labor and Industry
Author: Wilkins, 1996

Performance measures were established in 1993 in response to the governor's challenge to agencies to measure results and report performance so that he and the legislature could effectively allocate and manage scarce financial resources.

Lessons Learned
1. You need the support of agency leadership for this change to happen, even if top elected officials make the decision to measure performance.
2. Designate a coordinator. You should not rely on managers to implement this type of change.
3. Provide quality performance measures training for managers and line staff.
4. Line staff acceptance is essential for success. A typical reaction is fear.
5. Think program results, not internal activities.
6. Incorporate performance measurement into the agency's strategic vision as the tool that measures progress toward achieving the goals.
7. Make performance reporting a routine element of daily operations.
8. Performance measurement needs time.

Case 10. Development and Use of Outcome Information in Government: Oregon Department of Transportation
Author: Bowden, 1996

The Oregon Department of Transportation developed performance measures in response to budget reductions and dissatisfaction with government accountability.

The effort began in 1988 as a pilot project that combined performance measures with a gain-sharing program.

Lessons Learned

1. The entire organization needs to be involved to achieve change.
2. Management must lead and reinforce the value of the effort.
3. Employee union organizations must be involved and kept informed.
4. Performance measures should be directly linked to organizational goals and direction.
5. Programs should be reviewed with internal auditors or with an independent party and corrections made accordingly.
6. The value of performance measures is related to their use.

Case 11. Strategic Budgeting in Texas: A Systems Approach to Planning, Budgeting, and Performance Measurement

Author: Merjanian, 1996

In the late 1980s, Texas was facing fiscal stress and budget shortfalls. There was no sense of mission and little goal setting. In addition, there was lack of accountability, which was leading to a crisis of confidence, and little decision-making data available to address the concern.

Lessons Learned

1. Successful agencies are characterized by sustained commitment of management teams, as well as meaningful participation by agency employees (for buy-in) and external stakeholders.
2. Performance data must be used in tangible ways. There must be a constant connection between information and action.
3. Development of outcome measures takes time and patience.
4. Although performance measurement systems are often imposed on agencies, there is little understanding as to the use of performance measurement information as a management strategy and the process to produce them. The benefits to using performance measures by the agency must be stressed.
5. There is a need for continued training and orientation, and creative use of information.
6. Performance measures, in particular outcome measures, are threatening to governmental organizations and elected officials. There is a need for commitment to overcome these challenges.
7. Incentives for effective participation and later for performance are important to keep the system moving forward. Penalties should be used sparingly, especially in the early phase, because of the data and time limitations required for system change.
8. Limit the amount of information presented to decision makers according to their needs.

9. Report regularly and publicly; this is essential to ensure system longevity and usefulness and in raising public awareness of and support for reform efforts.

Case 12. Utah Tomorrow
Author: Cannon, 1996

A performance measurement system was launched in 1990 by the Utah Tomorrow Strategic Planning Committee as a way to convince elected officials and public managers that there was a need for change.

Lessons Learned
1. All players must be involved in the process from its inception. Top leadership must constantly reinforce support.
2. Agency training must be incorporated early in the process.
3. There is a need for continued public involvement.
4. There should be a focus on media awareness.
5. Emphasis on voluntary participation may result in greater cooperation and a better product in the long run.
6. Developing a meaningful system takes time.
7. The information needs to be used and leaders need to show that it is being used.

Case 13. Integration of Business Plan, Strategic Plan, Customer Service Plan, Unit Self Assessment, and Employee Performance Appraisals, Washington State Department of Labor and Industries
Author: Christenson, 1996

The development and implementation of a quality initiative to help transform the agency into a competitive world-class organization began in 1990. The original plan emphasized the need for cultural changes to stay competitive in terms of customer service and quality products.

Lessons Learned
1. The connections of the different pieces are difficult for staff and executives.
2. Some employees may not see performance measures as a critical part of their daily work lives. As a result, performance measurement might be viewed as an add-on, making it difficult to obtain commitment.
3. The pace of change may seem very difficult.
4. It is difficult to convey the idea that no matter what the measurement requirements are for the federal government, the agency also needs to measure something else.

Part II

BUILDING THEORY IN SUPPORT OF PRACTICE THROUGH A MIXED METHODS APPROACH

Chapter 3

Theoretical Framework

The underlying argument of this book is that to advance the practice and theory of performance measurement in public organizations, we must move beyond the simplistic views of performance measurement as a rational activity without abandoning the rational goal of informed decision making. I approach this task by making two interrelated assumptions. First, effective utilization of performance measurement information involves the distinct stages of (a) the initial adoption of a performance measurement system and (b) the implementation of the system wherein the information yielded is actually used. The second assumption is that the two major perspectives used in understanding performance measurement and its use in performance management—the rational/technical perspective and the political/cultural perspective—need to be integrated for both general and specific reasons, the specific reason being that each perspective is most useful for explaining different aspects of the two stages. The general reason is that no attempt at developing theory would be complete without taking into account the contributions of each of these perspectives.

To develop the implications of these assumptions and the empirical work related to them, I begin with a general discussion of knowledge utilization that emphasizes the need to recognize that the utilization of performance measurement information is as a process. Then I address separately the rational/technocratic and political-cultural perspectives. To address each conceptual area, I present the hypotheses that are entailed. The chapter concludes with a summary that describes an integrated model of performance measurement and the methods used to further elaborate this model, which include examining moderated and mediated relationships. It is important to note that the process used here to build the model of utilization of performance measurement information is a general one that offers constructive advice on developing more adequate theoretical frameworks in other areas of public administration and nonprofit management.

Deconstructing Utilization

To begin with the examination of utilization of performance measures as a process, performance measurement was defined earlier as knowledge and innovation. What follows is an intuitively appealing theoretical framework for the understanding of the utilization of performance measurement. This framework builds on evidence from practice and the wealth of ideas advanced in different areas of study of organizational life. For example, one evident, yet rarely discussed and studied, phenomenon is the apparent disconnect that exists between having developed a performance measurement system and actually using the information. Relevant to understanding this apparent disconnect is what Cronbach et al. (1980) distinguished in program evaluation as policy adoption and program implementation. These authors noted that when policies are being adopted, there is a tendency to gain a larger audience and there is a greater mobilization of political interests in support of the policy. But when the policy has been adopted and the activities to execute the policy are implemented, controversies that did not surface earlier become more apparent. Similarly, Beyer and Trice (1982) developed this distinction when they argued that knowledge utilization is a behavioral process with two stages, adoption and implementation. They said that these two stages are similar to those often observed in the adoption and implementation of change and innovation. A review of studies of the practice and prevalence of performance measurement in the public sector reveals that the *adoption* (knowledge as capacity for action) of performance measures does not necessarily lead to their *implementation* (knowledge converted into action). Thus, we can assume that there are some organizational factors that may be responsible for this. Moreover, the factors that lead to adoption may be different from those that affect implementation. These assumptions can be tested using the following hypothesis:

> *Hypothesis 1: Utilization is composed of two distinct stages, adoption and implementation, each affected differentially by contextual factors.*

There are, as shown in Table 3.1, at least five distinctions underlying why we can expect the relationship to be contextual, and for different factors to affect these two presumed stages. First, there is the notion of knowledge as capacity for action versus knowledge converted into action. Adoption implies that the organization has the capacity (knowledge) to act. A capacity to act does not mean that activities will actually be devised and take place as a result of this capacity. Implementation, on the other hand, means that the capacity has been used to carry out the policy or make a decision. Therefore, implementation implies action on the part of those making use of the information.

Second, there is the notion of symbolic versus concrete action. Policies can have both symbolic and concrete effects. However, due to political factors, policies for change are not necessarily expected to be implemented. Thus, organizations may satisfy a policy requirement for using performance measurement information by

Table 3.1 Summary of Characteristics of Adoption and Implementation of Performance Measures

Adoption	*Implementation*
Knowledge as capacity for action	Knowledge converted into action
Symbolic action	Concrete action
Compliance	Real behavior
Internal consequences	External consequences
Risky	Riskier

focusing on adoption. Implementation, on the other hand, requires that organizations undertake some activity or have people working to implement the knowledge. These can range from dissemination of the information to reallocating resources and changing organizational processes. Third, a related point is that the adoption of performance measurement (i.e., developing performance measures) alone can qualify as compliance with regulations. That is, although the organization may comply by putting a performance measurement system in place, this compliance may have no effect on behavior. Implementation, on the other hand, may require the organization to change they way things are done. One example of this change might be instituting an incentive mechanism to encourage achievement of stated goals and to reward those who reach stated levels of performance. Thus, whereas adoption permits conformance to form or compliance, implementation is more about real behavioral change.

Fourth, while adoption of performance measures affects and involves internal stakeholders (managers and nonmanagers), the effect of implementation goes beyond the organization, affecting and being affected by external stakeholders. An example of implementation having an external consequence would be when performance knowledge supports calls for eliminating aspects of a program that has a substantial or very vocal constituency. The constituency might decide to mobilize to block the change. Likewise, external stakeholders can influence the organization if the performance knowledge shows that the organization is not fulfilling its mission. They may demand changes in the organization. Therefore, even though interest groups (informal groups composed of management and nonmanagement employees) can prove effective for gaining initial support for the performance measurement effort and avoiding conflicts, external interest groups (elected officials and citizens) and unions will be essential in pushing or inhibiting action. Thus, because of the consequences, adoption can be conceived of as having an internal impact, whereas implementation could have an external impact.

Lastly, because of the different audiences involved, adopting performance measures may be risky because of the possible course of action that performance measurement information may suggest, but the real risk is in implementing evidence-informed decision making based on the measures. For example, if performance measurement information is used as an accountability hammer, when organizations report that a program is operating inefficiently or ineffectively, the possible actions may include budget cuts, program restructuring, and even reorganization.

Given these five characteristics, I argue that we should not view the utilization of performance measurement as a monolithic concept. Instead, it is important to disaggregate the concept and view it as a multistage process with different stages affected differentially by contextual factors. Such an approach would allow us to formulate context-sensitive recommendations for promoting utilization.

But a model of utilization of performance measurement would not be complete without the examination of the relationship between the two stages discussed above. Further elaboration of the relationship between these two stages is necessary. One important argument that will be made throughout this chapter is that when it comes to change and innovation, adoption does not necessarily lead to implementation. This argument is as applicable to performance-based management (PBM), and performance measurement in particular, as it is to technological or any other policy innovation. Nevertheless, without adoption there cannot be implementation. Therefore, one needs to take the hypothesized effects of factors affecting implementation one step further to determine how these factors work along with adoption in explaining implementation. As such, it is hypothesized here that adoption is an intervening or mediating mechanism; thus:

> *Subhypothesis 1a: The effects of the factors that affect implementation are also channeled through adoption.*

To be certain, finding out if the different theories and their associated factors described throughout these pages help explain the adoption and implementation of performance measures would be useful. However, focusing on this alone would be a limiting approach. The more interesting finding would be how each of these theories and factors work together in a model. The examination of mediating processes that produce estimated effects is an excellent approach for this purpose (Judd and Kenny, 1981).

Performance Measurement Adoption and Implementation as Knowledge Utilization

As illustrated in the literature and the American Society for Public Administration's (ASPA) case studies of government and governmental organizations experimenting with performance measurement, internal and external accountability, and the need for knowledge in management decision making are central to the impetus for performance measurement. However, in the social sciences, and the policy sciences in particular, information for decision making has been criticized for being excessively rationalistic. The result, contend critics, is that the information goes unused. Indeed, the study of knowledge utilization itself came about because of a deep disenchantment with what some viewed as rationalistic policy research. More specific to the topic of this book, performance measurement as an analytical tool for decision making in the public sector also confronts questions of utilization.

Although the state of the art of performance measurement is often said to be well advanced, the question remains as to why measurement of performance indicators appears not to be widely used. This question leads to another important question: What policies should facilitate knowledge use? Historical evidence suggests that external political pressure plays a role in the behavior of organizations. Often political changes have dictated whether policy analysis, knowledge production, is needed and what modes of analysis should be used (de Leon, 1988). Furthermore, these political changes, argued de Leon (1988), tend to create a demand for the application of science to actual social problems that validated the problem orientation criteria forwarded by its advocates. The mandates to use Zero-Based Budgeting (ZBB) or Planning Programming Budgeting System (PPBS), and more recently Government Performance and Results Act (GPRA) and the Program Assessment Rating Tool (PART), can be seen as examples of policy that affect the kinds of analysis that public organizations are expected to engage in and also embody the value system of their advocates.

As can be concluded then, the arguments, critiques, and hypotheses advanced particularly in the field of policy development are quite relevant to our understanding of utilization of performance measurement. In that performance measurement is a tool for the creation of knowledge that can be used for making decisions that affect programs, and thus affecting policy at both the microlevel (organization) and macrolevel (systemwide), it falls under the realm of policy sciences and particularly policy analysis. Therefore, the issues affecting the policy sciences, as well as the growing skepticism that began in the decade of the 1970s, when many wondered about the significance of the policy sciences, should be part of the analytical framework for those interested in studying the utilization of performance measurement information.

An important concern in the policy sciences has been the short-run and long-run usefulness of social sciences and research for social problem solving (Lindblom and Cohen, 1979). According to F. Fischer (1994), critiques range from an attack on its dominant methodological orientation, empiricism that rules out social and political evaluation, to "an attempt to locate an interest in sociotechnical control within social science methodology itself." This questioning of the use of scientific and technical knowledge made utilization research of crucial relevance for public decision making (Wingens, 1990). Ironically, knowledge utilization itself is often discussed or understood primarily in technical terms, which generally assumes the separation of politics from administration. Thus, F. Fischer (1994) argued that a theory of organization must take into consideration the political environment in which public organizations operate. Politics has a role in shaping organization's practice. Moreover, evidence from the work of Pettigrew (1973), Pettigrew et al.

(1992), and Pfeffer (1981, 1983) has shown that in reality politics and administration are intertwined. Thus, we should also expect knowledge utilization to mirror this relationship.

In addition, Pettigrew et al. (1992) have called attention to another important factor in organizational life. They have stressed the central role that organizational culture has in framing what occurs in organizations. Even though performance measurement is supposed to measure and guide an organization's productivity and improvement, it may be argued that political factors, both external and internal to the organization, as well as cultural factors provide the context for utilization of performance measurement information. The political paradigm has a larger focus on more cultural aspects of organizations and also is largely concerned with organizational conflict. The rational paradigm has tended to focus more on formal factors such as structure, but also includes factors such as resources and technical capacity.

Here these two views are reconciled recognizing their difference in emphases. This reconciliation is modeled in Figure 3.1. In the sections ahead I discuss the components of this model.

The Knowledge Utilization Framework

While not complete, the knowledge utilization literature provides a useful foundation for understanding the utilization of performance measurement information. Since the beginning of the 1970s, there has been an explosion of research trying to explain the use or lack of use of social science research. In spite of the proliferation of utilization studies, some have argued that utilization research theory remains underdeveloped, with no utilization theory proven to have explanatory

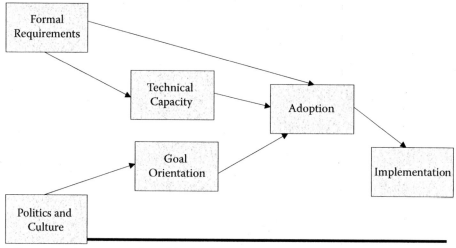

Figure 3.1 A conceptual model of utilization of performance measures. Adapted from de Lancer Julnes (2004).

power based on empirical testing (Wingens, 1990; Landry et al., 2001). Indeed, the large body of research on knowledge utilization consists mostly of normative studies and case studies "cohabitating with a rather small pool of quantitative studies" (Landry et al., 2001). According to Dunn and Holzner (1988), the study of research utilization proceeded under four broadly accepted theses about the nature of contemporary knowledge systems. But a lack of satisfaction with the explanations they provided elicited an ongoing debate regarding the need to find causal explanations for knowledge utilization (Dunn and Holzner, 1988; Stehr, 1992).

This lack of satisfaction with current models may be due to what Rich (1991) has characterized as an unfortunate practice of researchers: failing to consciously build on the research of others. As a result, claimed Rich, the "wheel" has been reinvented on many different occasions. This lack of attention to what others have done contributes to the proliferation of inadequate theories and does not help in the elaboration of suggestions for improving practice. This lesson is not going to go unlearned here. In fact, what is being presented in the following pages and has been argued throughout this book thus far is the need to integrate this knowledge to come up with more viable and sustainable models for promoting knowledge use in the context of performance management.

To begin the integration, I examine here the dominant model of inquiry in knowledge utilization, the two communities metaphor (Wingens, 1990; Nelson et al., 1987; Dunn, 1980). It should be noted that other bodies of theories have been drawn from to guide knowledge utilization studies, as well as to promote intervention strategies, but the two-communities theory remained dominant (Jacobson, 2007). The term *two communities* evolved from Snow's (1959) cultural conception of the difference between those in the natural sciences and those in the humanities (Wingens, 1990). Snow (1959) writes:

> *The non-scientists have a rooted impression that the scientists are shallowly optimistic, unaware of man's condition. On the other hand, the scientists believe that the literary intellectuals are totally lacking in foresight, peculiarly unconcerned with their brother men, in a deep sense anti-intellectual, anxious to restrict both art and thought to the existential moment. (p. 5)*

The differences between these two groups are based on what Snow termed the "two cultures." By definition, the two-communities metaphor is based on cultural differences. It is a metaphor that has allowed researchers to draw conclusions about nonutilization based on the differences between the social science and policy-making communities (Dunn, 1980).

While Dunn (1980) argued that the two-communities metaphor is useful because the problem of knowledge use is fundamentally cultural, Wingens (1990) argued that it was precisely that culturalistic view about knowledge that did not allow the development of sound theory building in the field of utilization research. The simultaneous presumption and explanation for lack of utilization is the weakness of the two communities (Wingens, 1990). As such, he advocated the development of a system theory that will go beyond individualistic behavior and orientations and that takes into consideration the context of use.

Conspicuously missing from all of the models or approaches to understand knowledge utilization is the role of politics. Cohen (1977) has lamented that "despite the fact that utilization would seem to be greatly influenced by organizational features, there exists no discrete body of knowledge explicating the relationship between organizational characteristics and research utilization and implementation." Holzner and Fisher (1979) have argued that knowledge utilization occurs in political arenas and stressed the need to investigate the different arenas surrounding knowledge utilization. With a few exceptions (notably the work of Elliott and Popay [2000], Hanney et al. [2003], and Lester and Wilds [1990] which draw from theories in political science and policy studies), the literature of knowledge utilization has continued to overlook the political arena by only focusing on explaining utilization/nonutilization based on cultural differences between the researchers and the users. Likewise, because the cultural focus has been almost exclusively on individual's perceptions of knowledge, researchers have also overlooked organizational culture.

To remedy the lack of attention to these factors two decades ago Sunesson and Nilsson (1988) called for a sociological analysis of the context where the use of research takes place. This context is what the authors call utilization context. In their case study of welfare departments in 15 Swedish cities and towns, utilization context was defined as an organizational concept that refers to the different control, power, and conflict patterns that affect the way research is used in the organization. Power and conflict patterns of different utilization contexts seemed to decide the way knowledge and research were used in the organizations they studied. These patterns of power and conflict are what the political model of organizational theory tries to bring to light.

In a more recent study of knowledge utilization at mental health government organizations, Oh and Rich (1996) attempted to develop an integrated model of knowledge use, including the political factor. In their study, Oh and Rich interviewed 60 federal and 419 state and local policy makers in a representative sample of 18 states. They developed and tested a model that included:

1. Organizational characteristics (defined in terms of the decision maker's position in the organization and the presence of organizational incentive systems)
2. Environmental factors (whether the policy issues were familiar to the decision maker)
3. Decision maker's characteristics (measured in terms of attitudes toward social science information, need for information, and perceptions of policy making as a political activity)
4. Characteristics of information (referred to source—internal or external, amount of information received, content of information, and type of information—statistical data, program evaluation, demonstration projects, and policy analysis)

The authors selected two policy areas within mental health: service provision and financing. These two areas were selected, according to the authors, to represent two different modes of decision making: the political and the technical. The service area is perceived as being one where the political mode of decision making is the preferable choice. In this mode, decision making is primarily achieved by compromise and bargaining. In contrast, the financial area is perceived as the technical mode of decision making. In this mode, operating work is complex; thus, it necessitates the expertise of highly trained professionals.

Yet, the study underplayed the influence of politics and did not pay explicit attention to organizational culture. The authors operationalized the role of politics by creating two questions based on a 5-point scale. They asked respondents how much they thought decisions are made through political activities and whether they (respondents) based their decisions on the findings of research rather than compromise with other stakeholders. The study found that information utilization is directly and indirectly affected by a variety of factors and not a unitary set of factors defined by a single perspective. Political perception, in particular, was found to have a statistically negligent effect on information utilization in the financial area, and a larger effect ($b = .214$, or 21 percent probability) in the service area. According to the author, these findings indicate that in the service area of mental health, information is more likely to be used as a political resource. These findings may be interesting because they appear to support the notion that in the more "rational" world (in this case financial services) politics do not have a place, but is more prevalent in the "softer" world of service provision. It will be argued in the pages ahead that theory and empirical evidence supports the view that politics plays a major role even in seemingly rational processes. This is also supported by other findings and methodological choices highlighted Oh and Rich's (1996) work. First, the authors found that stakeholders seem to have a major role in the process of knowledge utilization. This role is further examined in the research conducted to answer the questions guiding this book. Second, Oh and Rich's findings highlighted that knowledge utilization in public organizations is more dynamic and complex than previously acknowledged. Thus, to get as accurate a picture as possible of this concept, multiple perspectives are needed.

Finally, Oh and Rich also used position of respondents as an explanatory variable. The authors explained that a variety of norms and behaviors are expected for people in positions at different levels in the organization. Thus, for example, decision makers in different positions use information to define problems differently, and those at higher levels in the organization's hierarchy are expected to have different perspectives than those at lower levels. Furthermore, explained the authors, decision makers tend to use information that comes from internal sources because they trust it and think that it will support the organization's goals (Oh and Rich, 1996). A parallel claim can be made here.

Given the current demands for more accountability in government and for demonstrating results, those at higher levels in the organization may tend to protect their organization by saying that performance measures have been adopted and implemented. Such statements would make the organization look good because decision makers will be perceived as responsive to demands. Therefore, those at higher levels, who are ultimately responsible to the public, may have a vested interest in showing that their organization is doing that which is supposed to help them advance their organization's goals. This incentive may not be there for lower-level employees. To account for this possibility, position of the respondent will be used here as a control variable.

Certainly Oh and Rich (1996) and other scholars, have made important contributions to the improvement of the theory in the field of knowledge utilization. However, while it is important for the field to identify the different factors that affect the process of knowledge use, I argue that a reconciliation of the rational and political paradigms will prove more fruitful in helping to move the field forward. With that in mind, I explain below why, when elaborated in terms of the two stages of knowledge utilization claimed in this book, the rational factors will be more important for adoption and the political-cultural for implementation.

The Rational Model of Organizational Innovation and Change

A cursory review of the traditional organizational theory quickly reveals that managerial tools such as program evaluation and performance measurement, and the changes that they bring about when adopted and implemented, are often discussed within the realm of managerial goals as presented by the rational model and its modern variants (Cronbach et al., 1980; Howard and Schneider, 1994). The rational model views organizations as instruments for efficient goal attainment (Fischer, 1986). The orientation of this model is mechanistic in that organizations are conceived as being made of different parts that can be modified by applying rational planning based on scientific analysis to achieve the efficiency of the whole (Gouldner, 1959).

Performance measurement has largely been based on the rational model and positivistic methodology (e.g., operation research, cost-benefit analysis, econometrics regression). Mann (1986) criticized some of the assumptions embedded in these approaches. Particularly relevant here is his contention that one of the assumptions that must be overcome is that "because organizational change is a matter of rationality, policy decisions or directives will automatically elicit desired behaviors."

Nonetheless, the rational model has offered many insights about change in organization. The insight here is that in line with the rational-political contrast, the more formal and symbolic the rational factors, the more they will affect adoption. The more concrete these factors, the more they will affect both. Therefore, one can hypothesize the following:

Hypothesis 2: Rational factors will have a greater impact on adoption than on implementation.

I illustrate this by beginning with those rational factors that are more formal and sometimes symbolic. Thus, the first factor to be addressed is formal requirements, the second is goal orientation, and the third is resources.

Formal Politics as Rationality: External and Internal Requirements

In citing Croly (1909) and Weyl (1912), Martin (1992) stated that the progressive movement, one of the earliest examples of the role of politics in administration in American history, followed the notion that with help from government the political and economic wealth of the nation would rise. This belief was widely held and was described by Martin (1992) as one of the more overpowering expressions of unity and optimism ever seen in the American political system. This optimism culminated with 75 percent of the voters in 1912 selecting a progressive candidate.

In spite of its clear political impact, the progressive movement has been often interpreted as an expression of support for the separation of politics and administration. Administration was viewed as a technical question, and politics was thought of as a malady that inhibited administration (Goodnow, 1900; Bouckaert, 1992). Though the premises of the politics/administration dichotomy was that there would be a nonpartisan administrative state where policies were determined by politicians and executed efficiently by neutral administrators, practice showed this dichotomy to be nothing more than an illusion.

The New Deal programs that followed the Great Depression are examples of how politics, wanted or not, continued to exert its influence on administration. The President's Committee on Administrative Management (1937) was driven in significant part by a political goal to give the president more power. Furthermore, the adoption of Keynesian theory as the dominant paradigm, which states that an unregulated economy is not self-correcting but needs the guidance of governmental policy, is a telling example of how formal politics affects the activity of public organizations.

Another example is President Lyndon Johnson's 1965 order requiring the Department of Health, Education, and Welfare to implement the Planning Programming Budgeting System (PPBS) as practiced in the Department of Defense (deLeon, 1988). One can also argue that during the Reagan administration politics also motivated the strong concern for cutting costs, which in turn contributed to the present emphasis on improving and measuring public productivity and performance. Reagan's Executive Order 12552 provided for a more comprehensive productivity improvement program whose goal was to have a 20 percent increase in productivity by 1992 (Rich and Winn, 1992). Furthermore, another executive order (No. 12291), which institutionalized cost-benefit analysis as a must-do for agencies proposing rules with an estimated cost to the economy of $100 million or more, makes it clear that political involvement in the form of requirements has a place in an organization's performance and accountability improvement efforts.

Likewise, more recently the GPRA legislation has focused on institutionalizing mechanisms such as strategic planning and the specification of goals and objectives that are aligned with the mission of the organization. This, state Simeone et al. (2005), reflects Congress's desire to apply "principles of accountability to the provision of public goods and services." Certainly we can logically argue that these are desirable practices for management, but we can also argue that they have political implications. GPRA, as well as previous and current efforts to make government more accountable and efficient, has followed a number of political "sound bites," which include the late former president Reagan's aphorism: "Government is not the solution to our problem; government is the problem." The efforts have also been inspired by practices such as Total Quality Management (TQM) adopted in the private sector, and the suggestions of the popular book *Reinventing Government*, whose focus was on making government run more like a business.

Furthermore, in that performance measurement initiatives such as GPRA are part of government efforts to cut expenditures, the clear implication is that efficiency improvements will lead to decreasing the budget and thus managerial power (Flynn, 1986; Cavalluzzo and Ittner, 2003). The possibility of such outcomes could become a disincentive for managers to support performance measurement initiatives. Related, there has been a demoralizing trend in American public administration, particularly during times of economic downturn, that has caused strident calls to reassess public bureaucracies and to mandate change. As Caiden (1991) has pointed out, the blame for anything that goes wrong is often placed in the "dead hand of bureaucracy." He suggests that there is a perception of poor performance, "daily annoyances of irksome restrictions, cumbrous red-tape, unpleasant officials, poor service and corrupt practices." With these assumptions on their backs, how can public agencies be expected to view performance management initiatives and demands for more and better performance in a positive manner and react in a technically rational way?

For all these reasons, one can credibly argue that the environment in which public administration operates is political. A parallel argument can be made for nonprofit organizations, particularly regarding the impact that external politics in the form of pressure to adopt a particular way of analysis has on these organizations. Specifically, the pressure comes from large donors who have been increasingly requiring grantees and contractors to adopt outcome-based performance management processes.

Rainey (1997) has argued that even formal authority always operates in a political context. It is exercised through formal, rule-making, or legal authority. This, however, may weaken or bolster it in practical terms. The result is that even when policy is formulated, its implementation is not necessarily ensured. And even after the policy is formulated, and programs implemented, the continuity is not guaranteed by how successful the program is running. This is illustrated by the case of the National Drug Control Policy and its experimentation with performance-based management. Simeone et al. (2005) reported that even though the program was found by third parties to be exemplary and in spite of "broad acceptance, a project that began as a 10-year program ended within four years of implementation."

Furthermore others have suggested that policy makers do not necessarily expect policies for change to be implemented (Korman and Glennerster, 1985; Pettigrew et al., 1992). There are several reasons for this. One of them is that for elected officials, and particularly congressional and state legislators, their main concerns and motivation, which is reelection, are set in a short-term horizon. This is incompatible with the performance measurement mandates such as GPRA, which requires long-range decision making (Jones and McCaffery, 1997). Another reason is that, in general, policies are enacted to satisfy some party pressure, or require their supporters to compromise so much to get the votes, that they leave them too vague and void of details on how they should be implemented (Long and Franklin, 2004).

Thus, according to Korman and Glennerster (1985), public servants "know that they need not strain themselves too hard to achieve results." They are able to satisfy a law or administrative regulation (external requirement) for using performance measures by focusing only on policy adoption (developing the measures) and collecting information without effectively implementing the policy (actually using the information). This phenomenon is what was referred to earlier as "symbolic action," and substantiates the claim that there is a difference in the way different factors affect adoption and implementation of performance measurement information. Therefore, one would expect that a law or administrative regulation (external requirements) requiring public organizations to use performance measures will have minimal effect on the adoption and implementation of performance measures. However, we can also expect the following:

Subhypothesis 2a: Formal requirements will have more effect on adoption than on implementation.

In essence, given the arguments presented above, the expectation is that if external requirements do indeed influence adoption, this effect represents a symbolic commitment to the utilization of performance measures. This expectation is supported by empirical findings of previous innovations in government such as PPBS, Management by Objective (MBO), and ZBB, which, for the most part, were adopted for the sake of gaining legitimacy by conforming to external expectations, but did very little in the way of improving decision making and performance, as envisioned by proponents of these initiatives (Cavalluzzo and Ittner, 2003). Thus, according to Cavalluzzo and Ittner (2003), while the development of results-oriented performance measures will continue to increase, it will have very little effect on encouraging organizations to use the information, improve accountability, or improve performance.

Conversely, the experience of public organizations with performance measures suggests that it is when organizations voluntarily decide to use performance measures that the system is more successful. In the State of Utah, the Utah Tomorrow Strategic Planning Committee concluded that if they were to mandate performance measurement, it would cause the agencies to move slowly (Cannon, 1996). Voluntary cooperation of the agency, rather than an external requirement coming from outside the agency, would lead to a better product in the long run. Likewise, a more recent study of Utah Tomorrow suggests that agency leadership's commitment appears to be even more important in predicting the staying power of these initiatives than external requirements (de Lancer Julnes and Mixcoatl, 2006).

It is also the case that formal requirements lead to internal requirements. But the argument being made here is that the greater the proximity of these internal requirements to those affected by them, the more that these requirements tend to be more specific and concrete than external ones. Thus, whether or not this apparent commitment is in response to an external requirement, agencies that have internal policies for performance measurement can be expected to have more commitment than agencies without such policies. Therefore, we can expect that an internal policy (self-imposed requirement) that requires the organization to have performance measures will have a stronger effect than an external policy. This internal requirement may represent buy-in and an important commitment to make performance measurement work. As a result, it should facilitate implementation through the mechanisms that it may help to create to put this internal policy into practice. Because of this, we can posit that given their proximity:

> *Subhypothesis 2b: Internal requirements will have a stronger effect on adoption than external requirements.*

In that an internal requirement is dependent on leadership's commitment to the effort, the ephemeral nature of agency leadership, particularly for appointed leaders, make implementation heavily dependent on the leaders' ability to stay even after a change in administration. Therefore, unless performance management has been institutionalized, once the leader in charge of the effort leaves, the effort is likely to fade away.

Guiding Actions through Goals: A Rational/ Technocratic Perspective

Although the relationships that were hypothesized in the previous sections are a step beyond what previous studies have done to understand and explain innovation and change in organizations, a refined model of utilization of performance measures like the one being developed here would not be complete without the more concrete rational/technocratic factors. These factors have implications for the utilization of performance measurement. Therefore, instead of undermining the importance of these factors, I put them in their appropriate context—within a cultural and political organizational framework. Indeed, even purely political theories of organizational behavior do not seek to exclude rationality or the role of technical considerations in their explanation of what goes on in organizations. What they do is argue for putting such considerations within the realm of the political paradigm (Fischer, 1986).

One of such rational/technical considerations is organizational goals. Goals and objectives are instrumental to PBM. In fact, a well-managed organization is said to be one where actions are guided by its goals and objectives, which should in turn reflect the organization's mission. In the rational model, organizations are presumed to be goal oriented, with goals guiding everything the organization does. Furthermore, those conducting the case studies highlighted in Chapter 2 of this book indicated that the mission and strategies for achieving organizational goals are often developed and modified because of the organization's interest in performance measurement (Blanche-Kapplen and Lissman, 1996; Bryant, 1996; Berry and Ikerd, 1996; Curcio, 1996). This reciprocal relationship is reflected in the arguments presented in Chapter 1 of this book and the model of PBM depicted in Figure 1.1 earlier.

Similarly, in program evaluation, Attkisson et al. (1978) found that for evaluation to be useful there must be a consensus on program goals. The assumption is that organizations will reach a consensus on goals, and that these are going to be clear goals, and therefore will lead to knowledge that will be more likely to be used. However, as explained in Chapter 2 of this book, organizations often encounter difficulties when they attempt to become goal oriented, developing clear and objective goals that are agreed upon by all and using those goals to develop strategies for achieving stated goals. These difficulties are magnified when one considers political aspects such as conflict and culture, which tend to limit the effect that a goal orientation can have on any process of change and innovation, including that of utilization of performance measurement information. A goal orientation may be important in helping the organization start the process, and although necessary for continuation of the effort, it will not be enough to implement and sustain it. Thus, the effect of goal orientation will be more evident at the adoption stage of performance measures. That is:

> *Subhypothesis 2c: Organizations with high goal orientation are more likely to adopt than those with low goal orientation.*

Organizational Resources as Technical Capacity

As suggested by Howard and Schneider (1994) in their critique of what they referred to as a technocentric (or rational/technocratic) approach, which is deeply rooted in the traditions of scientific management, the adoption of performance measures and the subsequent utilization of the information would be considered a purely technical issue. In that traditionally one of the goals of performance measurement has been to increase efficiency, the expectation is for experts to be in charge of managing the system. There is not much room for meaningful participation of other employees, nor does this technocratic view recognize the conflicts that could arise from introducing such a change in the organization, as suggested by the political and cultural model mentioned above. Interestingly, the idea of experts in charge is also consistent with the two-communities metaphor discussed earlier, which separates the producers of knowledge ("the experts") from the consumers of knowledge.

Using the computerization of a workplace as an example of an innovation, Howard and Schneider (1994) stated that in the technocentric model:

> *The goal of workplace technological change is to increase efficiency by mechanizing production and reducing labor costs. And the design and implementation of new technical systems is the special responsibility of technical specialists. (p. 121)*

As a result, in the case of performance measurement, according to the rational/technocratic model, the development and use of information will depend on whether certain conditions, such as experts in charge, managerial control, systematic standardization, and work fragmentation and mechanization (the principles of scientific management), are present.

For our purposes, the rational/technocratic conditions, which represent available organizational resources, a concrete influence on the process of change, are operationalized as a technical capacity that includes commitment of resources (people, time, etc.), management trained in the latest techniques (Grifel, 1994), and frequency of access to information as well as use of benchmarks and availability of valid data (Wilkins, 1996; Weidner and Noss-Reavely, 1996; Berry and Ikerd, 1996; Holzer and Halachmi, 1996). The importance of these factors is illustrated by the experiences reviewed earlier of public organizations that have experimented with performance measurement. The experiences called attention to the importance of committing resources, having staff devoted to evaluation of performance measures, and collecting adequate data.

Moreover, consistent with the assumptions of the rational/technocratic view, the Iowa Council of Human Investment and Minnesota's Department of Labor and Industry came to the realization that having the technical knowledge of how to conduct and implement performance measurement was critical to their success in developing and implementing such systems (Weidner and Noss-Reavely 1996; Wilkins 1996). This kind of knowledge can be acquired through systematic training or by having adequate access to information on performance measurement. Furthermore, experience shows that organizations also turn to available information to learn how to develop performance measures (Tracy, 1996).

Therefore, as suggested by the rational/technocratic model, technical capacity plays a critical role, but it also has the distinction of being a concrete factor. And as a result, we should expect capacity to have an important influence on adoption and implementation. This leads to:

> *Subhypothesis 2d: Organizations with a high level of technical capacity are more likely to adopt and implement than organizations with low levels of capacity.*

Mediating Effects

The overall assumption here is that factors identified by the rational model will have an important role. However, because these factors influence a process that takes place within organizations, and this process is particularly influenced by politics and culture, it is also safe to speculate that some of these rational factors may mediate the effect of other factors influencing the process of adoption and implementation of performance measures.

That is, they may be in part the result of pressures, such as requirements, interest groups, and culture. Thus, in addition to their expected direct effect, they will have an intervening or mediating effect on adoption and implementation of performance measures. In other words, goal orientation and technical capacity can very well be affected by the impetus for performance measurement when supported by requirements, politics, and culture. Therefore one can hypothesize the following:

> *Subhypothesis 2e: Goal orientation and technical capacity will be partly explained by the influence of requirements, politics, and culture.*

The Political-Cultural Model

The debate about the significance of politics in organizations is part of a larger debate about constructing a more adequate theory of organizations. The rational view presented above assumed that the interests of all employees, management and nonmanagement, could be aligned relatively easily with the interests of the organization. An ensuing political critique was that conflict is inherent in organizations and must be given a central place in organizational theory. Specifically, scholars like Pfeffer (1981, 1983), Pettigrew (1973), Fischer (1986), and Howard and Schneider (1994) have argued that politics is central to organization behavior, and have criticized the rational perspective for neglecting the role of context and powerful groups within organizations. Such neglect has led to myths about the rational nature of problem-solving processes in organizations.

In the rational model of organizations, a key assumption is that policy decisions and legal mandates will automatically lead to the desired action. Furthermore, it assumes that organizations that are goal-oriented and have resources available will pretty much have no excuse to not follow through on these mandates. These assumptions are challenged here. The argument that I'm developing in this book is that while such factors may be sufficient for adoption, the follow through to implementation requires the presence of other factors necessary to support effort. Thus, for example, it was alluded to earlier that when there are conflicting interests groups in the organization, actual implementation will be affected by these interest groups. Therefore, successful implementation will require devising strategies for appropriately channeling the effect of interest groups.

Organizational culture is another important aspect of organizational theory that has a direct impact on the likelihood of success of PBM. Organizational culture, a key component of the focus of the political model of organizations, serves as a shaper of belief systems (Pettigrew et al., 1992). In referring to their study of change in the British National Health System, Pettigrew et al. (1992) emphasized that the recognition that culture can shape and not just reflect organizational power relationships directs attention to the ground rules that structure the political processes within the different organizational units, and "the assumptions and interest which powerful groups shielded and lesser groups may only with fortitude challenge."

Sometimes the culture of an organization has to change in order for innovations such as PBM to achieve their full potential. This was noted more than a decade ago by Marshall (1996), when reviewing the experience with performance measurement of Prince William County. Ten years later, in 2006, Prince William County received a certificate of distinction from the International City/County Management Association (ICMA) Center for Performance Measurement. This award recognizes communities that incorporate performance measurement into the management of their jurisdictions. Prince William County sustained its effort, and PBM became part of what the county does; it is part of the management culture.

The British National Health System and the Prince William County examples highlight the saliency of organizational politics. The argument to be explored below is that because of the perceived risk and potential impact that implementing performance measurement information could have on the various interest groups, an organizational culture that reflects an openness to change will be particularly important in encouraging the actual use (implementation) of performance measures. The overall argument is:

> *Hypothesis 3: Politics and culture will have a greater effect on the implementation stage of the process of performance measurement utilization than on the adoption stage.*

As with the rational model described above, which began with more formal factors and led to more concrete factors, in this I will begin with those political factors that are more in line with the rational goal orientation and move toward those that emphasize conflict.

Interest Groups

Internal Politics

Organizational change produces conflicts, which are often resolved by internal political processes such as the formation of interest groups or coalitions, bargaining, and side payments (Fischer, 1986; Mann, 1986; Harvey and Mills, 1970; Pfeffer 1981, 1983). Understanding how these political processes affect organizational change should be of particular concern for those trying to bring change in an organizational setting.

According to Fischer (1986), modern administrative techniques tend to obscure the social origins and political implications of an organization's goals. In that respect, since the late 1970s alternative approaches have been used to reformulate organizational theory in explicit political terms. The focus of the political model is to bring together the "full array of competing interests into organizational theory" (Fischer, 1986). Practice provides evidence for the need of such an approach to theory building. For example, in her account of the use of outcome information in Prince William County, Marshall (1996) stated that because of the resources and time that need to be allocated and the commitment necessary to develop a performance measurement system, managing for results is political. Furthermore, as long as information (in our case performance measurement information) is used as an instrument or basis for changing power relationships within or among institutions, generating information is a political activity (Rich and Oh, 1994). Furthermore, control over knowledge and information shapes politics in organizations.

Thus, management scholars have warned against the dangers of overlooking power and politics within organizations (e.g., Yates, 1985). In that respect, the political model focuses on the power structures that underlie both the formal and informal structures of the organization and how these structures shape the operations of the organization as a whole. Power, as defined by Dahl (1957), is the ability of one person to make another do something that the latter would not have done otherwise. And Pfeffer (1981) defines organizational politics as the activity undertaken by individuals and groups "within organizations to acquire, develop, and use power ... to obtain ... preferred outcomes in a situation in which there is uncertainty or dissensus about choice." Therefore, to understand the internal patterns of organizational politics, it is essential that we recognize that exercising formal authority is not the only expression of politics; there are other ways to influence behavior that can also be considered organizational politics. Political influence in the political model is a dynamic, multidimensional phenomenon that moves vertically and horizontally. Indeed, influence is the "currency of organizational change" (Fischer, 1986).

One way to exercise influence is through the creation of interest groups and coalitions within organizations. Although cooperation is essential when instituting new policies, it is not spontaneous and must be developed. The introduction of innovation inevitably imposes change, which in many cases results in resistance. In particular, "any significant change demands that existing ways of thinking about and talking about what we do be overturned; dominant views must be usurped" (Carnall, 1995). As a result, new structures are erected by those who fear change and those seeking change to meet the new demands. The experience of the Department of Labor in Minnesota clearly shows that fear is a typical reaction of line staff. But "when they understand that performance measurement can help them accomplish their job and do it more efficiently, they often become more interested in its potential" (Wilkins, 1996). This experience is not unique to performance measurement. At a recent meeting, a secretary of a state department of human services said that instituting personnel and new strategies for improving services at her agency was an uphill battle. While some employees welcomed the new ideas, others did not get interested until they were convinced that these strategies would make their jobs much easier. Thus, change opens and closes opportunities for competing groups. Interest groups may emerge to protect existing resources and to exploit new access to power (Fischer, 1986). Likewise, political processes such as coalition formation, bargaining, and side payments are often used to resolve these conflicts brought about by the need to adapt to change (Harvey and Mills, 1970).

Moreover, in his study of the innovative decision-making activity of a computer firm, Pettigrew (1973) pointed out that innovative decisions are a special source of political behavior because of their impact on the organization's distribution of resources. Pettigrew defines political behavior as "behavior by individuals, or in collective terms, by sub-units, within the organization that makes a claim against the resource-sharing system of the organization." The resources could be salaries, promotion opportunities, capital expenditure, new equipment, or control over people, information, or new areas of a business. Certainly, any kind of resource reallocation is a political issue because inevitably some will perceive themselves as losers and others will be perceived as winners.

Managers are key actors in the struggle over resources; thus, having their support is crucial when it comes to the implementation of change. Managers have the ability to provide resources, focus organizational goals and strategies on the innovation, use their political weight to motivate support for the innovation, or derail activities of individuals and coalitions who resist it.

At the same time, it would be naïve to overlook the fact that as with line staff, managers may feel anxious about change and innovation and the need to adapt. They may see change and innovation as highly ambiguous, and their reactions will depend on how they perceive the change and innovation will affect their jobs, status, and personal ambitions (Mumford and Ward, 1966). This fear may not be ill-founded. As explained by Pettigrew (1973), when adopting technological innovations, "the changes computer technologists recommend may alter the functions of management and perhaps eliminate some management positions altogether. Therefore, unlike normal staff advisers, the new specialist represents a threat to the job and power positions of many line managers." An example of such an outcome in the public sector can be found in Oregon. One of the results of adopting and implementing performance measurement at the Oregon Department of Transportation was the elimination of one-third, or 400, of all management positions (Bowden, 1996). This may be a positive result for the organization as a whole; however, it is doubtful that the line managers involved perceived it as such.

Thus, as suggested by Rainey (1997), because organizations are composed of interdependent systems, whenever there is a significant change that may alter organizational life, dealing with uncertainty becomes an important task. As a result, F. Fischer (1994) argues that coalitions with interest groups have emerged as a way for managers to gain control and influence over the possibility of conflict by means of improved communication, participation, and improved supervision. He adds that in reality these internal interest groups are used as a way to indoctrinate workers to management's point of view, a rather cynical interpretation of managerial action. This is not necessarily the position I take here. After all, working with these interest groups and creating a venue for collaboration that emphasizes mutual gain is likely the only way to obtain the necessary buy-in from those who may be affected the most by the change being introduced in the organization.

Indeed, Patton's (1978) findings in his study of the utilization of evaluation research showed that if there is any hope for evaluation results to be utilized, the evaluation process must include the identification and involvement of all relevant decision makers and information users. That is, individuals for whom information makes a difference, who are willing to share responsibility for the evaluation and its utilization, who can use the information, and who have questions they want to have answered, should be part of the process. Likewise, one of the lessons learned by Marshall (1996) was that involving internal stakeholders (such as management and staff) in the performance measurement efforts can lead to a greater understanding of the reasons for undertaking the effort and the consequences. This understanding can lead to more support for the effort.

Therefore, if it is true that forming coalitions could help to control internal conflict brought about by the uncertainty of change, one would expect these interest groups to have a positive impact on the utilization process. However, given that actions that may be taken as a result of performance measurement information could have an adverse effect on employees, we have to be prepared for other factors to dominate the implementation stage. Thus, we may find a strong positive effect on coalitions on adoption, but a smaller impact on implementation. We can hypothesize the following:

Subhypothesis 3a: Because of politics, internal coalitions (internal interest groups) will be important in the adoption of performance measures, but for implementation other factors are expected to predominate.

External Politics

The political model of organizations also contemplates the impact of external interest groups or stakeholders on organizational change. Those promoting changes in an organization should not only be concerned about getting buy-in of internal interest groups, but if the changes have any kind of external impact, it may be necessary to enlist the support of external stakeholders; otherwise, conflict and opposition may occur. Consider the conflict that may ensue if performance measures are implemented by using the information to cut a program, thereby affecting those who depend on the services and hurting someone's chances of reelection. Including these stakeholders in the process could avoid conflict and lead to better decisions that everyone can live with.

But there is another implication here that must be acknowledged. There is a reciprocal relationship because these external interest groups can affect what goes on in an organization, as suggested earlier by the discussion of formal requirements to develop and use performance measurement. Nonetheless, the focus here is not on these formal or legal mechanisms that political actors may use to influence behavior. Rather, the focus is on the relationship of these actors to the performance measurement effort as representative of the more concrete influences on the process of utilization.

Lessons from organizations that have experimented with performance measurement underscore that the success of a performance measurement system depends on the continued support from elected officials, and the continued involvement of the public (Bowden, 1996; Cannon, 1996, Weidner and Noss-Reavely, 1996; de Lancer Julnes and Mixcoatl, 2006). Thus, as a means of influence, the building of coalitions does not occur only within the organization, but also between members of the organization and external stakeholders. Carnall (1995) has cited the use of outside experts and consultants, working with external groups and stakeholders and opinion leaders, as important means of influence.

Noting a lack of implementation of performance measurement information by Utah legislators in their decision-making process, former Speaker of the House Nolan Karras stated that citizens needed to get involved in the strategic planning process. The former speaker believed that aggressive involvement of citizens would raise the political risk for legislators who do not support the effort and do not use the information. In Utah, citizens were involved in the earlier stages of development of this statewide strategic planning effort. However, after it moved to the implementation stage, there was little, if any, citizen participation.

If these assumptions are correct, we can expect to find that because of the expectation of conflict, and at times obstructive behavior, that change can cause, the following hypothesis is true.

> *Subhypothesis 3b: External coalitions (external interest groups) will be particularly necessary for implementation of performance measurement information.*

Unions as Internal and External Political Actors

Another important external political force in organizations that is often emphasized in the literature is unions. Unions are neither completely internal nor completely external political actors. This is due to their internal representation of members, their affiliation with national organizations, and their participation in the national agenda. They represent one avenue of a concrete form of influence that employees can use to affect decision-making in their organizations (Mechanic, 1962). According to some scholars, the role of unions has tended to be one that is characterized by opposition to change and innovation. In particular, Ammons (1992) has pointed out the tendency of unions to oppose technology or any innovation process that is considered disruptive or threatening to employees, thereby becoming a barrier to productivity improvement efforts in public sector organizations.

Nonetheless, Fischer (1994) has long criticized this view of unions. He says that such a view reflects "the human relation philosophy that portrays management as agents of cooperation, while unions, as external interlopers between management and workers, are the embodiment of social and political conflict." There are examples that suggest that unions may not always be the conflict-creating partners that their critics describe. One example is found in the accounts of the experiences with performance measurement of the Oregon Department of Transportation (Bowden, 1996). They found that support from unions can be gained by keeping them involved and informed of changes. Fiscal pressures and pressures for improving performance may also lead to union cooperation in reform efforts. For example, Holzer (1988) stated that due to fiscal pressures, municipal unions in New York City have long cooperated on productivity improvement programs.

But other examples also illustrate that whether the effect of unions on any type of organizational change is positive or negative will depend on the circumstances. For example, during the three-year-long tenure of Harold Levy as chancellor of New York City, cooperation between unions and the schools improved dramatically. The previous chancellor did not enjoy such cooperation because of a perceived lack of protection of union members who resisted former Mayor Rudolph Giuliani's confrontational policies. Thus, unions may feel justified in opposing change when it may bring about negative consequences to its members.

In the case of PBM, the issues of measurement and how the information is used may create anxiety for unionized workers. Therefore, if unions are indeed inclined to oppose practices that could disrupt or threaten employees, we expect to find that the level of unionization in an agency will have a negative impact on both stages of utilization of performance measurement information. But this effect should be particularly strong at the implementation stage. Therefore, we can expect to find the following:

> *Subhypothesis 3c: The negative impact of unions will be larger on the implementation of performance measures than on the adoption.*

However, as suggested by the conflicting accounts presented above regarding the role of unions, the effect of unions might not be as simple to discern as the sub-hypothesis 3c implies. This relationship may be more complex than posited. Thus, another way to explore the effect of employee unions is by testing their interaction with internal activities in support of innovation and change. Specifically, we can test the power of unions over less concrete organization activities such as internal interest groups that promote performance measurement. It can be hypothesized that if unions act as suppressors of innovation or changes that could potentially lead to negative consequences for employees, they will negatively interact with activities that could lead to negative consequences. Therefore, one would expect the following:

> *Subhypothesis 3d: The effect of internal political activities (internal interest groups) on adoption and implementation of performance measures is attenuated at higher levels of unionization.*

As informal groups that try to control conflict, internal interest groups will be less effective the more they are opposed by the more formal groups. In particular, because implementation deals with real consequences, one would expect that the potency in the effect of these groups will significantly diminish when they are opposed by more potent formal (external) groups, such as unions.

Organizational Culture

The concept of organizational culture and its pivotal role in any kind of organizational change was briefly introduced earlier. Before proceeding, any further research protocol dictates that we first define the term *organizational culture*. Unfortunately, there is no such thing as a single widely accepted definition of *culture*, and the term is used in diffuse ways by different scholars (Reichers and Schneider, 1990; Rainey, 1997). While some scholars define culture as something the organization *is*, others define it as something the organization *has* (Reichers and Schneider, 1990). Accordingly, the first definition studies culture under a native paradigm, seeking to explore and describe the deep structure of the organization. On the other hand, those who view culture as something the organization *has* focus on the examination of the system of shared meanings, assumptions, and underlying values, and the examination of the causes and effects of organizational culture. This latter definition is consistent with Schein's conception of culture. Schein (1992) states that the culture of a group is

> *a pattern of shared basic assumptions that the group learned as it solved its problems of external adaptation and internal integration that has worked well enough to be considered valid and, therefore, to be taught to new members as the correct way to perceive, think, and feel in relation to those problems. (p. 12)*

He has further argued that culture can be analyzed at different levels of degree to which the cultural phenomenon is visible to the observer. The levels range from the visible organizational structures and processes (artifacts) to the unconscious, taken-for-granted beliefs, perceptions, thoughts, and feelings (basic underlying assumptions—the ultimate source of values and action). Thus, norms, values, rituals, and climate are all manifestations of culture. And culture is a way of perceiving, thinking, and feeling in relation to the group's problems (Reichers and Schneider, 1990). Somewhere in the middle of the spectrum are the strategies, goals, and philosophies or espoused justifications used by an organization's members, which Schein referred to as espoused values.

The basic argument for studying culture is that because organizational culture shapes the way organizations react to innovation and change, an important question is to what extent organizational culture can be managed to achieve organizational goals. Indeed, the literature documents not only the importance of culture in organizations, but also managers' attempts to manage and change culture. Managing culture to create values and structures that support change is necessary because the introduction of anything that deviates from current practices often leads to denial, disbelief, and resistance. As has been suggested here for many organizations, performance-based management is not consistent with usual practices.

Therefore, building on the insights of Schein (1992, 1996) and Reichers and Scheneider (1990), culture is examined in the model developed here by including openness to change as one aspect of organizational culture that can be measured in the context of PBM. How open an organization is to change may be assessed by looking at existing structures, such as the presence of systems that reward innovation and risk taking, and by evaluating the perceptions of the attitudes of management and nonmanagement employees toward innovation, change, and performance measurement. As Rich (1979) asserted, organizational incentive systems can be used to control and facilitate use of information.

Based on the assumptions of the theory of organizational culture, one can then expect to find that an organization with a culture that supports change is more likely to adopt and implement performance measurement. Nonetheless, given the risk associated with performance measurement information (e.g., a program's performance may be deemed poor), for organizations that are truly open to change, the effect of culture should be greater on implementation. In the context of PBM, an openness to change can be measured by a positive attitude toward performance measurement and the presence of incentives for change. Thus, we can posit the following hypothesis:

> *Subhypothesis 3e: An openness to change will have a stronger impact on the implementation than on the adoption of performance measures.*

Even so, Reichers and Schneider (1990) have stated that culture should not be studied in isolation. In order for such studies to have significance for researchers and practitioners, it is necessary to study the relationship between culture and other variables. Thus, here I examine culture within the context of other organizational factors (i.e., requirements, organizational politics, rational/technocratic factors). As previously discussed, Pettigrew et al. (1990) have argued that culture shapes the way political processes operate when organizations are confronted with change. The implication is that culture operates as a moderator of behavior. That is, we may find different intensity levels of different responses to change due to culture. For example, we can test the assumption of Korman and Glennerster (1985) that cultural aspects of an organization may operate as catalysts for external requirements. The authors suggest that when organizations view external policies as symbolic, they would make little effort to implement them. When they are viewed as legitimate, they are more likely to be implemented.

Consequently, assuming that organizations with a culture that is open to change are more likely to view as legitimate an external requirements to have a performance measurement system, they are expected to be more likely to adopt and implement performance measures. Conversely, if the organization is not open to change, it will not adopt or implement performance measurement information. Thus, we can test the following notion:

> *Subhypothesis 3f: When organizations that are open to change are subject to external requirements, they will adopt and implement at a faster rate.*

The implication of this subhypothesis is that a positive interaction exists between change and external requirements.

Summary

A premise of the work presented here is that to increase the likelihood of success of PBM systems, we need to understand what factors influence the utilization of performance measurement information—adoption and implementation—and how. Five specific distinctions were made between adoption and implementation, which corroborated the argument that implementation does not necessarily follow adoption. As a result, based on the analysis of the rational and the political-cultural models of organizations, the main argument here is that adoption and implementation are affected differentially by factors particular to each of these paradigms.

Although performance measurement information (efficiency measures, outcome measures, and output measures) has been conceptualized here as knowledge, I also argued that the field of knowledge utilization is not adequate to provide answers to the questions driving the work presented in this book. As explained earlier, one of the reasons for this is the lack of a model of knowledge utilization that goes beyond the individualistic characteristics of knowledge producers and users. Further, even though performance measurement is often perceived and promoted as a technocentric activity, using a rational/technocratic model alone would also prove to be inadequate in explaining the adoption and implementation of performance measurement information in the inevitably political context of organizations.

Therefore, to adequately analyze the phenomena of utilization, I have drawn from the insights of the theories of organizational politics and culture to propose an integrated empirical model that will be furthered elaborated by analyzing proposed mediated and moderated relationships that may help to explain the broad concept of utilization. Elaborating the integrated model, which includes all of the factors discussed here, reflects the argument that to acquire an understanding of how public and nonprofit organizations operate, we need to go beyond simple models stressing covariation and look deeper for the mechanisms that produce the observed effects.

Three major hypotheses were put forth to reconcile the different insights used to develop this theoretical framework. These hypotheses can be summarized by the following broad statements:

1. The process of utilization of performance measurement is composed of at least two stages, adoption and implementation.
2. Rational/technocratic factors will have a preponderance of influence on the adoption stage of utilization.
3. Political-cultural factors will have a preponderance of influence on the implementation stage of utilization.

The factors within the rational/technocratic and the political-cultural models were presented in a progressive manner. The discussion began with an explanation of the more formal, and at times symbolic, factors and progressed to the more concrete factors. Thus, several subhypotheses were also discussed within each of these models. The three broad statements and their accompanying hypotheses (depicted in Box 3.1) suggest the expectation that each of the stages of utilization of performance measurement information will be differentially affected by each of the factors included in the rational and the political-cultural paradigm. They also suggest that utilization is, to some extent, a linear process when it comes to the two stages; adoption is necessary if implementation is to occur. As such, the process of utilization of performance measurement information will be expected to behave as suggested in the general model shown in Figure 3.1.

BOX 3.1: SUMMARY OF SUBHYPOTHESES RELATING TO THE EFFECT OF RATIONAL, POLITICAL-CULTURAL FACTORS ON THE ADOPTION AND IMPLEMENTATION OF PERFORMANCE MEASURES

Exhibit A. Hypothesized Effect of Factors on Adoption Compared to Implementation in an Integrated and Elaborated Model

Independent Factors	Dependent Factors		Subhypothesis
	Adoption	Implementation	(#)
Formal requirements	Higher/positive	Lower/positive	(2a)
Internal requirements	Higher/positive	Lower/positive	(2b)
Goal orientation	Higher/positive	Lower/positive	(2c)
Internal interest groups	Higher/positive	Lower/positive	(3a)
External interest groups	Lower/positive	Higher/positive	(3b)
Unions	Lower/negative	Higher/negative	(3c)
Openness to change	Lower/positive	Higher/positive	(3e)

Exhibit B. Effect of Internal Requirements Compared to External Requirements on Adoption and Implementation as Posited in Subhypothesis 2b

	Internal Requirements		External Requirements
Adoption	Higher	(than)	Lower
Implementation	Higher	(than)	Lower

Exhibit C. Nature of Effect of Interactions on Adoption and Implementation as Posited in Subhypotheses 3d and 3f

Interaction	Adoption	Implementation
Unionization and internal interest groups	Negative	Negative
Change and external requirements	Positive	Positive

Exhibit D. Elaboration of Models: Mediating Effect of Selected Rational Factors—Subhypothesis 2e

Independent Factors				Dependent Factors
	Lead to		Lead to	
Formal requirements	→	Goal orientation	→	Adoption
Coalitions (interest groups)	→	Technical capacity		
Openness to change	→		→	Implementation

Exhibit E.Elaboration of the Implementation Model: Mediating Effect of Adoption—Subhypothesis 1a

Independent Factors		*Dependent Factors*
	Lead to	*Lead to*
Rational factors		
Coalitions (interest groups) $\rightarrow$	Adoption $\rightarrow$	Implementation
Openness to change		

Chapter 4

Research Methodology

This chapter explains the methodological approach used for the survey study and follow-up interviews that serve as the major case example for this book. The discussion centers on strategies for data collection and analyses, rationale for selecting the various methods and techniques, and their advantages and disadvantages. It should be noted that the unit of analysis here is state and local government organizations. Thus, to collect data, employees of these organizational units were selected to participate in the study.

The research process used here was iterative, wherein each additional procedure built on the previous one. Such an approach is particularly useful in building sound theory that can help inform practice. After all, theory building has been defined as the "ongoing process of producing, confirming, applying, and adapting theory" (Lynham, 2002). The information presented in this chapter should be of particular interest to scholars or anyone wishing to assess the validity of the interpretations and conclusions reached here and the extent to which they can be applied to different situations in the performance-based management (PBM) context. Moreover, the discussion of the various methods and techniques can serve as a useful introduction for those new to research.

The chapter is organized in the following manner. First, there is a discussion of the survey methodology used for the mailed questionnaire. The reader will find a detailed description of the sampling techniques, the survey instrument, the mailing procedures, response rate, and a discussion of the strengths and limitations of survey research. The "Analysis of Quantitative Evidence" section describes the major data analysis techniques used, including factor analysis, scale reliability testing, multiple regression analysis, pattern matching, and path analysis.

The chapter then launches into a discussion of how a mixed methods approach, which combines qualitative and quantitative methods and techniques, helped to overcome the limitations inherent in the type of research presented here and increased confidence on the findings reported in subsequent chapters. Part of the discussion is focused on the various mixed methods strategies that were used for verifying and getting a greater understanding of the nuances of the survey findings. Finally, consideration is given to remaining concerns about the methodology.

The Survey: Collecting Quantitative Data

Sampling Techniques

In October 1996, the Governmental Accounting Standards Board (GASB) conducted a national survey seeking general information regarding the use of performance measures by state and local government entities across the nation. GASB sent out 5,013 surveys to its own members and individuals in mailing lists from the Government Financial Officers Association (GFOA), International City/County Management Association (ICMA), and National Association of College and University Business Officers. Of the 5,013 employees surveyed, 900 responded. To conduct the research discussed here, a list of names and addresses of these respondents was obtained from GASB. Because the unit of analysis is state and local government organizations, of these 900 potential contacts, only 500 were selected to participate in a survey conducted for the research presented in this book. Those not included in this research were respondents who worked for school districts, colleges or universities, and special authorities.

For the purpose of the survey study, respondents were classified into four different categories according to the following criteria:

1. The GASB survey had a question asking respondents to identify who should be contacted in their organization or department if further information regarding performance measures was needed. Of the 900 who responded to GASB's survey, 399 identified themselves as what can be classified as *self-nominated opinion leaders* for their organization or department. Of these 399, there were 296 who identified themselves as opinion leaders for their organization, and the other 103 self-identified as opinion leaders for their department.
2. For the same question described above, a large number of respondents also identified other individuals as opinion leaders for their organization. In total, 200 individuals were identified by the respondents as what can be classified as *volunteered opinion leaders*. Although in two instances those who fell under this classification scheme were already respondents to the GASB's survey, most of these individuals had not participated in the GASB survey. Some respondents identified opinion leaders for their specific departments. However, in the interest of resource conservation, only those identified for the entire organizational unit were included in this study.

3. Another group of respondents either (a) did not identify themselves as opinion leaders for their organization or department or (b) did not identify anyone else as an opinion leader. This group consisted of 105 respondents. This group was classified as *no opinion leader.*
4. In addition, a fourth group was selected. This consisted of 230 randomly selected individuals who received the GASB survey, but did not respond. This sample was stratified by type of organization (i.e., state or local government). To select these nonrespondents in the GASB survey study, the mailing lists used by GASB were obtained. The mailing lists identified those who had responded to the GASB's survey. Each nonrespondent (with the exception of those employed by school districts, colleges, or universities) was assigned a number. A table of random numbers was then used to select the sample. To ensure a large enough number of respondents from county and state governments (municipalities were well represented in the GASB's survey), a target sample size of at least 100 randomly selected county and state government respondents was set. As a result, once the normal random sampling method reached 130 (230 − 100) respondents, the researcher continued randomly selecting only county or state government respondents.

A total of 934 surveys were mailed to state and local government employees across the nation. Each group of respondents received the same survey content. Those selected for the study ranged in title from state auditor to city manager to county budget analyst. To differentiate among the four groups, while maintaining the anonymity of respondents, and to facilitate follow-up, each group's survey was differentiated by either the color of the survey sent (two colors were used—ivory for the 230 random sample and gray for the remaining 700) or the typeface used in the title printed on the first page of the questionnaire.

The Survey Instrument

As described above, data for testing the hypotheses were obtained by means of a mail questionnaire. The questionnaire was designed in several stages. The entire process, from the drafting of the questions to the mailing of the actual questionnaire, took approximately 10 weeks.

The first stage consisted of drafting questions based on the literature review. After this was completed, a number of individuals considered to be experts in performance measurement were asked to critique the survey questions. In particular, it was important to get their opinion about the validity of the questions. The experts tapped for this purpose included the assistant director of research at GASB in Connecticut and the principal of a performance measurement consulting firm for private and public organizations. For a number of years, GASB has been engaged in conducting research on and promoting the use of performance measures by state and local governments. The principal of the consulting firm had over 15 years of experience in performance measurement and improvement. Based on discussions with these experts and their critique of the instrument, questions were modified, deleted, or added. This was followed by another round of consultation with these experts.

The survey study discussed here deals with a number of concepts that cannot be measured directly or indirectly. The survey was attempting to measure what Babbie (1990) calls constructs, which are theoretical creations derived from observation. Spector (1992) has lamented that in many instances the constructs used in social sciences are "theoretical abstractions, with no known objective reality." This was not the case here. Certainly, the various theories discussed in the previous chapter guided the development of the theoretical framework for this book. As such, the framework was an important foundation for developing the constructs. But their development was also informed by the experiences of public organizations that have experimented with performance measurement and by the feedback received from the performance measurement experts that were consulted.

The decision on what type of questions to include in the survey instrument was also made in consultation with the expert advisors and the recommendations found in the literature. As the readers will note, for the most part the survey instrument consists of summated rating scale questions. This was chosen over single yes-no answers because of concerns with reliability, precision, and scope. Spector (1992) has argued that yes-no answers are inefficient, and single items do not produce consistent responses over time. These types of questions are also imprecise because they restrict measurement to only two levels; "people can be placed into only two groups, with no way to distinguish among people in each group." Moreover, as suggested by Spector, because of the broad scope of the many characteristics being measured here, it would be difficult to assess them with a single question. Another advantage of scales over single yes-no questions is that they provide more flexibility in the design of items and can help make the questions more interesting for the participants (Babbie, 1990). Box 4.1 provides a summary of the steps taken to develop the scales for the survey instrument.

After developing the scales a draft survey instrument was finalized and pilot tested. The pilot test consisted of surveying a group of 10 state and local government employees. The organizations in which these individuals worked had similar characteristics to those who were selected to participate in the survey. In addition to responding to the survey questions, the pilot test participants were asked the questions found in Box 4.2. Based on the answers to those questions, items on the survey were further refined and others were deleted. Particular attention was paid to the items that measured the constructs *culture* and *politics* because they seemed to generate the greatest concern among participants in the pilot test.

The final survey instrument developed for this study consisted of 60 open- and closed-ended items divided into six broad sections. The survey instrument, entitled "National Center for Public Productivity Survey on the Utilization of Performance Measures," is found in Appendix A, at the end of this book. The survey sections were:

BOX 4.1: SCALE DEVELOPMENT

1. **Construct definition**. Accomplishing this step required:
   - Identifying and specifying the concepts to be measured based on the theoretical framework developed.
   - Refining the concepts based on discussions with experts and practitioners. These concepts included: politics—internal and external interest groups, and formal politics—internal requirements and external requirements; rational/technocratic—resources, access to information, goal orientation; culture—openness to change (attitudes and encouraging risk taking); adoption; implementation; and utilization.

2. **Scale design**. This step consisted of:
   - Selecting the anchors or response choices. Three different response choices were selected:
     - Agreement: Asked respondents the extent to which they agreed with a statement.
     - Evaluation: Asked respondents to provide a rating indicating the extent to which certain activity had taken place in their organization.
     - Frequency: Asked respondents the extent to which each item had occurred.
   - Quantifying the responses. The scales ranged in value from 1 (the lowest) to 4 (the highest). To force a response, no neutral or middle category was included as a response option.
   - Writing the questions and statements or items that make up the scale.

1. Performance measurement: In this section respondents were asked about the development and implementation of performance measures, if members of the organization had access to "how-to" information on performance measurement, and if the organization was required to use performance measures.
2. Organizational orientation: The questions in this section pertained to the availability or presence of rational/technocratic factors—technical capacity.
3. Organizational groups: The focus of this section was to ascertain the existence and impact of coalitions (interest groups).
4. Organizational characteristics: This section included a number of questions that measured cultural and rational/technocratic factors.
5. Demographics: This section collected demographic information about the organization and the respondent.
6. Final comments: This section provided survey participants the opportunity to submit additional comments and information not covered in the other sections.

With the exception of the few questions asking for comments and most of the demographic data, respondents were asked to check boxes that described the extent

---

BOX 4.2: PILOT TEST EVALUATION QUESTIONS

1. How long did it take you to complete the survey?
2. Did you have any difficulty in answering the questions? If yes, please explain.
3. Were any of the questions unclear, ambiguous, or redundant? If yes, which ones?
4. Were the answer choices (i.e., scales) appropriate?
5. What questions would you delete?
6. What questions would you add?
7. What did you think of the overall format of the survey?

---

to which certain statements applied to their organization. The survey was printed on an 8.5-by-17-inch two-sided sheet folded in half.

Pilot test participants suggested that because of the nature of the questions asked, the researcher should have survey respondents answer the questions anonymously. Due to the questions that dealt with organizational culture and politics, pilot test participants believed that keeping the identity of the survey participants anonymous would encourage these participants to provide more candid responses to the survey questions.

Mailing Strategies

Response rate in mail surveys is an issue of concern. Participants may not feel as compelled to respond to questions as they would for surveys conducted over the telephone, for example, and thus may never return the completed survey. In an effort to help increase the likelihood of receiving more completed surveys, as suggested by Babbie (1990) and Fowler (1990), prospective respondents were contacted by mail before being sent the questionnaire. Approximately 10 days before the questionnaire was mailed, a letter was sent alerting prospective respondents about the research being conducted and letting them know that a questionnaire would follow.

However, some scholars have questioned the value of prenotifying prospective respondents on the grounds that people who are likely to return the completed questionnaires would do it anyway. For example, in a controlled study on the effectiveness of prenotification of respondents in the private sector, Chebat and Picard (1991) found that prenotification works when it is used in conjunction with some form of premium. According to the authors, this is consistent with a theory of cognitive dissonance that supports the argument that prenotification increased response rate among individuals with an internal locus of control. According to this theory, prenotification mentally prepares internally controlled individuals better than those externally controlled to respond to a mail questionnaire. It follows, then, that for those externally controlled, who would not complete the survey and return it, a reward is necessary. These arguments have merit. Therefore, to help remove this possible barrier for externally controlled individuals, survey respondents were offered a reward. Participants were told that upon completion of the study, and at their request, a copy of the research report would be sent to them.

Participants were also assured that because the questionnaire was to be filled out anonymously, their responses would be kept confidential and results would only be reported in the aggregate. To that end, as mentioned earlier, the survey instrument was designed without any type of individual identifiers. However, there was a need to have some way to follow-up with nonrespondents. Consequently, in addition to receiving the questionnaire, respondents received a postcard with the researcher's mailing address and the respondent's mailing label (containing a respondent's code for easier location in the mailing lists) affixed to the postcard. Respondents were asked to mail the completed questionnaire in an enclosed self-addressed envelope separate from the postcard. Thus, the postcard served two purposes. First, it let the researcher know whether the person had participated in the study and if further follow-up was necessary. Second, it allowed respondents to communicate that they wished to receive a copy of the results of the study once they were available.

The cover letter assured the respondents anonymity and asked them to complete the questionnaire whether or not they had a formal system of performance measures. The researcher's telephone number and e-mail address were also provided in case any of the respondents had questions concerning the study. In addition, respondents were provided with a sheet that contained the definitions of the various terms used in the questionnaire. The goal was to ensure consistency in the meaning that respondents attached to those terms. By the end of the study, a total of 10 survey participants had called for further information or clarification.

The whole package was mailed in first-class mail. No stamps were provided to respondents in the self-addressed envelope provided for returning the completed questionnaire or for the postcards. This allowed for significant savings in the cost of conducting the survey study.

Returned Questionnaires and Follow-Up Mailing

Approximately one week after the questionnaire was mailed, completed questionnaires and postcards began to arrive. Each questionnaire was assigned a response number and entered in a database. The postcards were checked off against the mailing list used. Fowler (1990) has pointed out that studies of early returned questionnaires have consistently shown that they tend to be biased and that a low response rate (20 to 30 percent) usually does not look like the sampled population.

Therefore, after a period of approximately three weeks, another mailing was done to those people in the mailing lists from whom no postcard had been received. The cover letter indicated that because their postcard had not been received, a new copy of the survey and a new postcard were being sent. The letter also stressed that their response was essential for the success of the study and reassured them of anonymity and confidentiality.

Response Rate

From a research design perspective, one of the most troubling areas in survey research is response rate, with mail surveys often associated with "the worst" response rate (Fowler, 1990). Thus, Fowler (1990) cautioned that carrying out a mail survey without procedures to ensure a high response rate is one of the worst design decisions that can be made. This is particularly important in light of the argument that those who return the survey early usually are biased regarding the subject matter.

Given the critical need of getting an adequate response rate, several decisions were made to ensure as high a response rate as possible. Some of these were discussed earlier and included making the survey anonymous, prenotifying survey participants, and sending another letter and copy of the survey to those who had not responded after a period of three weeks. Furthermore, the letterhead of Rutgers University's Graduate Department of Public Administration and the National Center for Public Productivity was used for the cover letters as well as for the return envelope and postcards. According to Babbie (1990), studies on response-increasing techniques consistently point out that university sponsorship tends to improve response rates.

After the first mailing, the overall response rate was 37 percent, or 347 out of 929 (932 surveys sent minus 3 returned by the post office as "undeliverable" as addressed). After the second mailing, the overall response rate increased to 55 percent, or 513. Although there are no statistically based rules for an acceptable response rate, Babbie (1990) says that at least 50 percent is generally considered adequate for analysis and reporting, with 70 percent or more being a very good response rate.

Strengths and Limitations of Survey Studies

Some of the limitations of the quantitative portion of the research presented in this book are inherent in both survey research methodology and research itself. Some others are specific to the subject matter. In designing a survey, researchers must take care to address as many of these limitations as possible. Likewise, consumers of research studies should not only take into account the limitations, but also pay attention to how the researcher addressed those shortcomings.

There are many advantages to using a questionnaire to collect data. These, according to Orlich (1978), include:

1. Many individuals may be contacted at the same time.
2. A questionnaire is less expensive to administer than is using an interview technique.

3. Each selected respondent receives identical questions.
4. A written questionnaire provides a vehicle for expression without fear of embarrassment to the respondent.
5. Responses are easily tabulated (depending on design of instrument).
6. Respondents may answer at their own convenience.
7. There is no need to select and train interviewers.
8. Persons in remote or distant areas are reached.
9. Interviewer biases are avoided.
10. Uniform data are gathered that allow for long-range research implications.

These characteristics of questionnaires also help researchers ward off possible issues with reliability and response rates.

Furthermore, Babbie (1990) has stated that survey research has all the characteristics of science. Therefore, it is a valid method of inquiry. The characteristics of survey research include logic, determinism, generality, parsimony, and specificity. These can be described as follows (Babbie, 1990):

Survey research is logical; it follows the logic of science.

Survey research is deterministic; the fact that it seeks a logical model conveys the deterministic notion of cause and effect.

Survey research is general; its ultimate goal is to generalize to the population from which the sample under study was selected.

Survey research is parsimonious; scientists can discriminate in terms of the importance of the many variables to their disposal.

Survey research is specific; a strength and weakness, the method itself forces survey research to be specific.

As with any other data collection approach, survey research has several limitations. As researchers consider a data collection approach, they must include in their deliberation an assessment of limitations and weight them against the strengths. The goal is to implement a design that takes advantage of the strengths of the method and has strategies for minimizing the weaknesses or limitations. Orlich (1978) summarizes the disadvantages of using a questionnaire to collect data as follows:

1. The investigator is prevented from learning the respondent's motivation for answering questions.
2. Respondents may be limited from providing free expression of opinions due to instrument design.
3. The collection of data from individuals who cannot read, write, or see is prevented.
4. The return of all questionnaires is difficult to achieve.
5. Complex designs cause poor responses or none.
6. The investigator is prevented from learning what causes poor returns.

7. The names and current addresses of the target population are often not available.
8. A question may have different meanings to different people.
9. There is no assurance that the intended respondent actually completed the instrument.
10. Selections of the sample, per se, may cause biased results: i.e., the sample is not representative of the universe.
11. The questionnaire asks for outdated information.
12. Respondents may not complete the entire instrument.
13. Too much data are requested, thus, only an incomplete analysis is provided by the investigator.
14. Poor designs (open-ended questions) may lead to data that cannot be merged for the systematic analysis.
15. The topic is trite or simply insignificant.

In addition, there are other concerns related to survey research and the subject matter that merit some attention. From the perspective of some organizational culture scholars, Schein (1992) in particular, survey methods, and especially those that emphasize quantitative research methods, are not an effective way to study organizational culture. Schein identified several problems. First, he argued that such surveys only measure aspects of organizational climate or its norms. Thus, data are artifacts that need to be deciphered and interpreted as would any other artifact. Second, designers of the questionnaire have no way of knowing which of the many dimensions of culture to build into the questionnaire. Thus, he or she will need a long and elaborate survey. Third, stated Schein, not all cultural dimensions are equally salient or relevant to a given group's functioning. And fourth, questionnaires assume that the responses will be responsible and accurate. Thus, concluded Schein, questionnaires are useful tools for getting at an organization's climate and norms of behavior, but not to the cultural assumptions as he defines them.

Reichers and Schneider (1990), on the other hand, have criticized culture scholars' emphasis on qualitative research methods (in particular in-depth case studies) and their total disregard of quantitative approaches. The authors have argued that this emphasis explains the scarcity of research on culture. They especially point out that it takes more resources to conduct qualitative research. In addition, Reichers and Schneider disagree with Schein (1992) in that cultural concepts cannot be measured through surveys. They believe that shared meanings and assumptions can be assessed through questionnaires that have been developed for the particular organization or subgroup under study and derived from in-depth interviews with key actors. Moreover, argued Reichers and Schneider, this type of methodology allows for multivariate analysis of the antecedents and consequences of particular cultural forms that may help advance the knowledge about organizational culture.

Both of these arguments were considered here. Thus while the research that forms the basis for this book did attempt to get to some aspects of culture that are relevant to the topic of performance-based management and performance measurement, I do not claim to have a full picture of all of the cultural dimensions of the organizations studied.

Analysis of Quantitative Evidence

Once the survey data were collected, a number of statistical techniques were used to analyze them. What follows provides a description of these techniques. Although in some instances there are specific references to the statistical analysis program (SAS), the analytical concepts and procedures discussed here apply regardless of the software used for analyses.

Factor Analysis for Scale Validation

As discussed above, to conduct the survey, a questionnaire that consisted of a number of multiple-item, summated rating scales (Likert scales) was developed. These scale items represent variables that are believed to measure a smaller number of underlying constructs or unobserved variables. That is, groups of observed variables are correlated with one another because they are influenced by an underlying (unobserved) factor (Hatcher, 1994). These underlying factors are the hypothetical variables that are actually being measured. The underlying factor logic is derived from a philosophical belief that there are real qualities in the world that cannot be measured directly (Julnes, 2007).

Factor analysis was used to validate the scales or constructs used in the survey. Factor analysis is widely used in the social sciences because its concern with the underlying structures contributes to parsimony, a desirable quality in social sciences research (Rummel, 1970; Hatcher, 1994). Although the general constructs were specified in advance, both confirmatory and exploratory factor analyses were used. With confirmatory factor analysis one must know what variables load on what factor. Exploratory factor analysis, in contrast, is used to determine the number of separate components (or dimensionality) that might exist for a group of items (Spector, 1992).

The factors derived by the factor analysis come from the analysis of the pattern of covariation among items (Spector, 1992). Items that tend to correlate strongly with one another tend to form one factor. This relationship conveys the idea of convergent and discriminant validity (Spector, 1992). When items correlate highly, they are assumed to reflect the same construct, which is the same as having convergent validity. On the other hand, when items have low intercorrelation, they are assumed to measure different constructs, which is the same as discriminant validity.

Some may ask why use factor analysis and not principal components analysis. The answer is that choosing one technique over the other depends on the purpose of the study. Like factor analysis, principal components analysis is a data reduction technique. But because the interest here was to identify underlying factors, factor analysis was deemed more appropriate. Principal components analysis, unlike factor analysis, focuses on obtaining an artificial variable that is a linear combination of observed variables (Hatcher, 1994). In contrast, factor analysis assumes that an identified hypothetical latent (unobservable) variable is responsible for the covariation between two or more variables. Thus, while a factor is a hypothetical, unobservable variable, a principal component is an observable linear combination.

For those interested, Box 4.3 depicts the quantitative models for analyzing data using factor analysis and principal components analysis. The formulas and the accompanying explanation further illuminate the differences between these two techniques.

Steps in Factor Analysis

A thorough treatment of factor analysis is beyond the scope of this book. Therefore, the steps involved in conducting factor analysis are only briefly outlined here. This information should be sufficient to provide the reader with a basic understanding of the technique and allow for the assessment of its appropriateness for analyzing the data collected through the survey instrument. Before describing these steps, however, we should heed Spector's (1992) advice on two issues that must be addressed when conducting factor analysis. The first deals with the appropriate number of factors that best represent the items; the second deals with the interpretation of the factors. Spector suggests that even though factor analysis is a mathematical procedure, these issues are best addressed based on the researcher's subjective judgment and statistical decision rules.

The steps in factor analysis are iterative:

Step 1: Initial extraction of factors. The number of factors extracted equals the number of items analyzed. The first factor usually accounts for most of the variance, with each succeeding factor accounting for progressively smaller amounts of variance. Each factor, however, accounts for the variance that has not been accounted for by the previous factor. Moreover, each factor is uncorrelated (orthogonal) with all the other factors. In this step, communality (squared multiple correlations) and eigenvalue (amount of variance that is accounted for by a given factor) estimates are obtained.

Step 2: Determining the number of factors to retain. Several options exist that can help to make the decision of how many of the initial factors should be retained. One option, which Hatcher (1994) considers less appropriate for factor analysis than for principal components, is the eigenvalue criterion. This particular option entails selecting those factors with an eigenvalue of 1.00 and above. Another option is the scree test, which is a graphical representation of

BOX 4.3: QUANTITATIVE MODELS FOR SCALE VALIDATION

The quantitative model for *factor analysis* is

$$X_1 = v_{j(1)}CF1_{(1)} + v_{j(2)}CF2_{(2)} + v_{j(i)} CF_{(1)} + e_j \qquad (4.1)$$

where:

X_1 = observed variable

$v_{j(i)}$ = regression weight (or factor loading) for $CF_{(i)}$

CF = common factor

As can be observed in Equation 4.1, observed variable X_1 is a linear combination of common factors, $CF_{(i)}$, and unique influences, $e_{(i)}$ (Julnes, 2007; Hatcher, 1994). The observed variables are weighted sums of the underlying factors included in the factor model. The sum also includes an error factor that is unique to the variable—also called unique factor.

Equation 4.1 is very similar to multiple regression. In fact, the variable X in Equation 4.1 replaces Y in multiple regression, and the latent variables (factors) $CF_{(i)}$. As such, explains Hatcher (1994), generally in factor analysis one would expect a different set of weights and a different predictive equation for each set of variables.

The quantitative model for *principal components analysis* is as follows in Equation 4.2:

$$PC_{(i)} = w_{(i)1}X_{(1)} + w_{(i)2}X_2 + \ldots + w_{(i)j}X_j \qquad (4.2)$$

where:

PC = the first component extracted

$w_{(i)j}$ = the weight or regression coefficient for the observed variable as used to derive the principal component 1

X_j = the subject's score on the observed variable

Although it is possible to determine where a subject stands on a principal component by summing the subject scores on the observed variables being analyzed, this cannot be done in an exact manner with factor analysis. The reason for this is that factors are unmeasured latent variables. Nonetheless, it is possible to arrive at estimates of standing (Hatcher, 1994).

the eigenvalues associated with each factor. Additionally, there is the option of retaining factors based on the proportion of variance accounted for. Finally, the analyst can decide how many factors to retain based on the interpretability criteria, which focus on interpreting and verifying that the interpretation of the retained factors makes sense based on what is known about the constructs under investigation.

Step 3: Rotation to a final solution. Rotation is a linear transformation on the factor solution. The purpose is to produce clusters of items based on various mathematical criteria (Kim and Mueller, 1978; Spector, 1992). This rotation procedure could be either orthogonal (resulting in uncorrelated factors) or oblique (resulting in correlated factors). It has been suggested that oblique solutions are better than orthogonal solutions (Hatcher, 1994). The reason for this is that the rotated factor pattern matrix derived from oblique rotation is more likely to display a simple structure and will be more helpful in determining what names should be assigned to the factors. Nevertheless, this does not make orthogonal rotation useless. Hatcher (1994) has also explained that in many research situations an orthogonal rotation is desirable. Again, the final decision will depend on the interest of the researcher.

Step 4: Interpreting the rotated solution. At this point, one looks for variables that have high loadings on that factor. A high loading means that the variable is measuring that factor (Hatcher, 1994). Spector (1992) has suggested that a minimum value between .30 and .35 is required to consider that an item "loads on any factor"; Hatcher (1994), however, suggests a value of .40.

Step 5: Creating factor scores or factor-based scores. In this stage, one must calculate where subjects stand on the factor(s) that has been obtained. A *factor score* is the subject's actual standing on the underlying factor; an *estimated factor score* is an estimate of a subject's standing on that underlying factor. True factor scores are never determined because of the error associated with the unique component to each variable (Hatcher, 1994). Therefore, suggested Hatcher, one should always refer to factor scores as "*estimated* factor scores" (1994).

These estimated factor scores (a linear composite of optimally weighted variables under analysis) can be automatically obtained when using SAS by specifying the command in the PROC FACTOR statement. Another possibility, which is considered less sophisticated than the former, is to compute factor-based scales. These are variables that estimate subject scores on the underlying factors without an optimally weighted formula. They are created by adding the values of the variables that make up the factor. Once factor scores have been created, they can be used in subsequent analysis such as correlation and regression.

Strengths and Limitations of Factor Analysis

One of the major strengths of factor analysis is data reduction or parsimony. Factor analysis allows for the reduction of a number of variables to a more manageable number. Another major strength is that because it seeks to analyze covariance rather than variance, as long as there are "underlying influences that have common effects on variables," factor analysis should find the covariance (Julnes, 2007).

As with the strengths, Julnes (2007) suggests that the causes of concern or limitations of factor analysis follow from the way the approach works. He summarizes these concerns in terms of:

1. Indeterminacy: Arises because there will always be alternative factors that would produce the same observed covariation among the variables measured.
2. Instability across methods: Refers to the different methods for estimating factors.
3. Instability from small changes in the data: If data are randomly divided into two parts, or if data are collected at two points in time, the resulting estimated factors can differ markedly.

While the first two concerns are essentially part of the method, to minimize the latter and avoid overinterpretation, some researchers use factor-based scores rather than factor scores in subsequent analysis.

In addition, Spector (1992) warns that the results of factor analysis are a function of the items entered. Thus, explained Spector, the proportion of variance accounted by factors depends on the number and nature of items entered. Subscales with more items tend to produce stronger factors (larger proportion of variance explained). Conversely, subscales with too few items tend to produce weak factors.

Testing the Reliability of Scales

Once the scales are obtained through factor analysis, they must be checked for reliability. Reliability in scale construction is often referred to as internal consistency, or how well the identified scale reflects a common underlying factor (Hatcher, 1994; Spector, 1992).

Although not the only statistic available in the social sciences, the most often used statistic to assess internal consistency is the coefficient alpha, developed by Cronbach in 1951 (Spector, 1992; Hatcher, 1994). The quantitative model for coefficient alpha is shown in Box 4.4, Equation 4.3.

What the coefficient alpha does is to provide the lowest estimate of reliability that can be expected for an instrument (Hatcher, 1994). In general, all things being equal, the magnitude of this coefficient will be high, depending on the items included in the scale and whether or not the items that constitute the scale are highly correlated with one another. To Hatcher (1994), a reliability coefficient less than .70 is not adequate. However, this is only a rule of thumb, and in the social sciences literature researchers have reported coefficient alphas well below .70.

Another way to check reliability is to conduct a test-retest reliability. This procedure consists of administering the same instrument to the same sample of subjects

BOX 4.4: SCALE RELIABILITY TESTING

$$r_{xx} = \frac{(N)}{N-1} \frac{(S^2 - \sum S_i^2)}{S^2}$$

(4.3)

where:

r_{xx} = coefficient alpha

N = number of items constituting the instrument

S^2 = variance of the summated scale scores

$\sum S_i^2$ = as of the variances of the individual items that constitute this scale

at two points in time and computing the correlation between the two sets of scores. One major disadvantage associated with this procedure is that it requires additional resources, such as time and money (Hatcher, 1994). Therefore, using an index of internal consistency is a fine alternative.

Multiple Regression

After testing the scales for reliability, the results of the factor analysis procedures were ready to be used to test all the hypotheses posited in Chapter 3. Testing the hypotheses entailed conducting multiple regression analyses.

The basic difference between simple and multiple regression is that the former only considers one independent or predictor variable at a time. In contrast, the multiple regression model contains a number of predictor (independent) variables. The formula for a simple regression model and the formula for a multiple regression model are stated in Box 4.5, Equation 4.4 and Equation 4.5, respectively.

Two of the hypotheses posited in Chapter 3 of this book required testing for moderating or interaction effects (see subhypotheses 3d and 3f). In a moderated relationship, we assume that multiplicative causal relation of the form $y = x_1 + x_2 + x_1 x_2$ exists. Thus, moderation implies that the intensity and direction of the relationship between a dependent and an independent variable (or construct, as is the case for some of the variables used here) is contingent upon the presence or level of another independent variable (or construct).

A moderated relationship can be of two types: reinforcement (or synergistic), and interference (or antagonistic). The first type, reinforcement (or synergistic), occurs when the slope of the response function against one of the predictor variables increases with higher levels of the other predictor variable (Neter et al., 1996). The second type, interference (or antagonistic), results when the slope of the response function against one of the predictor variables decreases for higher levels of the other predictor variable. When one of the predictors is a dichotomous (1, 0)

BOX 4.5: REGRESSION ANALYSIS

Simple regression analysis:

$$Y_i = \beta_o + \beta_1 X_i + \varepsilon_i \qquad (4.4)$$

where:

Y_i = the value of the response (dependent) variable in the ith trial

β_o and βX = parameters

X_i = a known constant, namely, the value of the predictor variable in the ith trial

ε_i = random term

$i = 1, \ldots, n$

For *multiple regression analysis*, the model is stated as follows:

$$Y_i = \beta_o + \beta_1 X_{1i} + \beta_2 X_{2i} + \ldots + \beta_k X_{ki} \varepsilon_I \qquad (4.5)$$

variable, the former relationship is called ordinal interaction and the latter disordinal interaction.

Model Elaboration: Pattern Matching

Another approach used here to analyze the evidence was pattern matching or elaboration. The point of elaboration is to test the implications "of prospective causal mechanisms in order to generate an elaborate pattern of prediction" (Mark, 1990). In pattern matching, an empirically based pattern is compared with a predicted one or with several alternative predictions; the results of such analyses can help to strengthen the internal validity of the study (Yin, 1989). Campbell (1966) considered pattern matching between theory and data an optimal way for achieving scientific understanding. In a pattern match, the value of the conclusions derived from data is strengthened if the pattern of results predicted by the theory is found in the data (Marquart, 1990). Conversely, more complex patterns provide more evidence for internal validity. In citing Trochim (1985), Marquart states that "greater effort on construct validity through conceptualization can lead to more precise, refined patterns of outcomes and thus improve internal validity."

One of the most common ways for pattern matching or elaboration is to conduct some form of causal modeling (see the path analysis discussion below). For example, one can make use of mediators or mediating variables. Mediating variables are those through which "the treatment has its effect on other outcomes of interest" (Mark, 1990). James and Brett (1984) have defined the effect of mediation as the influence of an antecedent being transmitted to a consequence through the influence of an intervening mediator. A mediation model has the form of $x \rightarrow m \rightarrow y$, where x is the antecedent, m is the mediator, and y is the consequence (James and Brett, 1984). This is a causal model that assumes both additive and linear causal relations. This model implies that all of the influence from x on y is transmitted by m. But this need not be the case all the time. The effect of x can also be direct (of the form $x \rightarrow y$). Thus, x may have both direct and indirect effects.

Elaboration can also be conducted without a hypothesized mediator (Mark, 1986, 1990; Reichardt, 1988). For example, there is elaboration with respect to the cause, and pattern matching that involves conceptual replication with respect to outcomes (Mark, 1990). In the latter, stated Mark, different process theories predict different patterns across two or more independent variables. In the former, the researcher uses the *purification approach*. The goal of the purification approach is to attempt to decompose a treatment and isolate the component(s) that is responsible for the desirable effect (Mark, 1990). Thus, if there is a causal effect, it should emerge through these manipulations.

Path Analysis

The elaboration of the models for adoption and implementation of performance measurement information allows for the building of an estimated path model (estimated causal model). In a path model, a variable hypothesized to have an effect on another variable is linked with a straight arrow (path) pointing in the hypothesized direction. As explained by Davis (1985), "in a linear system, the total causal effect of Xi on Xj is the sum of the values of all the paths from Xi to Xj."

Regression coefficients are used here as path coefficients. Some argue that standardized coefficients are more appropriate when we wish to make comparisons (see Welch and Comer, 1988). Others argue against such practice. For example, Achen (1982) has argued that "standardized betas do not measure the theoretical or potential power of the variable, which is usually the researcher's first interest." Standardized betas measure the spread of a variable on the spread of the dependent variable in a sample, and not the effect of each additional unit of the independent variable on the dependent variable. In addition, this practice destroys comparability across and within samples. For the sake of clarity and to satisfy multiple demands, both standardized and unstandardized coefficients are reported here.

A path model decomposes the total causal effect into direct and indirect effects. The direct effects are calculated by regressing all the variables (those that precede the dependent variable and those that intervene or mediate the relationship between the dependent and independent variables). For example, a direct effect is graphically represented by an arrow going directly from the dependent to the independent variable (of the form $x \rightarrow y$). The value of this path, as explained earlier, is a regression coefficient.

In contrast to direct effects, indirect effects are a result of the sum of the product of the coefficients from the independent variable to the dependent variable through intervening variables (of the form $x \rightarrow m \rightarrow y$). In this example, the value of the indirect path from x to y is obtained by multiplying the coefficient from $x \rightarrow m$ by the coefficient from $m \rightarrow y$.

As suggested by Davis (1985, the effects in a path model can be summarized as follows:

a) Total Estimated Causal Effect = effect after controlling for all priors
b) Direct Effect = effect after controlling for all priors and intervenors
c) Indirect Effect = a − b (due to intervenors)

"Priors" refer to the preceding variables. In the formula above, x is the prior and m is the intervenor.

Addressing Limitations

Further Elaboration and Model Verification

Given the strengths and shortcomings of survey research, one needs to devise appropriate strategies to take advantage of strengths and minimize the weaknesses. With this in mind, the earlier section on survey methods discussed the strategies that were used to design and distribute the survey instrument. The procedures addressed concerns of reliability, validity, response rate, and practical concerns such as cost. Here I focus on other approaches that sought to improve the quality of the quantitative study and the interpretability of the findings in an effort to make it suitable for theory building and informing practice.

The strategies discussed here addressed some of the concerns about quantitative research raised by some scholars, notably Schein (1996) and Guba and Lincoln (1989). Specifically, following the advice of King et al. (1994) on what they consider to be rigorous methodology, the strategies used here are based on a combination of positivistic (quantitative) and interpretivist (qualitative) methodologies. This mixed methods approach, which consists of collecting and analyzing data, integrating the findings, and drawing inferences using both qualitative and quantitative approaches or methods in a single study, has proven to be useful when it comes to refining the hypotheses, communicating and explaining quantitative findings, assessing context and probing the limits of generalizability, and checking validity (Mark et al., 1997). But most importantly, a mixed methods approach helps us achieve scientific understanding (Campbell, 1966).

Moreover, those in favor of a mixed methods approach have argued that qualitative research and quantitative research not only complement and enhance each other, but add substantive content that neither method could create alone, and this helps to correct for biases that each methodology suffers from separately (Lin, 1996). A qualitative piece can also help this research go beyond the plausible to the causal explanation. Qualitative research seeks to understand what people do and tries to find connections between the who, what, where, how, and why (Lin, 1996; Kaplan, 1992). It also tries to find out how people understand what they do or believe.

King et al. (1994) concurred that qualitative studies are particularly important when trying to make causal inferences because of the ambiguous results that are often obtained in a quantitative study. When citing a study by Putnam and his colleagues on regional politics, King et al. pointed out that by following their quantitative studies with detailed case studies of the politics of six regions, Putnam and his colleagues were able to gain an intimate knowledge of the internal political maneuvering and personalities that have had an impact on the regional politics.

On the other hand, Guba and Lincoln (1989) disagree, arguing that it is not possible to effectively combine quantitative and qualitative methodologies. This argument is based on the notion that each of these two methodologies rests on what they believe are diametrically opposed principles. They argue that, on one hand, the quantitative methodology follows the notion that reality exists and can be observed; qualitative methodology, on the other hand, follows the notion that reality is constructed by each person.

Mark et al. (1997) note that these discussions about the qualitative and quantitative paradigms and methods are commonplace and range from conciliatory and integrative to confrontative and separatist. From my perspective, it is best to err on the side of conciliation and integrate methodologies. Given that the goal here was to develop an understanding of attitudes, behaviors, and structures that can help explain the adoption and implementation of performance measures, and from that understanding develop theory and suggest ways to improve practice, the mixed methods approach seemed to be the most appropriate.

In this book, the implementation of a mixed methods approach is reflected in the use of the following strategies. First, a content analysis of the published cases of government entities experimenting with performance measures was conducted (the summary of these case studies is found in Chapter 2 of this book). The content analysis of these cases revealed patterns and themes that were useful in building the theoretical framework, refining the hypotheses to be tested, interpreting the open-ended answers of the questionnaire, and providing examples that helped explain the dynamics revealed by the quantitative findings. For example, the case studies revealed the centrality of organizational politics and the need for organizations to change their culture in order for performance measurement to be successful.

A second strategy was to use a pattern-matching logic for data analysis. This approach was explained earlier in the "Analysis of Quantitative Evidence" section of this chapter. A third strategy was analyzing and incorporating the comments made by the respondents in the open-ended questions of the survey. This added a great deal of richness to the discussion of findings.

Finally, to further elaborate and verify the findings of the quantitative model, telephone interviews were conducted in 1999 with a randomly selected sample of individuals who were part of the sample that received the mail questionnaire in 1997. The interviews permitted further inquiry into what it means to adopt and implement performance measures. This follow-up also allowed for the emergence of patterns and themes that helped to further enhance the findings of the earlier survey and provided more insights into the mechanisms responsible for the utilization of performance measurement as suggested by the quantitative study. Furthermore, the approach helped to identify challenges to the process that were not uncovered by the mailed questionnaire and also gave respondents the opportunity to suggest ways in which performance measurement efforts could be supported.

The selection of the respondents was as follows. First, a random subsample of 75 was selected from the list of those who were included in the mailed survey. Of these, 25 randomly selected individuals were contacted by mail to alert them about the follow-up study. Of these, 18 agreed to participate when contacted by telephone.

A structured-interview format was used for the 20- to 40-minute interview. The length of the interview was dictated by whether or not the organization had a performance measurement system. Obviously, it took less time to interview individuals in organizations that did not have a comprehensive performance measurement system. The interview instrument consisted of a few closed-ended questions and a larger number of open-ended questions. This instrument is shown in Appendix B, at the end of the book.

For the most part, a combination of quantitative and qualitative techniques was used to analyze the interview data. The quantitative approach consisted of tabulation of responses based on the themes and patterns that had emerged through the analysis of the responses.

Possible Remaining Concerns

Even after following a rigorous methodology, research studies may still run the risk of having certain characteristics that some could view as weaknesses. For example, with regard to survey methodology, many scholars have written about the trade-off between response rate and number of questions asked in a survey instrument (e.g., Babbie, 1990; Orlich, 1978). As a result, there is a possibility that not all plausible measures of the dependent and independent variables were collected here. Nevertheless, given the manner in which the survey instrument and the theoretical and methodological framework on which it was based were developed, it is safe to assume that the measures collected are a good representation of the factors that may be responsible for the success or failure of performance measurement efforts.

Another issue related to the survey study described here concerns the efforts in maintaining anonymity. Although many steps were taken to ensure that respondents would remain anonymous, some respondents viewed the questions on demographics as an attempt to obtain information that could potentially help identify them. This appeared to be of particular concern for state agency employees. Some of them made comments to this effect, and others opted to leave most of the demographic questions blank. Items left unanswered may pose some problems during the data analysis stage. In particular, quantitative techniques (especially regression analysis) discount all observations with missing values on the variables under analysis. This can dramatically reduce the number of usable responses. Fortunately, here the response rate was good and not all demographic information was needed to test the various hypotheses.

Finally, the fact that the data obtained through the survey and follow-up interviews are based on self-reported information may raise some additional concerns for some readers. With self-reported data there is always the potential for respondents to overstate their responses. Respondents may have a desire to protect their organization or to make their organization appear to be conforming to current expectations. As a result, one cannot totally discount the possibility that the relationships studied here may have been somewhat distorted by such responses. Yet, given the multiple sources of evidence and the different analytical techniques, the potential for distortion is probably minimal. Nonetheless, as was explained in the previous chapter, to assess the possibility of distortion, one independent variable was used as a control in the regression models. As will be explained in the chapters ahead, as tested here, there appeared to be little, if any, bias.

Summary

In this chapter I have described the methodology used for conducting the survey and interviews that will be discussed in the chapters to come. I described a methodology that is based on a mixed methods approach, one that combines quantitative and qualitative methods for collecting, analyzing, and interpreting data. As discussed in the preceding pages, these methods complement each other. Each one helps address the weaknesses of the other as well as provide more support for the findings of the other.

The practice of combining quantitative and qualitative methodologies is not without its critics. However, as argued here, this combination of methods, which reaches beyond traditional methods of inquiry, allows for richer studies and provides more confidence in the findings, thus helping to build better theories. The practice of performance-based management is in need of sound theory. A good theory is useful. Therefore, better theories translate into better suggestions for improving practice. The work presented here is a step in that direction.

Chapter 5

Survey Data Description and Preparation for Hypotheses Testing

This chapter describes the preliminary findings of the mail questionnaire and provides information regarding the steps taken to prepare the data for hypotheses testing and building the model of utilization of performance measurement information. The data analyses are based on the answers of 513 respondents (a 55 percent response rate). The chapter is divided into three sections.

The first section introduces the variables that were used in subsequent analyses. This is then followed by another section based on the results of descriptive statistics and includes descriptions of the survey participants and their organizations, as well as a discussion of the findings of the descriptive statistical analysis of the independent and dependent variables. The third section presents the results of the initial multivariate analyses conducted to prepare the data for hypothesis testing. For this purpose the data were subjected to factor analysis, which helped to identify the constructs needed for testing the hypotheses of interest.

The discussion of the results of factor analysis procedures also includes information about the Cronbach coefficient alpha, the scale reliability tests performed on identified factors. As explained in the previous chapter of this book, this test was conducted to determine the statistical appropriateness of the constructs suggested by factor analysis. A summary is provided at the end of the chapter.

BOX 5.1: DESCRIPTION OF DEPENDENT VARIABLES

Dependent Variables	*Type*	*Question Number*
Construct Measured: Adoption		
Developed efficiency measures	L	I. 3a
Developed outcome measures	L	I. 3b
Developed output measures	L	I. 3c
Construct Measured: Implementation		
Efficiency measures used	L	I. 4a–f
Outcome measures used	L	I. 5a–f
Output measures used	L	I. 6a–f
Construct Measured: Utilization		
All dependent variables	L	I.3a–f

Note: L = Likert scale: 1–4.

Variables

The unit of analysis, as specified in Chapter 4, is state and local government organizations. These government organizations were classified as (1) an entire municipal government, (2) an entire county government, or (3) an entire state department/agency. Data were gathered from individuals working for these organizations.

In Boxes 5.1 and 5.2, I show the main variables used here. The boxes do not contain all the variables for which data were collected through the mail questionnaire. Only the variables used in the multivariate quantitative analyses are included. The box also shows the question number and section of the survey instrument associated with each variable.

Where appropriate, the variables are grouped by the construct that they are supposed to measure. Thus, for example, Box 5.1, which depicts the dependent variables, also includes the constructs *adoption, implementation*, and *utilization*. Box 5.2 lists the independent variables and control variables. As the reader will recall from the discussion in Chapter 4, constructs are used in instances when the concepts of interest cannot be directly observed. In addition, as was the case of some of the concepts used here, constructs are particularly useful when it comes to capturing and representing concepts that are multidimensional.

The boxes also provide information on the level of measurement and type of variable. As indicated in Boxes 5.1 and 5.2, with a few exceptions, the variables

BOX 5.2: DESCRIPTION OF INDEPENDENT VARIABLES

Independent Variables	*Type*	*Question Number*
Measure: Requirement		
External requirement (law/administrative regulation)	C	I.7a–b
Internal requirement	D	I.7c
Construct Measured: Politics		
Management promotes	L	III.3a
Management forms groups	L	III.4a
Employees promote	L	III.3b
Employees form groups	L	III.4b
Solicit consultant	L	III.1
Constituents involved	L	III.2
Elected officials promote	L	III.3c
Elected officials form groups	L	III.4c
Construct Measured: Culture		
Management implements	L	IV.3
Management views	L	IV.4
Nonmanagement accepts	L	IV.5
Nonmanagement understands	L	IV.6
Reward improving	L	IV.7a
Reward risk taking	L	IV.7b
Construct Measured: Rationality		
Access to information	L	I.1
Management attends conference	L	I.2a
Nonmanagement attends conference	L	I.2b
Commit resources	L	II.1
Assign staff	L	II.2
Assign department	L	II.3
Collect data	L	II.4
Use benchmarks	L	II.5
Management trained	L	II.6
Guided by goals	L	II.7

Communicate strategies	L	II.8
Efficiency mission	L	IV.2c
Other Organizational Characteristic		
Percent unionized	R	V.2d
Control Variables		
Government entity type (state, municipal, county)	D	V.1a
Position	O	V.1c

Note: C = composite index: 0–2; D = dichotomous: 0, 1; L = Likert scale: 1–4; O = ordinal; R = ratio.

used in the survey study are Likert scale type items, which are used to measure underlying factors or constructs. As will be discussed later in this chapter, these underlying factors were identified through factor analysis. They were then used in regression analysis to test the hypotheses developed earlier.

The reader will notice that in Box 5.1 there is an additional dependent construct—utilization. This particular dependent factor will be used to demonstrate that when we conceive of utilization of performance measurement as a single concept, the process of how independent factors work is to a large extent confounded. Such analyses may suggest interventions that may not be as effective as was hoped for. And although the analysis may not be entirely useless, it may help us achieve only a limited understanding of an otherwise complex process. Furthermore, given the main hypothesis, which states that "utilization is composed of two distinct stages, adoption and implementation, each affected differentially by contextual factors," it is important to analyze the effect of these contextual factors on utilization. Such analysis serves as an important comparison for testing the robustness of the findings of the main hypothesis.

The position of respondents and government (or organization) type are used as control variables. Position is used in part to make this study comparable to previous knowledge utilization studies. It is also used because of the possibility that people in different ranks may have different perceptions of what goes on in their organizations. As a result, if we do not take into account their position, we may end up with conclusions that are based on biased responses.

Another control variable used here is government entity type. According to Weiss (1979), organizational characteristics tend to affect an institution's openness to knowledge. Referring to institutions in the legal and school systems, Weiss asserted that each differed in its utilization of knowledge. Related, in their study on knowledge utilization within the mental health sector, Oh and Rich (1996) differentiated by policy area and found different patterns of knowledge utilization when comparing the different types of policy area. In the mail questionnaire discussed here, such differentiation was captured by looking at the type of government entity the respondent worked for. As can be observed in question 1a of Section V in the questionnaire (see specific questions in Appendix A, the survey instrument), individuals were asked whether they worked for a state agency, municipality, or county. Then each of these three response choices was coded as 0 or 1, depending on the answer, 0 = no and 1 = yes. Organization type is used here as a control variable. For the purposes of control, only two of these responses can be included in a statistical model. The other one must serve as the reference control variable. For this reason, "state" was chosen as the reference.

Data Description

Characteristics of Respondents and Their Organizations

The data showed that about 57 percent (289) of the respondents worked for municipalities; 23 percent (118) said that they worked for county governments; and around 20 percent (101) worked for a state agency or government. Of 497 who answered the question asking for the region in which their organization was located, 9.5 percent, or 47, were located in the Northeast; 26.6 percent, or 132, were in the Midwest; and 25.2 percent, or 125, were in the West. The largest representation was from the South, with about 38.8 percent, or 193 respondents.

Table 5.1 depicts demographic characteristics of the organizations and the respondents. The table shows that the average number of full-time employees (FTEs) was 3,047 (n = 489). The mean rate of unionization for those who answered (n = 477) was 35 percent, and the mean operating budget was $833 million.

The characteristics of the respondents, as depicted in Table 5.1, are as follows: the average number of years respondents had held their current position was 6.3 years; the average number of years respondents had been working in the public sector was 16 years. Although there is a relatively larger variation in this last variable, these individuals' time in their current position and their length of time serving in the public sector indicate that their level of knowledge is more than adequate to assess the dynamics the survey tried to tease out.

The majority of the respondents who answered the question on what position they held were in the director or management-level category. Of 480 who answered, 335, or 69.8 percent, were in this category. The position category with the least number of respondents was the assistant level, with approximately 9 percent, or 45, checking this response choice. Staff level was the second highest category, with 100, or 20.8 percent of respondents. The position distribution can be worrisome to some. Certainly those at the highest level of the organization may have a higher stake in the performance measurement process, and thus might be more inclined to

Table 5.1 Demographic Characteristics of Participating Organizations and Respondents

	N	*Mean*	*Standard Deviation*
Organization			
FTEs	489	3,047	12,913
Operating budget (in millions)	471	833	4,392
Percent unionized	477	35%	37%
Respondent			
Years in position	502	6.3	1.2
Years in public sector	500	16.0	8.3

give responses that make the organization look good. On the other hand, one could argue that these individuals have a more global view of the performance measurement process in their organization and, as a result, can provide a more accurate picture of what is going on in the organization. Furthermore, it is possible that the bias and associated threat to validity that this distribution may have caused was lessened by the sampling scheme that was used for selecting the survey participants.

Dependent Variables: The Utilization of Performance Measures

Prevalence of Measures: What Has Been Adopted?

Table 5.2 shows the frequency distribution of the three variables that were used to measure the concept of adoption. These variables measured the extent to which efficiency, outcome, and output measures had been developed for programs in the organization. To ensure reliability of the responses, respondents were given the following definitions for each performance measure:

- Efficiency measures relate the amount of input to the amount of output or outcome.
- Output measures refer to the amount or quantity of service provided.
- Outcome measures refer to the results of services provided.

As can be observed in Table 5.2, the responses show that efficiency measures and outcome measures are developed with less frequency than output measures

Table 5.2   Extent Performance Measures Had Been Developed (Adopted) for Programs in Respondents' Organization

Variables	For None	For Some	For Many	For All	Total
Efficiency measures	135	249	87	33	504
(percent)	(26.8%)	(49.4%)	(17.3%)	(6.5%)	
Outcome measures	131	224	107	42	504
(percent)	(26.0%)	(44.4%)	(21.2%)	(8.3%)	
Output measures	104	175	154	72	505
(percent)	(20.6%)	(34.7%)	(30.5%)	(14.3%)	

for programs in public organizations. This suggests a level of increasing difficulty as organizations move from measuring inputs (which are usually readily available) to measuring outputs (which tend to be the bulk of what organizations report) to measuring outcomes and efficiency measures (which tend to be more politically loaded and more difficult to assess). The table indicates that of 505 who responded, 154 (about 31 percent) said that output measures had been developed for many programs, while 72 (or about 14 percent) said that they had been developed for all programs. Compare these responses to the extent to which outcome measures and efficiency measures had been developed.

Table 5.2 reveals that a significant difference appears to exist between the level of development of output measures and that of efficiency and outcome measures. Notice that out of 504 respondents, only 87 (17.3 percent) said that efficiency measures had been developed for many programs, while 33 (or about 7 percent) said that they had been developed for all programs. The table also shows that of all respondents, 107 (or about 21 percent) said that outcome measures had been developed for many programs, and only 42 (or about 8 percent) said that they had been developed for all programs. Thus, to summarize, the data show that comparatively outcome measures had been developed less extensively than output measures. Compared to efficiency measures, more respondents stated that outcome measures had been developed for programs in their organization.

Extent of Implementation of Measures

Tables 5.3 to 5.5 show data about the extent to which the three types of performance measures were being used for strategic planning, resource allocation, program management, monitoring and evaluation, and reporting to internal management,

Table 5.3 Frequency of Use of Efficiency Measures

Variables	Never	Sometimes	Frequently	Always	Total
a. Strategic planning (percent)	205 (41.0%)	214 (42.8%)	62 (12.4%)	19 (3.8%)	500
b. Resource allocation (percent)	150 (29.6%)	218 (43.0%)	107 (21.1%)	32 (6.3%)	507
c. Program management, monitoring, and evaluation (percent)	141 (27.9%)	244 (48.2%)	90 (17.8%)	31 (6.1%)	506
d. Reporting to internal management (percent)	137 (27.2%)	229 (45.4%)	100 (19.8%)	38 (7.5%)	504
e. Reporting to elected officials (percent)	149 (29.4%)	244 (48.2%)	84 (16.6%)	29 (5.7%)	506
f. Reporting to citizens or media (percent)	183 (36.2%)	243 (48.1%)	62 (12.3%)	17 (3.4%)	505

elected officials, and citizens or the media. These variables measure the concept of implementation. As can be observed in the tables, most of the responses fall in the *never* or *sometimes* categories. But something else is evident in these tables. The pattern found in the previous analysis on the types of performance measures adopted is also apparent here. That is, the information in these tables shows that compared to output measures, efficiency and outcome measures are less often used for each of the activities listed. This pattern shows consistency, and therefore reliability, with the responses to the questions discussed above.

Other patterns are also noticeable. The information in the three tables suggests that performance measures are less used for strategic planning and reporting to citizens and the media than for other activities. For example, Table 5.3 shows that 41 percent of those who responded stated that efficiency measures are never used for strategic planning purposes. Also, the data show that 36 percent of the respondents stated that their organization never reports efficiency measures to citizens or the media. Consistent with the pattern found on adoption, the tables here also show that outcome measures appear to be used more than efficiency measures but less than output measures. As shown in Table 5.5, only about 29 percent of those who responded stated that output measures are never used for strategic planning in

Table 5.4 Frequency of Use of Outcome Measures

Variables	Never	Sometimes	Frequently	Always	Total
a. Strategic planning (percent)	162 (32.3)	197 (39.2)	108 (21.5%)	35 (7.0%)	502
b. Resource allocation (percent)	130 (25.7%)	207 (40.9%)	125 (24.7%)	44 (8.7%)	506
c. Program management, monitoring, and evaluation (percent)	130 (25.7%)	224 (44.4%)	113 (22.4%)	38 (7.5%)	505
d. Reporting to internal management (percent)	130 (27.8%)	221 (43.8%)	108 (21.4%)	45 (8.9%)	504
e. Reporting to elected officials (percent)	126 (24.9%)	236 (46.6%)	103 (20.4%)	41 (8.1%)	506
f. Reporting to citizens or media (percent)	154 (30.7%)	240 (47.8%)	83 (16.5%)	25 (5.0%)	502

their organization. Furthermore, only 25 percent said that their organizations never report output measures to citizens or the media.

Moreover, output measures, according to the survey respondents, were used by managers more often than outcome and efficiency measures for managing, monitoring, and evaluating the performance of their programs. Likewise, they were more frequently reported to elected officials than any other measure. Citizens, on the other hand, were less likely to hear about performance than elected officials, and when they did get the information, it was about organizational outputs.

Adoption and Implementation in State and Local Government Organizations

A large number of the respondents in organizations at the state level said that they had adopted performance measures. Of those who responded, 56 percent said that their agency had all three types of performance measures for many or all programs. In contrast, only 30 percent of respondents from county agencies and 26 percent from municipalities stated that all three measures had been developed for many or all programs.

Table 5.5 Frequency of Use of Output Measures

Variables	Never	Sometimes	Frequently	Always	Total
a. Strategic planning (percent)	143 (28.5%)	203 (40.5%)	115 (23.0%)	40 (8.0%)	501
b. Resource allocation (percent)	100 (19.8%)	177 (35.1%)	170 (33.7%)	57 (11.3%)	504
c. Program management, monitoring, and evaluation (percent)	104 (20.6%)	191 (37.8%)	165 (32.7%)	45 (8.9%)	505
d. Reporting to internal management (percent)	94 (18.7%)	199 (39.6%)	157 (31.2%)	53 (10.5%)	503
e. Reporting to elected officials (percent)	97 (19.2%)	216 (42.9%)	145 (28.8%)	46 (9.1%)	504
f. Reporting to citizens or media (percent)	127 (25.2%)	234 (46.4%)	112 (22.2%)	31 (6.2%)	504

Table 5.6 Average Levels of Adoption and Implementation of Performance Measures by Government Entity Type

	State	County	Municipality
Adoption	56.00%	30.00%	26.00%
Implementation	46.05%	26.54%	24.92%

Interestingly, as can be observed in Table 5.6, even though a large percentage of respondents from state agencies stated that they had implemented performance measures, there was a significant difference (about 10 percent) between the percentage saying that the measures had been adopted and those saying that they had been implemented (used frequently or always). The gap between adoption and implementation was not as wide for county and municipalities, suggesting that once they adopt performance measures, they are more likely than states to implement them.

Independent Variables

Rational/Technocratic Variables

The questions in the survey dealing with the rational/technocratic factors focused on assessing the organizational capacity to adopt and implement performance measurement systems based on available resources. Respondents were presented with a series of statements that determined the extent to which their organization had each one of a set of elements (or variables) in place. These elements are believed to be important in the performance management effort. The response anchors for these statements were to a: great extent, considerable extent, limited extent, and not at all. The frequency distribution of the answers provided by the respondents is depicted in Table 5.7.

Of the eight statements, in all but three the respondents stated that their organizations either did not have these elements in place or had them only to a limited extent. The responses appear to indicate that a good percentage (35 percent) of organizations collected data that were useful for measuring performance. The individuals answering believed that these data were reliable and relevant for

Table 5.7 Frequency Distribution of Organizational Capacity for Performance Measurement

Variables	Not at All	Limited	Considerable	Great	Total
Commit resources (percent)	99 (19.3%)	304 (59.4%)	90 (17.6%)	19 (3.7%)	512
Assign staff (percent)	102 (20.2%)	308 (60.9%)	85 (16.8%)	11 (2.2%)	506
Assign department (percent)	187 (37.0%)	206 (40.8%)	84 (16.6%)	28 (5.5%)	505
Collect data (percent)	55 (10.8%)	275 (53.8%)	155 (30.3%)	26 (5.1%)	511
Use benchmarks (percent)	135 (26.6%)	296 (58.4%)	68 (13.4%)	8 (1.6%)	507
Management trained (percent)	147 (28.9%)	272 (53.4%)	70 (13.8%)	20 (3.9%)	509
Guided by goals (percent)	30 (5.9%)	211 (41.5%)	228 (44.9%)	39 (7.7%)	508
Communicate strategies (percent)	47 (9.3%)	268 (52.9%)	175 (34.5%)	17 (3.4%)	507

performance measurement. Thus, the data collection capacity seemed to be more prevalent than some of the other capacity-related variables. Likewise, the organizations represented, according to respondents, appeared to be fairly sophisticated when it comes to setting clear goals and objectives to guide action. Almost 53 percent of respondents stated that to a considerable extent their organization had goals and objectives in place. Goals and objectives are important components of a performance-based management system because they serve as the foundation for developing performance measurement indicators or measures.

However, even though these organizations may have had clear goals and objectives, it appears that they did not do as good of a job at communicating the strategies for achieving goals and objectives. The table shows that compared to the previous statement, the percentage of respondents saying that their organizations clearly communicated these strategies significantly declined, with only approximately 38 percent stating that this was done to a considerable or great extent. This may be related to a lack of technical managerial capacity in the area of performance management. Notice that few (approximately 18 percent) stated that managers were trained in management techniques such as Total Quality Management (TQM) or Management by Objective (MBO), both of which emphasize strategy and the connection of activity to desired results. Developing appropriate performance measures, collecting the appropriate data, analyzing the data, and implementing the results requires understanding of the technical aspects of this tool.

Benchmarking did not appear to be prevalent among the organizations represented. For the most part, respondents stated that benchmarking was used only to a limited extent (58.4 percent), with about 27 percent stating that it was not used at all. Likewise, only a few respondents indicated that their organizations had a special unit that focused on the evaluation of program performance, or that they had staff assigned to this task (approximately 22 and 19 percent, respectively). Benchmarking requires that organizations develop performance measures. It also requires that data be collected and compared with data across jurisdictions, units, or whatever the organization has chosen to benchmark with.

Not shown in Table 5.7 is a question also related to the rational/technocratic factors regarding the mission of the organization for which the respondents worked. Respondents were asked the extent to which they agreed that their organization's mission promoted efficiency, a rational/technocratic value at the core of traditional performance management measurement efforts. Approximately 80 percent of those who responded agreed or strongly agreed with the statement (396 out of 497).

The frequency and types of access that management and nonmanagement employees had to performance measurement-related information is shown in Table 5.8. As can be observed in the table, approximately 28 percent (or 189) of 497 respondents indicated that employees frequently or always received or had access to performance measurement information, and only approximately 9 percent stated that employees never had such access. In contrast, when it came to actually

Table 5.8 Frequency of Access to Information and Training on Performance Measurement

Variables	Never	Sometimes	Frequently	Always	Total
Receives information (percent)	44 (8.9%)	264 (53.1%)	129 (26%)	60 (12.1%)	497
Management attends (percent)	58 (11.4%)	352 (69.3%)	92 (18.1%)	6 (1.2%)	508
Nonmanagement attends (percent)	261 (52.6%)	209 (42.1%)	23 (4.6%)	3 0.6%	496

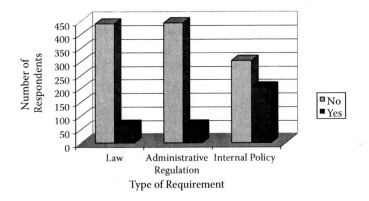

Figure 5.1 Requirements to use performance measures.

attending conferences and workshops on performance measurement, most respondents—261 (about 53 percent) of 508—indicated that nonmanagement employees never had access to such activities. On the other hand, managers were more likely to participate in conference and workshops, with only 11 percent (58 respondents) saying that management employees never attended. Nonetheless, the percentage of respondents saying that managers attended such workshops frequently or always is significantly low (18.1 and 1.2 percent, respectively) and is consistent with respondents' perceptions that managers in their organization are not trained in decision-making managerial techniques.

To assess the effect of formal rational factors, respondents were asked about the kind or requirements they had for using performance measures. These formal requirements were divided into external and internal. As shown in Figure 5.1, the results of the survey appear to indicate that external requirements are less prevalent than internal requirements. Of 510 of the respondents, 68 (about 13 percent) stated that their organization was required by law to have performance measures.

Of those who responded, 67 (or about 13 percent) stated that their organization was required by administrative regulation to have performance measures. Only 27 (5.3 percent) respondents stated that their organization was required by both law and administrative regulation to use performance measures. The total combined number of those saying that there was a law or an administrative regulation or both (external requirements) requiring the use of performance was 162.

In contrast to these external formal requirements, there seemed to be a preponderance of organizations with an internal policy requiring performance measures. A larger number of those who responded (205, or about 40 percent of 510) stated that their organization had an internal policy requiring the use of performance measures.

Internal and External Interest Groups

The political aspect of organizational life embodied in the formation of coalitions with and by interest groups was measured using an internal and external perspective. Participants were asked to evaluate the extent to which internal and external actors were involved in activities aimed at promoting and supporting performance measurement. The distribution of answers is summarized in Table 5.9.

The information in the table highlights the central role that managers play in the performance management effort. According to the respondents, in the organizations surveyed, management had taken the initiative to promote and support performance measurement and to form working groups (coalitions) to support the effort. Of those who responded, approximately 48 percent (or 243 [178 + 65]) said that to a considerable or great extent management had taken the initiative to promote performance measures. And about 34 percent (or 173 [123 + 50]) stated that management had formed working groups for that purpose. On the other hand, while employees appeared to be somewhat involved in promoting the efforts (44.6 percent of respondents said that they were involved to a limited extent), they seemed to be less likely to take on a more active role by forming groups to support performance measurement (53 percent of respondents stated not at all).

In terms of the impact of political activities that involve external actors, the respondents indicated that their constituents had some involvement in promoting accountability and efficiency (only 34.9 percent, 175, stated that citizens did not have any involvement in promoting accountability and efficiency). This information directs attention to two distinctive characteristics of public administration in the United States. First, it underscores the role of accountability and efficiency, two values that appear to be responsible for much of the performance improvement movements in the public sector. Second, it highlights the increasing trend of citizens' involvement in governance.

Table 5.9 Frequency Distribution of Answers to Variables Measuring Organizational Politics

Variables	Not at All	Limited	Considerable	Great	Total
Management promotes (percent)	43 (8.4%)	225 (44.0%)	178 (34.8%)	65 (12.7%)	511
Management forms groups (percent)	128 (25.0%)	211 (41.2%)	123 (24.0%)	50 (9.8%)	512
Employees promote (percent)	224 (44.2%)	226 (44.6%)	55 (10.8%)	2 (0.4%)	507
Employees form groups (percent)	270 (53.0%)	179 (35.2%)	51 (10.0%)	9 (1.8%)	509
Solicit consultant (percent)	273 (53.3%)	197 (38.5%)	36 (7.0%)	6 (1.2%)	512
Constituents involved (percent)	176 (34.9%)	243 (48.1%)	80 (15.8%)	6 (1.2%)	505
Elected officials promote (percent)	150 (29.6%)	246 (48.5%)	86 (17.0%)	25 (4.9%)	507
Elected officials form groups (percent)	266 (52.8%)	185 (36.7%)	39 (7.7%)	14 (2.8%)	504

Most respondents said that elected officials had taken the initiative to promote performance measurement, with only about 30 percent saying that elected officials had not at all done this. However, less than 50 percent said that elected officials had taken the more active role of forming working groups to promote the efforts. It appears that while elected officials may talk about and believe in the importance of such efforts, the how-to is left up to management.

Interestingly, the table shows that soliciting consultants to help develop and implement performance measures is not done very often. It is hard to draw a conclusion as to what the reason for this is. Yet, we can think of several possibilities. These include lack of resources, or the organization having personnel without the required knowledge or with little interest in developing and implementing a performance measurement system.

Table 5.10 Frequency Distribution of Variables Measuring Culture

Variables	Strongly Disagree	Disagree	Agree	Strongly Agree	Total
Management implements (percent)	9 (1.8%)	65 (12.7%)	318 (62.4%)	118 (23.1%)	510
Management views (percent)	26 (5.1%)	157 (30.8%)	258 (50.6%)	69 (13.5%)	510
Nonmanagement accepts (percent)	32 (6.3%)	260 (51.0%)	208 (40.8%)	10 (2.0%)	510
Nonmanagement understands (percent)	54 (10.7%)	278 (55.2%)	167 (33.1%)	5 (1.0%)	504
Rewards improving (percent)	78 (15.5%)	225 (44.7%)	177 (35.2%)	23 (4.6%)	503
Rewards risk taking (percent)	89 (17.9%)	268 (53.8%)	131 (26.3%)	10 (2.0%)	498

Organizational Culture

Table 5.10 summarizes the responses to the Likert scale items that were used to assess organizational culture and its impact on the utilization of performance measurement. Respondents were asked the extent to which they agreed with each of the statements presented and were given four response choices: strongly disagree, disagree, agree, and strongly agree. As noted earlier, these were forced responses in that respondents were not given an option to have "no opinion." But of course, as one can observe in the column showing the number of respondents, a small number of respondents chose not to respond to these questions.

The numbers in the table indicate that with the exception of the first item ("management implements" appropriate innovation and change), most answers fall in the disagree and agree categories. Also, as a percentage of the total, respondents tended to disagree more with those statements regarding nonmanagement employees' acceptance of change and understanding of performance measures. This is not an unexpected answer given the previous discussions of the findings on organizational politics, which depicted nonmanagement employees as less active in promoting the process and being less involved in activities to support the efforts.

An interesting finding shown in this table is that most respondents stated that their organization did not reward improving performance or risk taking. Of those who answered, 303 (or 60.2 percent [78 + 225]) did not agree with the first statement, while almost 72 percent (or 357 [89 + 268]) did not agree with the second. This is the kind of information that fuels criticisms of performance measurement and the whole accountability movement. Specifically, critics and opponents feel that focusing on performance measurement for accountability does not allow managers to focus on what they should be focusing on—managing. As a result, performance measurement can be a risky business given the perception that it could be used to punish those who do not appear to be achieving their goal, instead of encouraging them to find ways to improve.

There is even risk in doing too well. Certainly something not unheard of in government is that organizations (used here in the general sense to include departments, agencies, and programs) that become efficient in using their funds may actually face budget cuts the following year. As a result, we often witness a spending frenzy of savings at the end of the fiscal year. The somewhat wicked rationale of those in charge of making the budget allocations to these organizations is that they should continue to do well if their savings are taken away because they have already shown that they can do more with less or keep the same level of performance with fewer resources. Such practices create disincentives for performance improvement.

Multivariate Analyses

This section describes the results of the multivariate analyses that were used to analyze the variables included in subsequent analyses to test the hypotheses. The focus is on the results of the factor analysis procedure and the scale reliability testing that was performed.

Factor Analysis and Scale Reliability Testing

The Likert scale variables were examined with factor analysis using squared multiple correlations as prior communality estimates. The principal factor method, the most commonly used factor analysis approach, was used to extract the factors, and with the exception of the dependent variables, this procedure was followed with a promax (oblique) rotation. Then the scree test was used as part of the decision criteria for retaining factors.

As mentioned in the previous chapter of this book, factor analysis is an iterative process. Sometimes analysts have some idea of what variables should load on what factors, but other times they do not. Accordingly, suggested Hatcher (1994), when the results of the analysis do not corroborate expectations, one should return to the relevant literature, revise the initial model, and even find new ways of measuring the constructs of interests. Here, in most cases the results of the initial analyses of the survey data were consistent with expectations. However, in a few instances it was necessary to follow Hatcher's advice. I will not go over the details of the necessary iterations; instead, I will focus on the final factor analyses that led to the constructs used in subsequent analyses.

After the factors for subsequent analyses were identified, it was necessary to perform one more factor-related operation. As noted in the previous chapter, to use these factors in subsequent analysis it is necessary to obtained factor scores. There are a number of options as to how to obtain these scores. One of the options, which is considered a less sophisticated approach, is to add together the variables that load on the factor (factor-based scores). Another option, which is what was followed here, is to allow the computer program to calculate estimated factor scores. As discussed earlier, the resulting estimated factor scores are linear composites of the optimally weighted variables under analysis.

The preparation for further analysis does not end with the calculation of factor scores. The analyst must assess the reliability of the scales. Thus, subsequent to factor analysis, the scales were tested for internal consistency by calculating Cronbach's coefficient alpha. For this test, only those observations that had no missing values for the variables under analysis were included.

Dependent Variables and Corresponding Factors

The focus of the main research question of the survey study, namely, understanding why performance measures systems were not more widely used, called for a set of three different constructs—adoption, implementation, and utilization—to be used as dependent variables. Thus, having identified the constructs, conducting confirmatory factor analysis was the next logical step. With confirmatory factor analysis, not only do we need to know the number of factors (latent or unobserved variables) being assessed, but we also need to know which manifest variables load on which factors (Hatcher, 1994). Here, the number of desired factors was known, as well as which variables represented each of these factors.

The questionnaire items (variables) and the corresponding factor loadings for the dependent variables measuring adoption, implementation, and utilization are presented in Box 5.3. The numbers in the box show that the three dependent variables relating to the extent to which performance measures had been developed load on the factor labeled adoption. All of the factor loadings for the variables making up this construct are greater than .70. The same is true for the variables that form part of the underlying construct implementation. Having a high factor loading is part of the criteria used to determine which factors should be retained. Such a decision was not relevant for these dependent variables, but as will be explained later, it was relevant for the independent variables. Finally, with only one exception, all factor loadings on the utilization construct were greater than or equal to .70.

The final communality estimate numbers shown in the table refer to the sum of the communality for each observed variable. Communality refers to the variance in an observed variable that is accounted for by the common factors (Hatcher, 1994). Communality for a variable is calculated by squaring that variable's factor

BOX 5.3: UNROTATED FACTOR LOADINGS FOR UNDERLYING DEPENDENT FACTORS

Exhibit A. Unrotated Factor Loadings for Adoption

Item	Loadings
Developed efficiency measures	.84
Developed outcome measures	.88
Developed output measures	.90
Final communality estimates	**2.27**

Exhibit B. Unrotated Factor Loadings for Implementation

Item	Loadings
Use efficiency measures for:	
Strategic planning	.71
Resource allocation	.75
Program management, monitoring, and evaluation	.80
Reporting to internal management	.80
Reporting to elected officials	.79
Reporting to citizens or the media	.79
Use outcome measures for:	
Strategic planning	.81
Resource allocation	.82
Program management, monitoring, and evaluation	.85
Reporting to internal management	.86
Reporting to elected officials	.85
Reporting to citizens or the media	.83
Use output measures for:	
Strategic planning	.83
Resource allocation	.80
Program management, monitoring, and evaluation	.80
Reporting to internal management	.83
Reporting to elected officials	.84
Reporting to citizens or the media	.81
Final communality estimates	**11.82**

Exhibit C. Unrotated Factor Loadings for Utilization

Item	Loadings
Developed Efficiency Measures	.64
Developed Outcome Measures	.71
Developed Output Measures	.70
	.70

Use Efficiency Measures For:

Strategic Planning	.70
Resource Allocation	.73
Program Management, Monitoring, and Evaluation	.80
Reporting to Internal Management	.80
Reporting to Elected Officials	.77
Reporting to Citizens or the Media	.77

Use Outcome Measures For:

Strategic Planning	.80
Resource Allocation	.80
Program Management, Monitoring, and Evaluation	.85
Reporting to Internal Management	.86
Reporting to Elected Officials	.83
Reporting to Citizens or the Media	.81

Use Output Measures For:

Strategic Planning	.79
Resource Allocation	.79
Program Management, Monitoring, and Evaluation	.83
Reporting to Internal Management	.84
Reporting to Elected Officials	.81
Reporting to Citizens or the Media	.79
Final Communality Estimates	**12.89**

loadings for all retained common factors. For example, the loading for the variable *developed efficiency measures* on the factor *adoption* in Box 5.3 is .84. Squaring factor loading .84 yields .71. This means that 71 percent of the variance in that variable is accounted for by the factor *adoption*. In contrast, the communality for this variable on the factor *utilization* is only .41 (.64 squared).

Because only one factor was being retained for each set of dependent variables, the next step was to obtain the final communality estimate. This was accomplished by adding the square of the loadings for each variable on the factor.

The factor analysis for the dependent variables was then followed by the Cronbach scale reliability test. The coefficients of reliability for all three of the dependent constructs exceeded the recommended coefficient alpha of .70. The raw variables coefficient alpha for adoption was .84; both implementation and utilization had a coefficient alpha of .97.

Independent Variables and Corresponding Factors

Exploratory factor analysis was used to analyze all the variables comprising the general constructs—politics, culture, and rational/technocratic. The principal factor method was used to extract the factors. This procedure was then followed with a promax (oblique) rotation. The promax rotation consists of two steps. First, a varimax rotation is conducted. At this point, the factors extracted are uncorrelated. Then, the factors are rotated again, but this time this restriction is relaxed and factors are allowed to be correlated. The result is an oblique solution. For the most part, oblique rotations produce better results when the actual underlying factors are truly correlated and tend to provide a simpler structure (Hatcher, 1994). The factor loadings on a promax rotation matrix are standardized regression coefficients. Also known as pattern loadings, these coefficients represent the unique contribution that each factor makes to the variance of the observed variables (Rummel, 1970).

The decision of how many factors to retain for all the independent variables analyzed was based on the scree test and the interpretability criteria explained in Chapter 4 of this book. Thus, for example, the analyses yielded two meaningful factors for the *political* and *culture* variables. On the other hand, for the *rational/technocratic* variables, the analysis yielded three meaningful factors. Only these factors were retained for rotation. It should be noted that there is no established rule for what constitutes a high factor loading for a variable. Hatcher (1994) has suggested that a factor loading of .40 can be considered high. Spector (1992), on the other hand, has suggested anything between .30 to .35 or above. The suggestion of Spector was followed here. The results of the various factor analyses are shown in Box 5.4. The results of testing the reliability of the scales are shown in Box 5.5.

Rational/Technocratic

As mentioned earlier, the exploratory factor analysis on some of the variables (goal orientation and technical capacity) included in the overall concept of rational/technocratic yielded three different factors. These are shown in Exhibit A of Box 5.4. Each of these factors appears to measure three different concepts within the realm of the rational model.

BOX 5.4: RESULTS OF EXPLORATORY FACTOR
ANALYSIS WITH OBLIQUE ROTATION

Exhibit A. Independent Variables Relating to Rational/Technocratic Factors and Corresponding Factor Loadings (Standardized Regression Coefficients)

Item	Factor 1 Loadings	Factor 2 Loadings	Factor 3 Loadings
Committed resources	**.74**	.02	.10
Assigned staff	**.79**	.07	−.02
Assigned department	**.69**	.03	.02
Collect reliable data	**.62**	.17	.06
Use benchmarks	**.66**	.09	−.02
Management trained in applications	.22	.26	.22
Guided by goals	.08	**.77**	−.02
Communicate strategies	.02	**.82**	−.02
Mission promotes efficiency	.02	**.34**	.10
Access to how-to information	.07	.18	**.48**
Management attend conferences	.03	.00	**.68**
Nonmanagement attend conferences	.02	−.03	**.70**

Final communality estimates   **6.09**

Exhibit B. Independent Variables Relating to Politics and Corresponding Factor Loadings (Standardized Regression Coefficients)

Item	Factor 1 Loadings	Factor 2 Loadings
Management promotes	**.65**	.16
Nonmanagement promotes	**.74**	.00
Management forms groups	**.63**	.23
Nonmanagement forms groups	**.75**	.06
Constituents involved	.11	**.52**
Consultants solicited	.20	**.34**
Elected officials promote	.11	**.72**
Elected officials form groups	.02	**.76**

Final communality estimates   **4.20**

Exhibit C. Independent Variables Relating to Culture and Corresponding Factor Loadings (Standardized Regression Coefficients)

Item	Factor 1 Loadings	Factor 2 Loadings
Management implements change	.56	.09
Management views performance measures as important	.68	−.03
Employees accept change	.54	.09
Employees understand performance measures	.67	.00
Organization rewards performance improvement	−.04	.85
Organization rewards risk taking	.10	.79
Final communality estimates	**3.03**	

Because of the nature of the variables loading on factor 1 (above .30), this factor was labeled *resources*. The variables deal with the availability of monetary and nonmonetary resources. Factor 2, on the other hand, was labeled *goal orientation*. Notice that the variable *management trained in applications* had low loadings on all three factors. Its highest loading was on factor 2, goal orientation. The reliability test for this scale yielded a coefficient alpha that was above the minimum recommended .70 (see Box 5.4). Thus, even though the variable had a low loading on the factor, including it did not decrease the internal consistency of the scale. Yet, when

BOX 5.5: CRONBACH COEFFICIENT ALPHA FOR ALL INDEPENDENT FACTORS: RAW VARIABLES COEFFICIENT

Factor	Raw Variables Coefficient
Internal interest groups	.85
External interest groups	.76
Attitude	.73
Rewards	.87
Resources	.86
Goal orientation	.73
Access to information	.70

one allows the program to calculate the estimated scores, the effect of this variable (because it is optimally weighted) practically disappears. The last factor, factor 3, was labeled *access to information*.

Organizational Politics

As can be observed in Box 5.4, Exhibit B, the variables that loaded on factor 1 appear to represent internal political activities in the organization. The variables measure activity in support of performance measurement by management and non-management employees. Thus, factor 1, a hypothetical variable, greatly contributes to the variance of these four variables. Note that all four loadings are significantly higher than the recommended level.

On the other hand, the variables that loaded on factor 2 appear to better represent external political activities. This factor explained a significant portion of the variation on each of the four variables that loaded. These variables include activities with and by consultants, elected officials, and citizens in support of performance measurement. Accordingly, in subsequent analyses, factor 1 was labeled *internal interest groups* and factor 2 was labeled *external interest groups*.

Culture

Exploratory factor analysis revealed that the variables thought to measure only one concept, labeled *openness to change* in the hypothesis presented in Chapter 3 of this book, in reality measured two different aspects of culture. The rotated factor loadings are shown in Exhibit C of Box 5.4. The four variables dealing with aspects of acceptance and understanding of change, innovation, and performance measures loaded on one factor. The variables that dealt with the existence of an organization's culture that rewarded performance improvement and risk taking loaded on a second factor. As a result, the first factor was labeled *attitude* and the second was labeled *rewards*.

Yet, there is a certain technical limitation regarding the extent that the factor *rewards* measures what it is supposed to measure. The reason is that it has been recommended that scales have at least three variables (Hatcher, 1994). However, due to the high intercorrelation of these two variables (as shown by the coefficient alpha in Box 5.5) and their theoretical importance, it makes sense to use them as a factor and not as two separate variables.

Summary

The results of the descriptive analyses of the dependent variables provide empirical evidence to the accounts that public organizations have tended to focus on measuring and implementing output measures. Though output measures may be useful for some things, they provide limited information about the performance of organizations. For a number of audiences, including managers of programs, outcome measures and efficiency measures would be more useful and interesting. This is particularly the case when it comes to making value judgments about and suggesting improvement for performance. The findings also suggest that for a number of reasons, organizations may find it more difficult to develop and implement outcome and efficiency measures than output measures.

In terms of organizational characteristics that impact on the adoption and implementation of these measures, the data revealed that internal requirements to use performance measures are more prevalent than external requirements. A related issue is that although elected officials and employees are important actors in performance measurement efforts, to a large extent the success of such efforts depends on managers.

According to respondents, many organizations have not made the connection between success of performance measurement and a positive and supportive organizational culture. Few respondents thought that the organization rewarded improving performance and taking risks. Also, when it comes to allocating different types of resources that can support performance measurement efforts, most responses pointed to a lack of commitment. And although a good number of respondents agreed that their organizations collected performance data, the use of these data is limited.

Two types of factor analyses were conducted: confirmatory on the dependent variables and exploratory on the independent variables. The confirmatory factor analyses provided the bases for the factor scores of the three dependent variables—adoption, implementation, and utilization—to be used in hypotheses testing. The exploratory factor analyses identified several underlying constructs that influence performance measurement efforts.

Chapter 6

Modeling Causal Linkages

This chapter presents the findings of statistical data analysis conducted to test the hypotheses presented earlier in Chapter 3 of this book. The models for testing these hypotheses are shown in Box 6.1. The analyses consisted of running ordinary least squared multiple regressions on the variables and constructs (with their respective factor score for each observation) identified in the models. The residuals of all the regression models were analyzed to determine whether the specified regression models were appropriate. The analysis did not suggest any departure from the linear model. Also, the variance inflation factor method was used to detect multicollinearity. This procedure detects whether one predictor is an exact, or near-exact, combination of others. The analysis indicated that multicollinearity was not a problem in any of the models.

To avoid comparing apples and oranges and drawing erroneous conclusions, only those observations that had responses to all items included in the models were used in the multiple regression analyses. That is, observations with missing values for any one of the variables that formed part of the models being tested were not included in the analysis.

The chapter is divided into two main sections. The first section discusses the basic integrated models for adoption, implementation, and utilization, which do not include the more concrete rational/technocratic factors *goal orientation*, *resources*, and *access to information* as predictor variables. The second section deals with further causal modeling discussing the results of the analyses of the more comprehensive models. The point of presenting the findings in multiple sections is twofold. First, it shows that there is empirical support for the argument that although these concrete rational/technocratic factors are necessary for supporting performance measurement efforts, they are not sufficient to ensure the implementation of performance measurement information.

BOX 6.1: REGRESSION MODELS

The identified factors were used to specify the following regression equations. These models were used to test the hypotheses and subhypotheses stated in Chapter 3 and to develop an elaborated model of Utilization of performance measurement information.

■ The following set of equations were used to test the basic integrated models as specified in subhypotheses 2a, 2b, 3a, 3b, 3c, 3e, and hypothesis 3.
  – Model 1:
    Adoption = external requirements + internal requirements + internal interest groups + external politics + attitude + rewards + municipality + county + position + percent unionized
  – Model 2:
    Implementation = external requirements + internal requirements + internal interest groups + external interest groups + attitude + rewards + municipality + county + position + percent unionized
  – Model 3:
    Utilization = external requirements + internal requirements + internal interest groups + external politics + attitude + rewards + municipality + county + position + percent unionized
■ To test the interaction effects hypothesized in subhypotheses 3d and 3f, respectively, the following terms were added to the three models specified above:
  (1) (Attitude) * (external requirements)
  (2) (Percent unionized) * (internal interest groups)
■ This resulted in six new models shown in the tables ahead. Two models are for *adoption* (models 4 and 7), two for *implementation* (models 5 and 8), and two for *utilization* (models 6 and 9).
■ Following the logic of pattern matching, to strengthen the robustness of the models and to develop the path model, the basic integrated models were further elaborated in four different ways:
  1. Subhypothesis 2e was tested by regressing all the independent factors specified in models 1, 2, and 3 on *resources, goal orientation*, and *access to information*. The models used for this purpose were:
  – Model 10:
    Resources = external requirements + internal requirements + internal interest groups + external politics + attitude + rewards + municipality + county + position + percent unionized
  – Model 11:

Goal orientation = external requirements + internal requirements + internal interest groups + external interest groups + attitude + reward + municipality + county + position + percent unionized
- Model 12:
  Access to information = external requirements + internal requirements + internal politics + external interest groups + attitude + rewards + municipality + county + position + percent unionized
2. Then, these mediating factors were added to model 1, model 2, and model 3. This also allowed for testing hypothesis 2.
- Model 13:
  Adoption = external requirements + internal requirements + internal interest groups + external politics + attitude + rewards + municipality + county + position + percent unionized + resources + goal orientation + access to information
- Model 14:
- Implementation = external requirements + internal requirements + internal interest groups + external interest groups + attitude + rewards + municipality + county + position + percent unionized + resources + goal orientation + access to information
- Model 15:
  Utilization = external requirements + internal requirements + internal interest groups + external interest groups + attitude + rewards + municipality + county + position + percent unionized + resources + goal orientation + access to information
3. The next to the last step was to add the factor *adoption* to model 2. This represented the first step in estimating the path model and a further step in elaboration. The result was model 16:
- Model 16:
  Implementation = adoption + external requirements + internal requirements + internal interest groups + external interest groups + attitude + rewards + municipality + county + position + percent unionized
4. Lastly, the more concrete rational/technocratic factors were added to model 16 to determine the direct effects of these and all other independent factors and variables on *implementation*. The resulting model is shown below (this new model is an extension of model 14).
- Model 17:
  Implementation = adoption + external requirements + internal requirements + internal interest groups + external interest groups + attitude + rewards + municipality + county + position + percent unionized + resources + goal orientation + access to information

Note: Models 13 and 17 were used as the basis for the path analysis.

Second, it helps to demonstrate the validity of the main hypothesis that serves as the foundation for this book, guiding the survey study described here and the subsequent follow-up interviews:

Hypothesis 1: Utilization is composed of two distinct stages, adoption and implementation, each affected differentially by contextual factors.

The approach used serves to highlight the difference in magnitude and significance of the factors affecting adoption from those affecting implementation. All the multiple regression models used for testing this hypothesis were significant at less than the .01 level. Further evidence in support of this hypothesis is provided by the findings of the integrated models for the crude utilization construct. The results of the analysis show that this construct, which does not differentiate adoption from implementation, obscures the real effect of the predictor factors. In the pages that follow, whenever I discuss this crude utilization model, I'll always refer to it using lowercase. This is done to distinguish it from the overall concept of Utilization, which, as suggested in hypothesis 1, refers to both adoption and implementation.

The data analysis and presentation of findings are guided by three different types of pattern-matching approaches, discussed earlier in Chapter 3 of this book: pattern matching with respect to outcomes (adoption and implementation), elaboration with respect to the cause (the purification approach), and model elaboration with mediation. Thus, the presentation of the results is organized as follows. First, the discussion starts with an analysis of the results of testing subhypotheses 2a, 2b, 3a, 3b, 3c, and 3e, and hypothesis 3 in multiple regression models of the factors *adoption, implementation,* and *utilization*. The results of the analysis of the interaction effects hypothesized in subhypotheses 3d and 3f are also discussed in this section. The discussion highlights the elaboration approach with respect to the dependent constructs. That is, conceptual replication was conducted to assess the differential effect of the independent factors on adoption and on implementation. The assumption underlying this approach, as articulated by Mark (1990), is that different process theories predict different patterns across two or more independent variables.

Second, the results of the elaborated models with mediation are presented in the "Elaboration: Toward an Estimated Causal Model" section. In this section subhypotheses 1a, 2c, 2d, and 2e are tested. The section draws attention to the elaboration of the models by means of the purification approach. As discussed in an earlier chapter, this entails decomposing a treatment to isolate the components that are responsible for the effect. The last part of this chapter focuses on an estimated path model for adoption and implementation. Thus, the analyses and findings presented in this chapter can be understood as a series of steps taken to validate theory and to tease out relationships, which culminate with the estimation of causal relationships as depicted by a path model.

Table 6.1 Multiple Regression Model 1: Basic Integrated Model Explaining Adoption

R-sq	Adj R-sq	F Value	P > F	N
.5002	.4785	35.23	.0001	363

Independent Factors	Parameter Estimate	T Value	Prob > T
Intercept	.0436	0.272	.7860
External requirements	.1290	1.677	.0945
Internal requirements	**.5766**	**7.027**	**.0001**
Internal interest groups	**.3725**	**5.027**	**.0001**
External interest groups	.0332	0.464	.6431
Percent unionized	.0526	0.513	.6084
Attitude	.0403	0.648	.5174
Rewards	.0893	1.531	.1267
County	–.1667	–1.324	.1863
Municipality	–.2246	–1.911	.0568
Position of respondent	–.0794	–1.655	.0989

Basic Integrated Models: Deconstructing Utilization Using Pattern Matching with Respect to the Outcome

Earlier in Chapter 3, Box 3.1, Exhibit A and B, the hypothesized relationships between adoption and implementation and the set of independent variables (or factors) were summarized. These exhibits also included the expected behavior of these factors with regard to whether the impact would be positive or negative. The results of the regression models testing these subhypotheses are shown in Tables 6.1 to 6.3. Those factors that are significant at less than the .05 level are highlighted in bold.

The Impact of Contextual Factors

Formal Politics (External and Internal Requirements)

The theoretical argumentation developed earlier regarding the effect of external and internal requirements was supported by the evidence presented in Tables 6.1 and 6.2 (see subhypotheses 2a and 2b). The evidence shows that relative to the effect of internal requirements, the effect of external requirements on adoption and

Table 6.2 Multiple Regression Model 2: Basic Integrated Model Explaining Implementation

R-sq	Adj R-sq	F Value	P > F	N
.4874	.4729	33.47	.0001	363

Independent Factors		Parameter Estimate	T Value	Prob > T
Intercept		−.1300	−0.839	.4019
External requirements		.0953	1.284	.1999
Internal requirements		**.3874**	**4.894**	**.0001**
Internal interest groups		**.1838**	**2.571**	**.0105**
External interest groups		**.2696**	**3.899**	**.0001**
Percent unionized		−.1075	−1.087	.2777
Attitude		**.1373**	**2.288**	**.0227**
Rewards		**.1164**	**2.068**	**.0394**
County		.0295	0.243	.8081
Municipality		.1107	0.977	.3292
Position of respondent		−.0463	−1.001	.3176

implementation is very small. The effect of external requirements, as measured by the parameter estimate, is about .13 for adoption and marginally significant at less than the .10 level. Their effect on implementation was smaller (about .10) and non-significant. This finding holds in the crude utilization model shown in Table 6.3.

On the other hand, internal requirements, as predicted in subhypothesis 2b, had a strong and significant effect on both adoption and implementation. But as expected, the effect was larger on adoption than on implementation. The effect on the utilization construct was just as large. By looking at Table 6.1, one will notice that the parameter estimate of this variable in the adoption model was substantially larger than in the implementation model (.58 and .39 at less than the .01 level, respectively). The estimate for the crude utilization model is .42, also significant at less than the .01 level.

These findings clearly support the hypothesis and theoretical argument that when the policy to use performance measures comes from within the organization, performance measures are more likely to be adopted. Several explanations can be given for this phenomenon. One is that unless top management is committed to the effort, mandates will have little effect on the organization. Having an internal

Table 6.3 Multiple Regression Model 3: Basic Integrated Model Explaining Utilization

R-sq	Adj R-sq	F Value	P > F	N
.5115	.4976	36.85	.0001	363

Independent Factors		Parameter Estimate	T Value	Prob > T
Intercept		.1036	1.394	.1643
External requirements		.1036	1.394	.1643
Internal requirements		**.4290**	**5.408**	**.0001**
Internal interest groups		**.2170**	**3.030**	**.0026**
External interest groups		**.2530**	**3.652**	**.0003**
Percent unionized		−.0935	−.0935	.3459
Attitude		**.1325**	**2.205**	**.0281**
Rewards		**.1185**	**2.101**	**.0363**
County		.0051	0.042	.9664
Municipality		.0735	0.647	.5180
Position of respondent		.0526	−1.135	.2573

policy can be interpreted as some form of commitment from the top. Yet, others (e.g., Korman and Glennerster, 1985) have also suggested that public organizations do not necessarily think that they are expected to implement policies for change. Thus, while internal requirements may lead to adoption, as with external mandates, they do not necessarily compel implementation, but may facilitate the process.

Organizational Politics (External and Internal Interest Groups)

It was predicted in subhypothesis 3a that because of the uncertainty of whether the information is going to be misused or misinterpreted, internal interest groups in support of performance measurement would be particularly important during the adoption stage. As was suggested in the case studies reviewed, this uncertainty may cause fear in both management and nonmanagement employees, who are internal interest groups, and could lead to resistance. Such resistance may end up substantially hindering the adoption of performance measures. As implied by the organizational politics theories discussed earlier, one of the strategies to overcome uncertainty is to form coalitions with these interest groups. These coalitions would work together with management to support change efforts. Therefore, when these internal interest groups work in support of performance measurement efforts, adoption is more likely to occur.

Table 6.1 supports these assertions. Compared to the factor external interest groups, the factor internal interest groups is significant and primarily responsible for the adoption of performance measures. The parameter estimates for internal interest groups and external interest groups are .37 (significant at less than the .01 level) and .03 (significant at less than the .10 level), respectively. On the other hand, when it comes to implementation of these two factors, the one with the greatest influence is external interest groups (about .27 parameter estimate).

Compare these results to the crude utilization model presented in Table 6.3. The results convey that there is very little difference in the effect of these two factors. Thus, this confirms that this model which is based on the assumption that implementation automatically follows adoption, does not provide an accurate picture of the effect of these political processes. When we make this erroneous assumption, we are not able to get a clear picture of the way in which political factors affect both adoption and implementation of performance measures.

Unionization

It was hypothesized that as the level of unionization in an organization decreases, adoption and, particularly implementation (see subhypothesis 3c), increase. The analysis, however, found that the variable percent of unionized employees does not have a significant effect on either one of the models. But the direction of the effect is consistent with expectations in two of the three models tested. Note also that the magnitude of this factor is larger in the implementation model (–.11 parameter estimate) than in any of the two other models (.05 and .09 for adoption and utilization, respectively). Though not significant in this analysis, as will be shown later, unionization is a factor that must be considered by those promoting changes such as performance-based management and performance measurement in particular.

Culture (Attitude and Rewards)

The tables show that the two constructs measuring a culture that is open to change–attitude and rewards–have a small and nonsignificant impact on adoption (parameter estimates of .05 and .08, respectively). However, they have a significant impact on implementation (parameter estimate .14 for factor attitude and .10 for factor rewards, both significant at less than the .05 level).

These findings appear to corroborate the theoretical argument on which hypothesis 3 was based, which suggests that organizational culture facilitates use of performance measurement information. Therefore, the more the organization has a culture that embraces change and rewards taking risks, the more likely that implementation will occur. As for the crude utilization model, it can be noted in

Table 6.3 that both of these factors are significant in explaining the dependent variable. The factor attitude is significant at less than the .05 level with a parameter estimate of approximately .13. The factor rewards, with a parameter estimate of about .12, is also significant at the .05 level.

Control Variables (Organization Type and Position of Respondents)

Table 6.1 shows that in the basic integrated model for adoption, counties and municipalities are both negatively related to adoption. In this context, this means that relative to state-level organizations, respondents from county and municipal governments tended to say that they had not developed (adopted) performance measures. In contrast, respondents from state governments tended to say that they had. The parameter estimate for counties, however, is smaller than that of municipalities (–.17 compared to –.22, respectively). Also, counties are not significant, whereas the significance level of municipalities gets very close to the .05 threshold.

In the basic integrated implementation model, shown in Table 6.2, neither one of these variables is significant, but both are positively related to implementation. This means that relative to states, counties and municipalities are more likely to implement. When we assume that the factors that affect adoption are the same as those that affect implementation, as we do in the utilization model in Table 6.3, the effect of these two variables are confounded. It is not possible to differentiate effects, and answer the question of who is adopting and who is implementing performance measures.

The variable position of respondents was not significant in any of the three models (it approached the .10 significance level in the adoption model). Therefore, it appears that respondents in higher positions were not more likely than those in lower positions to say that their organization had adopted and implemented a performance measurement system. Thus, the negative effect of this factor implies that those in higher positions (here it ranges from directors and managers to assistant directors and assistant managers to staff level) tended to say that their organization had not adopted or implemented performance measures.

This suggests that, indeed, performance measures may not be used throughout the organization. And, if they are used, it only happens at the lower levels of the organization and there is no awareness of their use by top management. This could also be an indication of lack of coordination of performance measurement efforts within the larger organization (Newcomer and Wright, 1997). But most importantly, this raises the question of how performance measure efforts can be successful when there is not awareness at the top levels of the organization about their prevalence and use. As suggested by the experience of Texas (Merjanian, 1996), performance measures should be used regularly and publicly; this is essential to ensure system longevity and usefulness and in raising public awareness and support for reform efforts.

A related explanation for this finding is that individuals at the lower level (here, this includes analysts) could be the ones most involved and most knowledgeable as to the state of development of performance measures in the organization. It is not uncommon for organizations to designate someone to whom all performance measurement-related questions go, including the survey that was sent out for this study. The reasons for having a point person in these efforts made sense to Minnesota's Department of Labor (Wilkins, 1996, p. 7):

> *An agency cannot rely on its managers to implement this type of change without knowledgeable assistance.... Labor and industry used the earlier lessons and designated a knowledgeable coordinator who works with program managers and line-staff to develop their missions, goals, objectives, and measures. This assignment is a quality control measure that allows a single individual to assure consistency and continuity across program units in the construction of performance measures.*

Nevertheless, having an expert in charge does not negate the need to bring awareness about performance measures to all levels of the organization. This is the only way for performance measures to become something an agency does without having to think about it.

Moderation (Interaction) Effects

This section describes the results of testing subhypotheses 3d and 3f, which were based on interaction effects. Specifically, those hypotheses claimed that the level of unionization and attitude influences the extent to which internal interest groups and external requirements, respectively, affect adoption, implementation, and utilization. These hypotheses were tested using multiple regression models 4 through 9, discussed in Box 6.1.

Unionization and Internal Interest Groups

Tables 6.4 through 6.6 depict the results of testing the analysis of the effect of the variable percent of unionized employees on internal interest groups and the subsequent effects on adoption, implementation, and utilization.

It was expected that unions would have a negative impact on internal political activity promoting performance measures. The findings show that whereas the interaction effect is not significant in the adoption model (Table 6.4), it is significant in the implementation and utilization models (Tables 6.5 and 6.6). The effect on the dependent variable in all three models is negative, as expected.

The parameter estimate for the interaction effect is about $-.23$ and significant at less than the .05 level in the implementation and utilization models. This relationship tells us that whatever effect internal interest groups have on implementation is

Table 6.4   Multiple Regression Model 4: Explaining Adoption—With Interaction of Percent Unionized and Internal Interest Groups

R-sq	Adj R-sq	F Value	P > F	N
.5021	.4865	32.18	.0001	363

Independent Factors		Parameter Estimate	T Value	Prob > T
Intercept				
External requirements		.1214	1.573	.1167
Internal requirements		.5816	7.081	.0001
Internal interest groups		.3724	5.028	.0001
External interest groups		.0364	0.508	.6120
Percent unionized		.0516	0.504	.6148
Attitude		.0373	0.599	.5497
Rewards		.0897	1.537	.1251
County		−.1416	−1.109	.2682
Municipality		−.2079	−1.757	.0798
Position of respondent		−.0814	−1.695	.0909
Interaction Effect				
Percent unionized and internal interest groups		−.1253	−1.149	.2515

decreased as the level of unionization goes up. This reinforces the notion that internal (informal) interest groups working in coalitions represent abstract forces whose potency is diminished when more formal groups, such as unions, opposed them.

Attitude and External Requirements

The results of testing the effect of the hypothesized moderated relationships between attitude and external requirements on adoption, implementation, and utilization (models 7 to 9) were not significant. In addition, the hypothesized relationship did not hold. The expectation was that organizational culture (as measured by the factor attitude toward change) should serve as a catalyst for external requirement. That is, this relationship should have been positive (of the reinforcement or synergistic type). Instead, the relationship found was negative (of the antagonistic or

Table 6.5 Multiple Regression Model 5: Explaining Implementation— With Interaction of Percent Unionized and Internal Interest Groups

R-sq	Adj R-sq	F Value	P > F	N
.4944	.4785	31.20	.0001	363

Independent Factors	Parameter Estimate	T Value	Prob > T
Intercept	−.1531	−0.992	.3218
External requirements	.0813	1.098	.2730
Internal requirements	.3966	5.030	.0001
Internal interest groups	.1836	2.582	.0102
External interest groups	.2753	4.001	.0001
Percent unionized	−.1093	−1.111	.2674
Attitude	.1317	2.205	.0281
Rewards	.1171	2.091	.0373
County	.0755	0.616	.5382
Municipality	.1413	1.244	.2143
Position of respondent	−.0499	−1.083	.2794
Interaction Effect			
Percent unionized and internal interest groups	−.2300	−2.194	.0289

interfering type). This finding suggests that whether or not external policies are considered symbolic, their presence will overwhelm the effect of attitude toward change. Attitude becomes less important as organizations have no other choice but to adhere to the requirement. This point can be illustrated by a comment made by one of the respondents from a municipality. This person stated that although there is not complete buy-in from top management, "in order to receive some state aid, some level of performance measures must be utilized."

Another plausible explanation is that a requirement may trigger the change in attitude that is necessary for a successful performance measurement system. To this effect, a respondent, also from a municipality, commented, "My sense tells me that it's going to take an outright federal or GASB mandate/requirement before this city does more performance measures." Another respondent, from a county organization, stated that although they are in the early stage of performance measures, he

Table 6.6 Multiple Regression Model 6: Explaining Utilization—With Interaction of Percent Unionized and Internal Interest Groups

R-sq	Adj R-sq	F Value	P > F	N
.5180	.5029	34.29	.0001	363

Independent Factors		Parameter Estimate	T Value	Prob > T
Intercept		−.1282	−0.829	.4076
External requirements		.1282	1.209	.2274
Internal requirements		.1282	5.545	.0001
Internal interest groups		.1282	3.043	.0025
External interest groups		.1282	3.752	.0002
Attitude		.1270	2.122	.0346
Rewards		.1192	2.124	.0344
County		.0509	0.414	.6791
Municipality		.1039	0.913	.3621
Position of respondent		−.0562	−1.217	.2244
Percent unionized		−.0953	−0.966	.3346
Interaction Effect				
Percent unionized and internal interest groups		−.2285	−2.176	.0302

or she is convinced that "legal or grant related requirements would have accelerated the adoption [of performance measures]."

Section Summary: Basic Integrated Model

Box 6.2 summarizes the findings presented in this section. Exhibit A shows the results of testing the subhypotheses. The table contrasts the results of the analyses for adoption and those for implementation. Exhibit B displays the patterns that emerged in these analyses.

As can be concluded from the information in the box, there is a preponderance for more formal and symbolic factors to affect adoption. Adoption is more strongly influenced by internal requirements and internal interest groups. These factors seem to be consistent with the notion that adoption may represent symbolic action, as

BOX 6.2: SUMMARY OF FINDINGS AND PATTERNS FOR BASIC INTEGRATED MODELS

Exhibit A. Basic Integrated Models: Comparing Adoption to Implementation

Independent Factors	Subhypothesis	Adoption (Supported Yes/No)	Implementation Model (Supported Yes/No)
1. External requirements	2b	Yes*	Yes
2. Internal requirements	2b	Yes***	Yes***
3. Internal interest groups	3a	Yes***	Yes***
4. External interest groups	3b	Yes	Yes***
5. Percent unionized	3c	No	Yes
6. Interaction 5*3	3d	Yes	Yes**
7. Attitude	3e	Yes	Yes**
8. Interaction 7*1	3f	No	No
9. Rewards	3e	Yes	Yes**

* Significant at <.10 level; ** significant at <.05 level; ***significant at <.01 level.

Exhibit B. Emerging Patterns: Comparing Adoption to Implementation

Independent Factors	Adoption (Value of Parameter Estimate)	Implementation (Value of Parameter Estimate)
External requirements	Higher*	Lower
Internal requirements	Higher***	Lower***
Internal interest groups	Higher***	Lower***
External interest groups	Lower	Higher***
Percent unionized	Lower	Higher (negative)
Attitude	Lower	Higher**
Rewards	Lower	Higher**
County	Negative	Positive
Municipality	Negative*	Positive
Position of respondent	Negative*	Negative

* Significant at <.10 level; ** significant at <.05 level; ***significant at <.01 level.

argued earlier in Chapter 3. But one can also argue that even in cases when adoption actually reflects a genuine desire in the organization to have a performance measurement, it does not necessarily mean that implementation will follow.

In contrast, implementation is more strongly influenced by the political factors—internal interest groups, and unions (external because of their connection to organized interest outside the organization)—and having a positive attitude toward change, as well as having the appropriate encouragement and reward for improving and taking risks. This appears to indicate that more concrete mechanisms must be in place in order for implementation to occur. As the riskier of the two stages of the overall process of Utilization, this is an expected outcome for implementation. While adopting performance measures can have some consequences for the organization, the "real" and more direct consequences will be a result of implementing the information.

Elaboration: Toward an Estimated Causal Model

The analysis and findings described in this section represent one step further in elaborating the basic integrated models. This was done by introducing the rational/technocratic factors resources, goal orientation, and access to information as mediators. The analysis allowed for the elaboration of the models through the mediation process and pattern matching based on the purification approach.

The discussion that follows is based on the test of subhypotheses 1a and 2e. It should be noted, however, that subhypothesis 1a was tested in two steps as proposed in models 16 and 17, shown in Box 6.1.

Mediation and Model Purification

To begin this discussion, I first proceed to present the findings of the test of subhypothesis 2e. The proposition made was that the presence of the technical and rational organizational capacity for performance measurement, represented by the rational/technocratic factors, can be explained by organizational politics and culture, and the presence of requirements. The results are shown in Tables 6.7 through 6.9. These three multiple regression models (models 10 to 12) show the effect of all the independent factors on resources, goal orientation, and access to information.

The findings presented in the tables above need to be put in context to make better sense of the information. This context is provided by the findings of models 13 to 15, which represent the basic integrated models elaborated by including these rational/technocratic factors. These findings are shown in Tables 6.10 through 6.12. The tables also show the direct effect of these rational/technocratic factors on adoption, implementation, and utilization, suggested in subhypotheses 2c and 2d.

Table 6.7 Multiple Regression Model 10: Integrated Model Explaining Resources

R-sq	Adj R-sq	F Value	P > F	N
.6141	.6031	56.01	.0001	363

Independent Factors	Parameter Estimate	T Value	Prob > T
Intercept	.0016	0.012	.9905
External requirements	−.0220	−0.340	.7338
Internal requirements	.3335	4.833	.0001
Internal interest groups	.3338	5.358	.0001
External interest groups	.2292	3.805	.0002
Attitude	.1855	3.547	.0004
Rewards	0712	1.451	.1475
County	−.0738	−0.697	.4863
Municipality	−.0748	−0.757	.4493
Position of respondent	−.0438	−1.086	.2782
Percent unionized	.0354	0.410	.6818

In that the discussion will often refer to the terms *direct effect, indirect effect,* and *total effect,* it is prudent to review their meaning. These terms were presented earlier in Chapter 4 of this book (Davis, 1985):

a) Total Estimated Causal Effect = effect after controlling for all priors;
b) Direct Effect = effect after controlling for all priors and intervenors;
c) Indirect Effect = the difference of a − b (due to intervenors).

The Relevance of Resources, Access to Information, and Goal Orientation

As was expected, the analysis showed that to be successful in their performance measurement efforts, organizations need to have the technical capacity provided by rational/technocratic factors. Furthermore, Tables 6.10 through 6.12 show that as measured here, of the three rational/technocratic factors, the one with the biggest

Table 6.8 Multiple Regression Model 11: Basic Integrated Model Explaining Goal Orientation

R-sq	Adj R-sq	F Value	P > F	N
.4455	.4298	26.81	.0001	363

Independent Factors		Parameter Estimate	T Value	Prob > T
Intercept		.0715	0.463	.6435
External requirements		−.0205	−0.277	.7818
Internal requirements		.0367	0.465	.6425
Internal interest groups		**.2090**	**2.931**	**.0036**
External interest groups		.0757	1.098	.2728
Attitude		**.2720**	**4.546**	**.0001**
Rewards		**.2228**	**3.969**	**.0001**
County		**−.3053**	**−2.521**	**.0122**
Municipality		−.1117	−0.988	.3239
Position of respondent		−.0110	0.238	.8117
Percent unionized		.1260	1.277	.2026

impact in all three models is resources. The parameter estimate for resources ranges from about .34 for adoption to .39 for implementation and .40 for utilization, all significant at less than the .01 level. This is consistent with several of the comments made by respondents who attributed the inability of their organization to use performance measures to a lack of resources.

Another comment that corroborates this concern refers to the availability of quality benchmarks, which are part of the resources construct. Several of the respondents said that benchmarks are an important factor in the utilization of performance measurement. For example, a respondent from a county government commented that the lack of reliable, comparable benchmark information hampered his or her organization's ability to adopt performance measures.

The tables also reveal another important characteristic of the factor resources, one that is central to the discussion in this book. This factor has a differential effect. Tables 6.10 and 6.11 show that the effect of resources in the adoption model is smaller than in the implementation model (for obvious reasons, this effect is not apparent in the utilization mode).

**Table 6.9 Multiple Regression Model 12: Basic Integrated Model
Explaining Access to Information**

R-sq	Adj R-sq	F Value	P > F	N
.2887	.2685	14.29	.0001	363

Independent Factors	Parameter Estimate	T Value	Prob > T
Intercept	.1838	1.130	.2591
External requirements	−.0441	−0.565	.5722
Internal requirements	.0025	0.295	.7684
Internal interest groups	**.3290**	**4.381**	**.0001**
External interest groups	.0230	0.316	.7520
Attitude	.1108	1.758	.0796
Rewards	.0451	0.762	.4464
County	−.1595	−1.250	.2122
Municipality	**−.2310**	**−1.939**	**.0532**
Position of respondent	−.0107	−0.221	.8256
Percent unionized	−.0203	−0.195	.8456

The lack of access to pertinent information appears to hinder the development and implementation of performance measures. As indicated by the results, access to information is important particularly for implementation. This variable has a parameter estimate of .19, significant at less than the .01 level for implementation, versus about .13, significant at the .01 level for adoption. This differential effect is not appreciated in the utilization model, as shown in Table 6.12.

Goal orientation appears to be more important for adoption than for implementation. But the difference in its effect on each stage of utilization is not as marked as that of resources. The parameter estimate for adoption is larger and more significant than the estimate for implementation, but only by about 2 points (about .15 and significant at less than the .01 level, and .13 and significant at less than the .05 level, respectively).

Effect of Formal Politics (External and Internal Requirements)

In general, the findings of the mediated models, shown in Tables 6.10 through 6.12, are consistent with the results found by testing the basic integrated models. As

Table 6.10 Elaborated Multiple Regression Model 13: Basic Integrated Model Explaining Adoption with Rational/Technocratic Factors

R-sq	Adj R-sq	F Value	P > F	N
.5795	.5587	36.25	.0001	363

Independent Factors	Parameter Estimate	T Value	Prob > T
Intercept	.0019	0.060	.9521
External requirements	.1450	2.033	.0428
Internal requirements	.4564	5.804	.0001
Internal interest groups	.1879	2.577	.0104
External interest groups	−.0575	−0.848	.3968
Attitude	−.0755	−1.261	.2081
Rewards	.0274	0.495	.6206
County	−.0772	−0.654	.5133
Municipality	−.1535	−1.400	.1623
Position of respondent	−.0618	−1.386	.1665
Percent unionized	.0251	0.264	.7920
Resources	.3349	5.390	.0001
Goal orientation	.1447	2.688	.0075
Information	.1292	2.627	.0090

before, compared to external requirements, internal requirements have a stronger effect on the three independent variables: adoption, implementation, and utilization. Moreover, both external requirements and internal requirements have a stronger effect on adoption than on implementation.

However, as can be noted in these tables, while the parameter estimates for internal requirements have sharply decreased in all three models, this has not been the case for external requirements. The effect of external requirements on adoption not only has increased from about .13 to .15, but now it is also significant at less than the .05 level. The same pattern is evident in the utilization model. Now, although the factor external requirements is not as significant as the factor internal requirements, the change in the parameter estimates and significance indicate that external requirements exert a significant influence on adoption if the

Table 6.11 Elaborated Multiple Regression Model 14: Basic Integrated Model Explaining Implementation with Rational/Technocratic Factors

R-sq	Adj R-sq	F Value	P > F	N
.5985	.5836	40.02	.0001	363

Independent Factors		Parameter Estimate	T Value	Prob > T
Intercept		−.1751	−1.270	.2050
External requirements		.1150	1.743	.0823
Internal requirements		.2474	3.400	.0008
Internal interest groups		−.0368	−0.546	.5853
External interest groups		.1658	2.645	.0085
Attitude		.0092	0.166	.8679
Rewards		.0520	1.016	.3103
County		.1274	1.167	.2440
Municipality		.1988	1.960	.0508
Position of respondent		−.0257	−0.624	.5331
Percent unionized		−.1331	−1.511	.1317
Resources		.3918	6.813	.0001
Goal orientation		.1246	2.502	.0128
Information		.1939	4.58	.0001

other three rational/technocratic factors are present. This effect is less significant on implementation.

In contrast to external requirements, part of the effect of internal requirements on the dependent factors occurs through the three rational/technocratic factors. This can be verified by comparing the information in Tables 6.10 to 6.12 to that of Tables 6.1 to 6.3. The comparison will show that once the mediators were introduced, there was a sharp decline in the parameter estimate of this variable in all three models. The parameter estimates decreased from .58 to .46 for adoption, from about .39 to .25 for implementation, and from about .43 to .28 for utilization. This is further confirmed by the numbers in Table 6.7, where the results of a regression analysis showed that the variable internal requirements is one of two variables with the greatest influence on resources (about .33 and significant at less than the .01 level).

Table 6.12 Elaborated Multiple Regression Model 15: Basic Integrated Model Explaining Utilization with Rational/Technocratic Factors

R-sq	Adj R-sq	F Value	P > F	N
.6240	.6099	44.54	.0001	363

Independent Factors		Parameter Estimate	T Value	Prob > T
Intercept		−.1515	−1.106	.2695
External requirements		.1239	1.891	.0595
Internal requirements		.2844	3.934	.0001
Internal interest groups		−.0105	−0.157	.8753
External interest groups		.1457	2.339	.0199
Attitude		−.0005	−0.009	.9931
Rewards		.0512	1.007	.3145
County		.1070	0.986	.3247
Municipality		.1641	1.628	.1044
Position of respondent		.0814	0.773	.4399
Percent unionized		−.1206	−1.378	.1692
Resources		.4045	7.081	.0001
Goal orientation		.1330	2.687	.0075
Information		.1967	4.347	.0001

Effect of Organizational Politics (Internal and External Interest Groups)

The pattern discovered in the basic model presented earlier still holds here. As before, the factor internal interest groups has a strong and significant effect on adoption. Furthermore, the decrease in the parameter estimate (from .37 to .19) indicates that this factor not only has a direct effect on adoption, but its effect is mediated through all three of the rational/technocratic factors. That is, the factor internal interest groups has an impact on resources, goal orientation, and access to information (parameter estimates are .33, .21, and .33, respectively, all significant at less than the .01 level). These factors, in turn, have an impact on adoption. Thus, we can conclude that in addition to its direct impact on adoption, the variable internal interest groups has an indirect effect through these organizational capacity factors.

Table 6.11 shows that the effect of internal interest groups on implementation (which was expected to be small) not only has substantially decreased, but also has become negative and nonsignificant. The parameter estimate for this predictor factor decreased from a significant .18 to a nonsignificant −.04. This indicates that for implementation, most of the effect of internal interest groups occurs through the rational/technocratic factors.

Note also in the tables that the hypothesized relationship between the factor external interest groups and implementation still holds after the introduction of the rational/technocratic factors as mediators. Also, as was the case with internal interest groups, the direct effect of external interest groups has decreased from a parameter estimate of about .27 to .17, indicating that part of the effect of external interest groups on implementation is through at least one of these rational/technocratic factors. More specifically, Table 6.7 shows that the factor external interest groups has a direct effect on resources.

Regarding the crude utilization model, the findings in Table 6.12 show that practically no effect is attributed to internal interest groups on this dependent factor. Likewise, the effect of external interest groups is underestimated in this model. The inclusion of the rational/technocratic factors leads to a large decrease in the parameter estimate of external interest groups. The parameter estimate changed from about .25, and significant at less than the .01 level, to .15, and significant at less than the .05 level. These findings provide further support to the argument that when we assume that the factors that affect adoption affect implementation in the same manner, we attribute an undue effect to a set of factors without really gaining an understanding of what and how mechanisms work for adoption, and what and how mechanisms work for implementation. As a result, we gain little insights on how best to support performance management efforts.

Unionization

In the elaborated model the variable percent unionized exhibited the same behavior that was found in the basic integrated model. That is, the variable has a positive sign for adoption, but a negative one for implementation and utilization. This is consistent with the hypothesized relationship. However, the variable is not significant in this analysis.

Effect of Culture (Attitude and Rewards)

Whereas the factors attitude and rewards were significant in explaining implementation and utilization in the basic integrated models, after introducing the rational/technocratic factors their effect practically disappeared.

In the basic integrated model for implementation shown in Table 6.2, the parameter estimates for the factors attitude and rewards were .14 and about .12, respectively. For utilization, shown in Table 6.3, they were about the same. After the introduction of the rational/technocratic factors, the potency of these two factors sharply decreased. The effect of the factor attitude, in particular, decreased to about .01. And the effect of the factor rewards decreased to about .05.

These findings indicate that these two constructs do not have a direct effect on implementation and utilization. Rather, their effect is mediated through the three rational/technocratic factors, and because of this, they also have an indirect effect on adoption. This is illustrated in Table 6.8, which shows that the effects of the factors attitudes and rewards are particularly strong in explaining goal orientation (the parameter estimates are about .27 and .22, respectively, and significant at less than the .01 level). This is an appropriate finding because *goal orientation*, as defined here, refers to managerial attributes that one would expect to find in organizations that accept, value, and reward innovation and change, and that view performance measurement as an important part of the management process.

The findings of this analysis also indicate that the factor attitude helps explain resources (.19, significant at less than the .01 level, in Table 6.10). However, Table 6.9 shows that this factor has a smaller and less significant effect in explaining access to information (about .11, significant at the .10 level).

Control Variables (Organization Type and Position of Respondents)

As was the case with the basic model for adoption, in the mediated model shown in Table 6.10 the variables municipalities and counties continue to be negatively related to adoption. Thus, even after accounting for rational/technocratic factors, respondents from municipalities and counties were less likely to say that their organizations had adopted performance measures. Both of these variables, however, are not significant in this analysis.

In contrast, it was shown earlier that, although nonsignificant, those from municipalities and counties were more likely to say that they had implemented performance measures. They were positively related to implementation. The same pattern was true when the rational/technocratic factors were accounted for. Moreover, Table 6.11 shows that in this analysis, municipalities are significant at the .05 level (the parameter estimate is about .20) in explaining implementation. This result shows that because of the lack of technical capacity, municipalities are less likely to implement than states. However, once these barriers are removed, they are able to implement at a faster rate than states.

This explanation is corroborated by the findings shown in Tables 6.7 to 6.9. The findings show that both municipalities and counties have a negative parameter estimate in all three models explaining the rational/technocratic factors. This indicates that when the organization was a municipality or county, respondents were likely to say that they did not have in place the technical capacity that can be developed when organizations have the various rational/technocratic factors measured here.

As for the crude utilization model, the positive association that was found between counties and municipalities and the dependent variable in the basic model municipality was also found in the mediated model. Although in the basic model the variable was not close to being significant, in this elaboration it reached significance at the .10 level.

The other control variable—position of respondent—exhibits the same pattern that was found in the previous analysis. As can be observed in Tables 6.10 to 6.12, it is negative in all three models. Although this variable was found to be significant at less than the .10 level in the basic integrated model for adoption, this is no longer the case here.

Section Summary: Elaborated Models

The findings discussed in this section are summarized in Box 6.3. Exhibit A shows the results of testing the subhypotheses on adoption in comparison with implementation. Exhibit B shows the pattern that emerged in the elaboration analysis with respect to adoption and implementation.

I have conceptually replicated the effect of a model integrating requirements, politics, culture, and other relevant organizational characteristics on two nonequivalent dependent factors, and found their effect to be as predicted. I have also used rational/technocratic factors as mediators in these integrated models and found that the previously predicted effect, as well as patterns found in the earlier analyses, still held. This can be quickly ascertained by comparing the patterns in Box 6.3 to those shown in Box 6.2, and the predicted relationships depicted in Box 3.1 in Chapter 3. As can be noted, what I have referred to as more formal and symbolic mechanisms still continued to exert an important influence on adoption.

Elaboration has allowed for causal mechanisms to emerge. This has also allowed for the confirmation of the main hypothesis. Elaboration has further helped highlight the differential effect of the independent factors on adoption and implementation of performance measures.

An Estimated Causal Model of Adoption and Implementation

The observed variations in the effect of the set of variables and constructs when resources, goal orientation, and access to information were introduced in the three elaborated models indicate that the effects of original variables and constructs on the dependent factors are channeled in some cases through the three rational/

BOX 6.3: SUMMARY OF FINDINGS AND PATTERNS FOR BASIC INTEGRATED MODELS MEDIATED WITH GOAL ORIENTATION, RESOURCES, AND ACCESS TO INFORMATION

Exhibit A. Comparing Findings: Testing of Subhypotheses in Elaborated Models with Mediation

Independent Factors	Subhypothesis	Adoption (Supported Yes/No)	Implementation (Supported Yes/No)
1. External requirements	2a	Yes**	Yes*
2. Internal requirements	2a, 2b	Yes***	Yes***
3. Internal interest groups	3a	Yes***	Yes[a]
4. External interest groups	3b	Yes	Yes***
5. Percent unionized	3c	No[b]	Yes
6. Attitude	3e	Yes[a]	Yes
7. Rewards	3e	Yes[a]	Yes

[a] But negative effect.
[b] But positive effect.
* Significant at <.10 level; ** significant at <.05 level; ***significant at <.01 level.

Exhibit B. Emerging Patterns: Comparing Adoption to Implementation

Independent Factors	Adoption (Value of Parameter Estimate)	Implementation (Value of Parameter Estimate)
External requirements	Higher**	Lower*
Internal requirements	Higher***	Lower***
Internal interest groups	Higher***	Lower
External interest groups	Lower	Higher***
Percent unionized	Lower	Higher
Attitude	Lower	Higher**
Rewards	Lower	Higher**
Position of respondent	Negative*	Negative
County	Negative	Positive
Municipality	Negative*	Positive**
Resources	Lower***	Higher***
Goal orientation	Higher***	Lower***
Access to information	Lower***	Higher***

* Significant at <.10 level; ** significant at <.05 level; ***significant at <.01 level.

technocratic factors. At the same time, the fact that those rational/technocratic factors are significant in the mediated models indicates that they also have a direct effect on the dependent constructs.

The previous analyses helped to tease out the effects that different factors have under different circumstances. We are now ready to estimate the proposed path model for adoption and implementation shown earlier in Figure 3.2. However, to reveal the linkages and effects in such a model, adoption needs to be included in the mediated model explaining implementation (model 14, Table 6.11). As discussed earlier, there can be no implementation without adoption; therefore, any model that purports to explain implementation would be incomplete without considering the effect of adoption on implementation. Yet, judging from the patterns that emerged in the forgoing analyses, one can convincingly argue that to assume that implementation unconditionally follows adoption would be very bad and not lead to a good outcome.

Before moving to a full mediated model explaining implementation, it is necessary to show the results of extending model 2 (basic integrated model) by including adoption as a precursor to implementation. This procedure allowed for the isolation of the effect of adoption of performance measures when rational/technocratic factors are not present.

Tables 6.13 and 6.14 show the results of the analysis that includes adoption in the basic integrated model and mediated model explaining implementation. The discussion here proceeds in the following manner. First, there is a brief description of the patterns that emerged in model 16 (shown in Table 6.13) and how these patterns support the findings of the data analysis presented earlier. Then, results of model 17 (shown in Table 6.14) are presented, but only significant factors are discussed. Then, there is a discussion about the results of the analysis that combined the elaborated model for adoption, shown in Table 6.10, with the elaborated model for implementation, shown in Table 6.14, to estimate a path model. The discussion of the estimated path model is grounded on the direct and indirect linkages of the factors that have a significant impact on the adoption and implementation of performance measures as they emerged in models 13 and 17.

Discussion 1: Elaborated Model Explaining Implementation with Adoption as a Precursor to Implementation

Table 6.13 shows that, as was expected, adoption has a direct effect on implementation. The parameter estimate is large and significant. However, the table also shows that adoption is not sufficient to explain implementation. As with the earlier findings, the variable external interest groups has an important influence on implementation. Also, notice in Table 6.13 that the variable internal requirements loses its significance once adoption is taken into consideration. As shown in this particular

Table 6.13   Multiple Regression Model 16: Elaborated Model Explaining Implementation with Adoption as a Precursor

R-sq	Adj R-sq	F Value	P > F	N
.6346	.6231	55.41	.0001	363

Independent Factors		Parameter Estimate	T Value	Prob > T
Intercept		−.1525	−1.165	.2450
Adoption		**.5167**	**11.888**	**.0001**
External requirements		.0286	0.454	.6498
Internal requirements		.0893	1.250	.2121
Internal interest groups		−.0087	−0.140	.8890
External interest groups		**.2524**	**4.316**	**.0001**
Attitude		**.1164**	**2.294**	**.0224**
Rewards		.0703	1.471	.1422
County		.1157	1.124	.2619
Municipality		**.2268**	**2.354**	**.0191**
Position of respondent		−.0053	−0.135	.8930
Percent unionized		−.1347	−1.610	.1082

model, adoption is one of the mechanisms through which this particular variable works. This is consistent with the theoretical arguments and the explanatory power of internal requirements on adoption shown earlier.

Discussion 2: Elaborated Model Explaining Implementation with Adoption and Goal Orientation, Resources, and Access to Information as Mediators

Table 6.14 shows that the basic patterns uncovered in previous analysis are still valid. However, there are a few changes in the direct effect of some of the factors.

Significant Factors

As predicted, adoption is significant and has a strong effect on implementation. However, notice in Table 6.14 that the factor external interest groups continues to

Table 6.14 Multiple Regression Model 17: Full Elaborated Model Explaining Implementation with Adoption and the Three Rational/ Technocratic Factors as Mediators

R-sq	Adj R-sq	F Value	P > F	N
.6757	.6626	51.78	.0001	363

Independent Factors	Parameter Estimate	T Value	Prob > T
Intercept	–.1787	–1.440	.1508
Adoption	**.4056**	**9.097**	**.0001**
External requirements	.0562	0.940	.3476
Internal requirements	.0623	0.908	.3645
Internal interest groups	–.1130	–1.844	.0660
External interest groups	**.1892**	**3.348**	**.0009**
Attitude	.0398	0.797	.4259
Rewards	.0409	0.887	.3755
County	.1587	1.614	.1074
Municipality	**.2610**	**2.851**	**.0046**
Position of respondent	–.0007	–0.018	.9857
Percent unionized	–.1433	–1.807	.0716
Resources	**.2559**	**4.751**	**.0001**
Goal orientation	.0659	1.455	.1464
Information	**.1414**	**3.417**	**.0007**

have a significant and important effect on implementation (parameter estimate of about .19 and significant at less than .01).

We will see later that the negative direct effect of internal interest groups shown in Table 6.14 (parameter estimate –.11, significant at the .10 level) is more than offset by the positive indirect effect that it has through adoption and resources (see Table 6.15). The negative effect depicted in Table 6.14 indicates that adoption and the three rational/technocratic factors are acting as suppressor variables. As explained by Davis (1985), a suppressor variable is one that creates a negative path that suppresses the true positive net effect. Thus, this negative effect, for all practical purposes, is a noneffect.

Table 6.14 also shows that once adoption is taken into consideration, percent of unionized employees, which had been previously found to have a negative effect on implementation, not only continues to be negative, but becomes significant at the .10 level. The parameter estimate, however, is about the same as in the previous models explaining implementation.

The effect of type of organization, whether a municipality or county, is positive on implementation. In this model (model 17, Table 6.14), however, municipalities are significant at the .01 level, and counties are close to a significance level of only .10.

Resources and access to information also have a strong impact on implementation. But, the decrease in the parameter estimate for resources (from .39 in the isolated elaborated model, shown in Table 6.11, to about .26 in this model) indicates that part of the effect that the factor resources has on implementation is indirect through adoption. This is not inconsistent with the earlier findings. Rather, it shows the mechanisms through which resources work for implementation.

Further, the effect of access to information has decreased to about .14. This is an indication that the effect that was found in the earlier analysis of this factor on implementation was not direct. It was part of the causal effect.

Discussion 3: Estimated Path Model of an Elaborated Model Explaining the Adoption and Implementation of Performance Measures

The discussion that follows is based on Figure 6.1 and the accompanying information presented in Table 6.15. As mentioned earlier, this path model is a combination of the analyses of the elaborated mediated model for adoption shown in Table 6.10 and the elaborated mediated model for implementation discussed above and shown in Table 6.14. Before proceeding with this discussion, to make comparisons easier, I would like to call attention to Box 6.4. It contains information on the location of the results of the analyses showing the indirect, direct, and total estimated causal effects of the independent factors on adoption and implementation.

Direct Effects to Adoption and Implementation

Adoption

As discussed earlier, adoption has a direct effect on implementation. Nonetheless, the size of its coefficient validates the claim that even when adoption has occurred, there are other mechanisms that must be in place in order for implementation to follow.

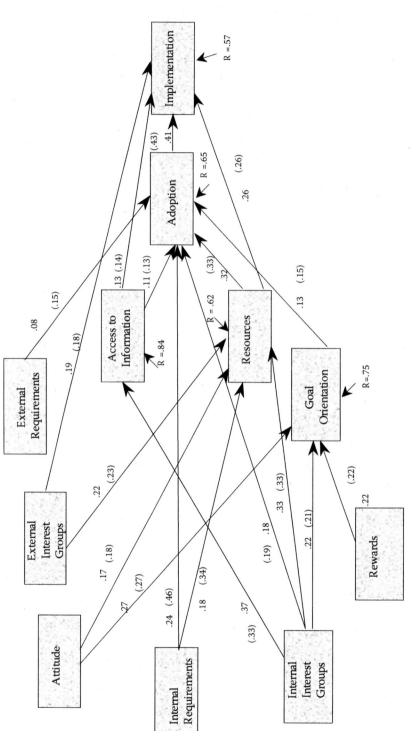

Figure 6.1 Estimated causal model of the process of utilization of performance measures. (Adapted from de Lancer Julnes

* All Factors Significant at < .05; the numbers are estimated regression coefficients--number in parentheses are standardized coefficients

R is the residual path coefficient or $(1 - R_2)^{1/2}$

Table 6.15 Indirect, Direct, and Total Estimated Causal Effects for Path Model Explaining the Utilization of Performance Measures[a]

Factor	Direct to Adoption	Indirect to Adoption	Total Est. Causal	Direct to Implementation	Indirect to Implementation	Total Est. Causal	Total Est. Causal for Model
1. Adoption				.41			.41
2. External requirements	.15		.15		Via 1 = .06	.06	.21
3. Internal requirements	.46	Via 8 = .11	.57		Via 1=.19		
					Via 8 =.09		
					Via 8, 1 = .05	.33	.90
4. Internal interest groups	.19	Via 8 =.11			Via 1 = .08		
		Via 9 = .03			Via 8 = .09		
		Via 10 = .04	.37		Via 8,1 = .05		
					Via 9, 1 = .01		
					Via 10 = .05		
					Via 10,1 = .02	.30	.67
5. External interest groups		Via 8 = .08	.08	.19	Via 8 = .06		

Table 6.15 Indirect, Direct, and Total Estimated Causal Effects for Path Model Explaining the Utilization of Performance Measures[a] (continued)

Factor	Direct to Adoption	Indirect to Adoption	Total Est. Causal	Direct to Implementation	Indirect to Implementation	Total Est. Causal	Total Est. Causal for Model
6. Attitude		Via 8 = .06			Via 8, 1 = .03	.28	.36
		Via 9 = .04	10		Via 8 = .06		
					Via 8, 1 = .03	.11	.21
7. Rewards		Via 9 = .03	.03		Via 9, 1 = .02	.01	.04
					Via 9, 1 = .01		
8. Resources	.34		.34	.26	Via 1 = .14	.40	.74
9. Goal orientation	.15		.15		Via 1 = .06	.06	.21
10. Access to information	.13		.13	.14	Via 1 = .06	.19	.32

[a] Path values were calculated from the parameter estimates shown in Table 6.14.

BOX 6.4: FINDING THE TOTAL ESTIMATED CAUSAL EFFECTS, DIRECT EFFECTS, AND INDIRECT EFFECTS FOR ESTIMATED CAUSAL MODEL

Dependent Factor	Total Estimated Causal Effect	Direct Effect	Indirect Effect
Adoption	Table 6.1	Tables 6.10 and 6.15	Table 6.15
Implementation	Table 6.2	Tables 6.14 and 6.15	Table 6.15

Formal Politics (Internal and External Requirements)

As depicted in Figure 6.1 and shown in Table 6.15, internal requirements has a direct effect on adoption, but not on implementation. The direct effect on adoption is .46 and significant at less than the .01 level. As noted earlier in Table 6.10, the effect of external requirements on adoption is about .15 (as measured by the parameter estimate) and significant at about the .05 level. (This represents the direct effect of this variable on adoption).

Organizational Politics (Internal and External Interest Groups and Unions)

As was shown in Table 6.1, the factor internal interest groups is important for the adoption of performance measures. This continued to be the case after introducing the rational/technocratic factors (see Table 6.10). Figure 6.1 and Table 6.15 show that the direct estimated causal effect of this factor on adoption is .19.

Earlier I mentioned that the negative effect of internal interest groups on implementation that was found in the analysis shown in Table 6.14 was not an important effect. We will see more on this in the next section, on indirect effects. But for now it is sufficient to mention that this particular effect is not included in the path model as a direct effect because it does not meet the .05 significance level standard.

The effect of external interest groups, as pointed out earlier, is significant at the implementation stage. Consistent with the findings shown earlier, as can be observed in Figure 6.1, the factor external interest groups has a direct causal effect on implementation. Its direct effect is .19, significant at less than the .01 level.

The percent of unionized employees was not included in the model because, as was the case of the effect of internal interest groups on implementation, it did not meet the .05 significance level criteria. However, if we were to include it, its effect, as shown in Table 6.14, is negative (–.14). As explained before, this suggests that as the percent of unionized employees increases, implementation decreases.

Rational/Technocratic Factors (Resources, Goal Orientation, and Access to Information)

Figure 6.1 shows that all the rational technocratic factors—resources, goal orientation, and access to information—have a direct effect on adoption. Of the three, the strongest direct effect, as shown in Table 6.15, is from resources (.33). The second strongest is goal orientation (about .15).

In contrast, the figure shows that only two of those factors have a direct effect on implementation. Table 6.15 shows that resources and access to information have a direct effect, with corresponding parameter estimates of .26 and .14, respectively. Also, the effect of goal orientation on implementation dramatically decreased once adoption was introduced. This indicates that the effect of goal orientation on implementation is through adoption.

Indirect Effects on Adoption and Implementation

Formal Politics (Internal and External Requirements)

As shown in Table 6.14, and consistent with the findings and arguments presented in previous sections, the factor external requirements has practically no direct effect on implementation and is not significant. Whatever effect external requirements has on implementation is indirect through adoption. Thus, the indirect effect of external requirements on implementation is just .06 (or [.15]*[.41]).

The effect of internal requirements on implementation, as shown in Tables 6.14 and 6.15, is through several paths. One of the paths is through adoption. Another is through resources, and the third one is through adoption and resources. Compared to the findings in Table 6.11, as can be observed in Table 6.14, once adoption was introduced in the model, the effect of internal requirements on implementation dropped from a significant .25 (as measured by the parameter estimate) to a non-significant .06.

Organizational Politics (Internal and External Interest Groups)

As noted earlier and depicted in Figure 6.1, the factor internal interest groups has direct and indirect effects on adoption. This indirect effect is due to its explanatory effect on adoption and on the rational/technocratic factors. Table 6.15 shows that the total direct causal effect of this factor on adoption is .19, its total indirect causal effect on adoption is .19, and its total estimated causal effect is about .38, as was shown in Table 6.1.

Figure 6.1 and Table 6.15 show that the estimated causal effect of internal interest groups on implementation is through six indirect paths. These paths include access to information, access to information and adoption, adoption, goal orientation and adoption, resources, and resources and adoption. As shown in Table 6.15, this effect is .28 which more than offsets the negative effect shown in Table 6.14. The total estimated causal effect, however, is about .17 ([.28] − [.11]), as made apparent in Table 6.2 (allowing for rounding errors).

The factor external interest groups has a minimal indirect effect on adoption through its explanatory effect on resources. This effect is .08. If we add its direct (nonsignificant) value −.06, its estimated effect is only about .02. On the other hand, in addition to its direct effect on implementation, the factor external interest groups has an indirect causal effect through two paths: resources (.06) and resources and adoption (.03). The total estimated causal effect of external interest groups on implementation is .28 (or [.19] + [.06] + [.03]).

Culture (Attitude and Rewards)

As discussed in the previous analysis of findings, cultural factors were not significant in explaining adoption and implementation. Their effect on these two dependent factors is mostly through their explanatory power on resources, goal orientation, and rewards.

Figure 6.1 and Table 6.15 illustrate the effect of attitude on adoption. If we were to add its nonsignificant direct effect (about −.08), as shown in Table 6.10, its total estimated causal effect would be .02. (Allowing for rounding errors, this value is equivalent to that shown in Table 6.1.)

The effect of attitude on implementation is through three paths: resources, resources and adoption, and goal orientation and adoption. The total indirect effect of change on implementation is .11.

The estimated path model shows that the factor rewards affects both adoption and implementation indirectly through its effect on goal orientation. As depicted in Table 6.15, the total indirect effect of this factor on adoption is .03. Its indirect effect on implementation is .01.

Summary

This chapter presented the results of the various statistical analyses conducted to test the main hypothesis and subhypotheses. The models tested were purposely specified to test for a differential effect of requirements, organizational politics and culture, and rational/technocratic factors on adoption and implementation of performance measures. The models were also specified to isolate the effect of each of these constructs. The predictions and findings held throughout the analyses, which concluded with the estimation of a causal (path) model for adoption and implementation of performance measures. The findings lead to the conclusion that the Utilization of performance measures is not a unitary concept. Utilization is composed of at least two stages, adoption and implementation, each differentially affected by a number of factors.

The field of knowledge utilization has not particularly addressed the differentiation between the *adoption* (capacity for action) and *implementation* (knowledge converted into action) of information. By using pattern matching to examine data from a survey, it was shown here that a number of factors, which were borrowed from different fields of studies, are useful in advancing our understanding of the use of performance measurement information. Moreover, pattern matching made making this differentiation of stages possible, highlighting the mechanisms through which these factors work.

The findings suggest that adoption is more heavily influenced by more formal and internal forces, while implementation is more heavily influenced by more external and concrete forces. The more symbolic forces appear to be satisfied with adoption, while the more concrete forces seem to be more responsible for implementation. In particular, in an organizational setting, the consequences of implementation can be more detrimental or real to specific members of the organization and stakeholders outside of the organization. Thus, this may be a risk that organizations would be less likely to take if they are not compelled to do so by the external and more concrete forces.

Part III

LETTING PRACTICE INFORM THEORY

Chapter 7

Interpreting Survey Findings

This book is based on the premise that performance measurement is a critical component of performance-based management (PBM). A quality performance measurement system can provide valid and reliable knowledge about the cost, quantity, processes, quality, and results of services provided. Such information can be used by organizations' internal and external stakeholders to make decisions or to guide actions. The literature, cases reviewed, and current research makes it clear that when done properly, performance measurement could be an effective tool for administration.

Yet despite the documented value of measuring the performance of public programs and services, as discussed earlier in Chapter 2 of this volume, performance measurement does not appear to be as prevalent as believed, and there are conflicting claims as to the extent to which the use of performance measures is pervasive in the public sector. Many organizations claim to have developed performance measurement systems, and some researchers say that the use of the information among these organizations is rapidly increasing. However, others question the validity of such claims, arguing that for many public organizations performance measurement is rather rudimentary, consisting of a few workload and output measures. And even in such cases, the actual use of the information is relegated to reporting.

Indeed, the empirical findings presented support the assertions made by skeptics. Output measures are more likely to be developed than outcome and efficiency measures, and even when organizations are able to adopt a performance measurement system, implementing the measures can become a very challenging task. As suggested by Posner and Fantone (2007), actually using performance information raises the risks for some actors, particularly when performance measures are intended to be used in the budget process. As a result, there is always the possibility that performance measurement will be perceived as benefiting one group and not another, thus increasing the political stakes. In addition, even though the information affords an opportunity to benchmark, praise, and reflect, because it inevitably leads to judgment, some will fear it and become defensive (Solberg et al., 1997; de Lancer Julnes, 2006). This occurs in spite of performance measurement often being touted as a rational activity, a desirable management tool. As will be discussed here, the fact is that the adoption and implementation of performance measures do not appear to follow a rational/technocratic logic. As such, the process is not as straightforward as proponents would like it to be.

Related to this, the empirical results presented in the previous chapters of this book and discussed here show that politics is an important factor for knowledge utilization, and performance measurement in particular. The political model of organizations thrives on the importance of interest groups as political factors in the organization. They provide the context for diminishing or enhancing the impact of other factors that affect any kind of change introduced in an organization. However, political factors have been neglected in the knowledge utilization theory. The extent of their inclusion has been limited to perceptions of how political an issue is, ignoring the concrete manifestation of these factors in organizations.

The work presented in this book focuses on determining the factors that influence performance measurement and what makes such efforts succeed in an organizational setting. The latter is a critical question if we are to develop context-sensitive recommendations for improving utilization of performance measures.

For this purpose, thus far I have presented empirical evidence that has resulted from analyzing data from a cross-sectional national survey of state and local government organizations. In what follows, I discuss this evidence and highlight the policy and practical implications that follow from these findings. A simplified summary of the findings that were presented in Chapter 6 of this book is shown in Figure 7.1. The columns of the figure identify two stages of Utilization, adoption and implementation. The rows represent the sources of influences. The circles and rectangles represent the locus of influences, external or internal. The smaller circles and rectangles imply lesser impact. The figure shows that adoption is more heavily influenced by more formal and internal factors, while implementation is more heavily influenced by external and more concrete factors. I will refer to this figure in the discussion below. For consistency with the previous chapter of this book, the discussion is structured around the pattern-matching approach that was used for data analysis.

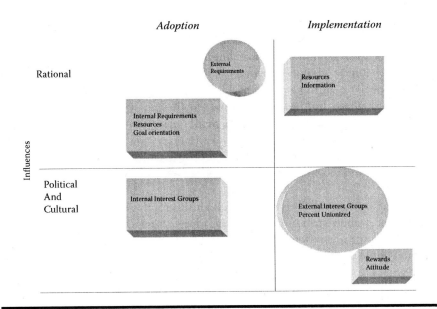

Figure 7.1 Influences on the Process of Performance Measurement Utilization. Circles represent external influences. Rectangles represent internal influences. The size of the circles and rectangles represents the amount of influence.

Differentiating the Stages of Utilization of Performance Measurement

As was evident in the various analyses presented in Chapter 6 of this book, central to our understanding of knowledge utilization, and particularly to performance measurement, is the distinction of adoption from implementation of performance measures. The need for making this distinction stems from Stehr's (1992) analysis of social science knowledge as being comprised of practical knowledge and action knowledge. These two components of knowledge utilization represent capacity for action and knowledge converted into action, respectively.

Thus, it seems appropriate that in the realm of utilization of performance measurement information, we make a parallel distinction between the adoption of performance measures as the capacity for action and the implementation of performance measures as the knowledge converted into action. Although the same factors may be involved in the process of utilization, as was shown by the survey data in the previous chapter of this book, the reality is that they may behave very differently at different stages. In one stage a set of factors may be more salient than others; in the next stage a different set may have more influence. Knowing this is valuable information in helping to advance the understanding of the process and to develop more focused strategies for supporting it in public and nonprofit organizations.

Formal Politics (External and Internal Requirements)

As suggested in Figure 7.1, internal requirements have a greater impact on the adoption of a performance measurement system than external requirements. These internal requirements represent internal policies that may reflect a more genuine desire to move an organization toward a culture of managing for results where performance-based management is the rule rather than the exception. External requirements, on the other hand, might be viewed as an imposition on the organization, and unless the right conditions are in place, they are less likely to inspire buy-in and elicit the kind of organizational infrastructure that is required for a successful performance measurement system. As a result, external requirements to use performance measurement may end up being perceived as something that simply creates more work, has no impact on the organization, and provides no value. Internal requirements, on the other hand, have more chances to achieve their purpose. Because of their nature (internal versus external), they would be more in tune with the organization's capacity for implementation. Alternatively, the findings here suggest that at the very least, internal requirements should help facilitate the mechanisms that lead to effective implementation of performance measurement information and thus help sustain PBM.

Threaded in the empirical findings and the experiences of those experimenting with performance measures is the notion that the success of performance measurement, or, for that matter, any type of change that's introduced in an organization, rests on a foundation of trust and commitment. As stated by one of the survey respondents key to this is obtaining buy-in, especially from top management; otherwise, mandated performance measures cannot work. This was also evident in the case of Minnesota's Department of Labor and Industry, reviewed earlier. Wilkins (1996) concluded that even when the top elected officials make the decision for state agencies to adopt performance measures, in order for the necessary changes to occur, the agency's top leadership must be committed to the effort. Related to this, it is important that agency leadership does not perceive the performance measurement effort as something that is being forced on the agency. Otherwise, it may lead to resistance and the effort may stagnate (de Lancer Julnes and Mixcoatl, 2006).

Nonetheless, we will find instances when there is not buy-in, but there is a policy mandating performance measurement, and the agency actually implements performance measurement information. This is particularly the case when the requirement is attached to monetary incentives. Take as an example the comment made by one of the respondents who stated that although there was not complete buy-in from top management, "in order to receive some state aid, some level of performance measures must be utilized." This comment highlights the tension that exists between compliance (which is closely related to adoption) and real behavior (which is more closely related to implementation). Compliance alone may legitimize an organization, showing that the leaders are responding to requirements. However, it does not necessarily lead to a change in behavior. This begs the questions: What should be a policy for mandated performance measures? That is, what kind of incentives will lead organizations not only to adopt a performance measurement system, but also to actually use appropriate performance measurement information to manage?

Questions like these are guiding current research at the federal level with regard to the Government Performance and Results Act (GPRA) and the Program Assessment Rating Tool (PART). For example, as she tried to understand what it would take to encourage managers to move away from the compliance mode toward using their performance measurement system to ask meaningful performance questions, Newcomer (2007) observed that although the progress seems slow, there is an increased interest among managers in learning about their organization. This is certainly encouraging, but we have reasons to believe that this desire for learning may not be enough to translate into action. A typical pattern among those who mandate performance measurement or any kind of policies for change is to do it without regard to the organization capacity to implement those policies. They seem to be particularly oblivious to the centrality of resources. And as a survey respondent from a state government commented, even when performance measures are mandated by statutes, the "effective and accurate implementation of any performance measures depends on the availability or non-availability of sufficient resources." This same sentiment reverberated in Newcomer's (2007) findings. Study participants believed that although their agencies are collecting evidence regarding program effectiveness as mandated, their managers are not likely to provide resources that could be used to evaluate program impacts. Thus, agencies end up with only partial information, far from the kind of information that they would need to make informed decisions about program changes.

Organizational Politics (External and Internal Interest Groups)

Consistent with the assumption that the potential for use of performance measurement information could be perceived as risky by some, and with the underlying need for buy-in from various actors, Figure 7.1 shows the differentiating effect of internal and external interest groups. While internal interest groups have an important positive impact at the adoption stage, external interest groups exert the greatest influence at the implementation stage. Even when the organization is mandated by law or statutes to use performance measurement, at the adoption stage the internal organizational groups have greater influence. At the implementation stage, however, when the use of the information is likely to expose the organization and touch actors outside of the span of organizational control, the internal interest groups may feel more vulnerable. Therefore, we see their uniquely large and positive contribution at the adoption stage, but small and at times negative contribution to implementation.

This empirically derived evidence is substantially corroborated by the experience of government organizations illustrated in the case studies that were reviewed and some of the open-ended responses from those who participated in the mail survey. For example, Marshall (1996) stated that one of the lessons learned by Prince William County, Virginia, was that because using performance measures represents a change in the organization, it is important that management and nonmanagement understand the reasons for undertaking the effort and the consequences of these efforts. In Minnesota, Wilkins (1996) realized that

> *line-staff acceptance of performance measures is essential for success. A typical reaction is fear when people hear the word "performance" because they think of the term as it affects them personally.... When line-staff understand that performance measures can help them accomplish their job and do it more efficiently, they often become more interested in its potential.*

Whether or not the consequences are perceived or real, it follows that the early inclusion of internal interest groups in organizational activities promoting performance measurement is a useful step toward developing a performance-based management culture. The value of their participation at the early stages of the performance measurement effort was echoed by some of the respondents to the survey, who stated that the success of performance measures is very much contingent on taking the time early on to work with line-staff to discuss the benefits of performance measurement and enlisting them in the efforts. Broad-based participation—stated Bryant (1996) in the case analysis of the Long Beach Police Department, is necessary given that the most successful measures are often those developed by the individuals that are responsible for doing the work.

In addition to line-staff, convincing and engaging top management early on is fundamental to success. For example, one respondent attributed the positive welcoming that a performance measurement program had in her organization to visible support and active engagement from top management. On the other hand, another respondent from a county government stated that when there is no support from top management, there is little chance for performance measures to be adopted and much less implemented. As stated by the respondent from a county government,

> *While there is desire from a small group to push innovation, we have not convinced nor affected the organization enough to witness results...I think that we need to convince our senior managers that there is benefit involved in establishing this type of system.*

Likewise, the failure of the mandated performance reporting law in Minnesota can be attributed to a large extent to managers not being supportive of the effort. The law was passed without the agency heads' input. As a result, suggested Jackson (1996), this did not help build the necessary support for the concept.

It was pointed out earlier that organizations may comply with the requirements for performance measurement, but as a respondent from a municipality stated, this is often nothing more than lip service and is not conducive to performance measurement becoming an integral part of the organization. Therefore, it appears that sometimes to move organizations in the desired direction, external actors need to exert pressure and provide support. Particularly important is the continued support and involvement of elected officials and citizens. The positive impact that elected officials can have in performance measurement is well documented (de Lancer Julnes and Mixcoatl, 2006; see also the case studies by Schwabe, 1996, and Weidner and Noss-Reavely, 1996, summarized in Chapter 2 of this book). For example, when governors not only require performance measurement but also model the behavior by using the information, this becomes an incentive for state agencies to use information as well. Statements of a number of survey respondents who attributed their inability to implement performance measures to the lack of support from the public and elected officials support this assertion. One respondent stated that even when the elected officials appear to show commitment to performance measurement efforts, when it is time to implement the information by using it as the basis to make program cuts, they refuse to do it. Another respondent attributed little, if any, use of performance measures in his municipality to lack of support from elected officials and citizens. The respondent stated, "Our elected officials and citizens do not like a lot of administration—[so] we run performance measures on a 'shoe string' and do not want to change that."

The strong impact that external interest groups exert on implementation supports the underlying argument shown in Figure 7.1, that to a great extent, the effect of internal interest groups on the process is more of the symbolic type. As suggested in Chapter 3 of this book, implementation leads to real consequences that go beyond the organization—thus the need for more concrete forces. For example, external stakeholders may be detrimentally affected by a decision taken due to performance measurement information, as would be the case if the information suggests cuts for a program that is inefficient and ineffective based on its stated goals, but that has a fairly vocal constituency. These external interest groups, as external stakeholders of the program, may affect the implementation phase of performance measures by opposing such implementation.

On the more positive side, performance measurement information may lead to the mobilization of external interest groups in support of changes to a program. For example, the information may show that program processes are not at the level they should be because of a lack of resources, causing significant delays and customer dissatisfaction. Involving external interest groups may help convince an otherwise unresponsive management that the allocation of resources, as suggested by the performance measures, is necessary to respond to citizens' (defined broadly) needs. They would demand accountability, and decision makers may feel under pressure to actually implement the performance measurement information.

As we delve into these findings, we are increasingly justified in concluding that even when there is a desire to implement performance measures in a public organization, the real push for implementation will often come from enlightened and involved external stakeholders (elected officials and citizens). For nonprofit agencies, implementation would require the engagement of the service recipients and funding agencies.

The secondary nature of the power of internal interest groups brings up another point. The findings regarding their impact on the process of utilization appear to be in line with the rational model. The factor internal interest groups was very important at the adoption stage, but not so at the implementation stage, which may reinforce the notion that forming coalitions with these groups is really a form of co-optation or appeasement, and thus is an abstract or formalistic gesture. As an internal factor, these coalitions do not seem to have much force as the organization moves toward the stage that entails real consequences—implementation. This perception of co-optation or appeasement is something that leaders of change efforts need to avoid because in the end they will need everyone to buy-in to ensure not just adoption, but also implementation and survival of the effort.

Culture (Attitude and Rewards)

A culture characterized by an openness to change, as demonstrated by a positive attitude toward change and reward systems that support risk taking, makes a difference at the implementation stage of performance measures, but appears to have little relevance at the adoption stage. This makes sense given the argument about the more abstract nature of adoption that was discussed in Chapter 3. For adoption, compliance may suffice to gain legitimacy, because it gives the appearance that the organization is being responsive to demands for accountability and transparency. Although compliance requires a great deal of effort, the real test in performance measurement is the implementation. This is the stage where consequences are real; therefore, the organization must be prepared for the challenges and risks.

This reality had to be confronted in the state of Minnesota. According to Jackson (1996), one of the lessons learned from attempting to comply with the state's mandated performance reports is that "[mandated performance reports] represent a change in thinking and a task that requires not only discipline but courage." The implication is that unless a willingness to take risks exists, performance measures will not be used even if they are mandated. Evidently, this was in the mind of one of the survey respondents who said that some elected officials in her municipality opt to ignore performance measures when the implementation of the information suggests program cuts. Cutting program funding in itself represents a real consequence, but for these elected officials, the consequences go beyond the organizational unit where the program changes are being suggested. The consequence might be losing the upcoming election because of a perceived lack of responsiveness to citizens' needs.

A related issue at the implementation stage is that unless the organization has a culture that not only accepts change but also does not punish apparent failures, performance measurement information will not be used in the manner intended. In particular, those organizations trying to get a PBM effort off the ground may find it impossible if there are fears that performance measurement information is going to be used as an accountability whip. The goal should be to get information to help improve the programs; to learn about where things are and what can be done to get them where we want them. This is an enduring lesson learned in Portland, Oregon, where Tracy (1996) found that "using measures for budget rewards/reductions or to promote or discipline managers is counterproductive because managers will resist or sabotage measurement systems that unfairly hold them responsible for outcomes they have only partial control over."

The quandary reflected in this lesson learned in Portland evokes the need for decision makers and policy makers to understand the limited direct effect that, despite the best intentions, government programs have on the overall desired outcomes for society. As a government employee told me during a telephone interview, you cannot control your clients once they leave. And you cannot control what happens to them out there. There are many other programs that have an impact on what you do. As a result, he said, managers are fearful of setting goals that cannot be achieved. Moreover, sometimes a program has an underlying logic that is faulty, and no matter how hard the agency tries, the desired program outcomes are never achieved.

On the other hand, having a culture that rewards risk taking encourages implementation of performance measures. In the analysis of strategic budgeting in Texas, Merjanian (1996) suggests that incentives are very important in stimulating participation in performance measurement. The trick is figuring out what is appropriate for the organization, at a level that can be sustained without discouraging those that do not appear to meet expectations. Although conflicting accounts can be found about the extent to which monetary rewards work, when properly done, they can be an incentive to use performance measures. Assuming that a performance measurement system has been properly developed, organizations can reward units for the performance of their program by giving more authority and flexibility over decisions relating to the budget or resource allocations. Other suggestions include that organizations implement gain sharing or shared savings (Osborne and Plastrik, 2000). The first entails giving employees a portion of financial savings. With the second, the organization is allowed to keep a portion of funds saved during a fiscal year. Nonmonetary rewards such as public recognition and celebrations of success are also an alternative that may encourage utilization. The bottom line is that the decision on how to reward for good performance or punish for underperformance must be carefully considered.

The Interaction of Unionization and Internal Interest Groups

The notion that internal interest groups represent more of an abstract internal influence on the process of performance measurement is supported by the finding that their impact is decreased as the number of unionized employees increases. The experience of some of the survey participants appear to further validate this finding by pointing out the particularly negative effect unions may have on implementation and utilization in general. Unionization, as suggested in the literature, appears to be a deterrent to innovation and change. In fact, some of the survey respondents cited unions as a negative influence on their ability to implement performance measures.

In particular, when asked what activity, group, or influence has affected the organization in the adoption and implementation of performance measures, a respondent from a county government stated that "unions tend to shy away from performance measures for evaluation, pay for performance, or any other measure that enhances quality." Another respondent pointed out unions' role in protecting employees as he said: "Union has been mixed in influence in general; publicly they support but if it results in a job action (reduction in staff for failure to perform) they resist."

However, the experience of the Oregon Department of Transportation suggests that although organizations wishing to move toward performance-based management should expect to encounter difficulties, unions do not necessarily represent an insurmountable threat. In their experience, the possibility of negative action from employee unions can be ameliorated if they are kept involved and informed (Bowden, 1996). Thus, giving the opportunity to union leaders and member employees to become active participants in the process early, and negotiating expectations and consequences up front, can help organizations achieve the necessary buy-in. At the same time, union members benefit as they become less of a threat and more of a partner in the process of change.

Elaboration toward an Estimated Causal Model: Model Purification and Mediation

The following discussion builds on the notion that performance measurement utilization is a process with stages. Henceforth, this process is referred to as the process of performance measurement Utilization. Now, although confirming the distinction of the two stages was valuable to our understanding of Utilization, further elaboration was necessary to improve the predictive abilities of the model for explaining the Utilization of performance measures. As a result, two other approaches were used after the initial differentiation of the stages of Utilization, model purification, and elaboration by means of mediation.

The initial models tested did not include goal orientation, resources, and access to information as predictor variables. The models used for elaboration and model purification did include these factors. This not only helped to validate the original predictions, but also helped create a better picture of how the whole structure of the final Utilization model works together. Furthermore, this made it possible to isolate the specific effect of each factor and the mechanisms through which they work. Conducting these different analyses and doing so in an iterative manner led to a model that, given the set of organizational factors, allows us to make better predictions of how organizations will fare in their performance management effort.

Rational/Technocratic Factors: Resources, Access to Information, and Goal Orientation

The quantitative analysis presented earlier showed strong evidence that the rational/technocratic factors resources, access to information, and goal orientation are necessary conditions for the success of the performance measurement process. Qualitative evidence provides further support to this conclusion. Many respondents to the survey attributed failure in their efforts to develop and implement a performance measurement system to the inadequacy of the resources allocated to this effort. For example, one respondent stated that not having the appropriate human and financial resources available in his or her municipality is an issue that limits their ability to develop a performance measurement system. Another, also from a municipality, stated that the cost of obtaining data is prohibitive, and expressed concerns about the competence of members of the organization to interpret the data. These comments speak directly to the need organizations have for a technical capacity that allows them to effectively undertake performance measurement.

Another important resource for organizations appears to be benchmarks. Several respondents mentioned that not having adequate benchmarks limits their ability to use performance measures. By providing a tool for comparison, benchmarks allow organizations to examine themselves in a comparable context against previous performance or that of other organizations. Although they do not tell an organization why programs are or are not performing like others', benchmarks can highlight areas for improvement. When properly done, benchmarks identify exemplary performance among peers, thus providing learning opportunities for those with performance below expectations. During the initial attempts to develop and implement performance measures, Catawba County experienced the frustration of not having benchmarks available (Berry and Ikerd, 1996, p. 4).

> *The lack of benchmarks was a major concern the first year. Many of the things to be measured had never been measured. There was no idea what the goal should be and in some cases there was no data available from any other organization to compare with. There continues to be a real inability to compare to anything other than what was accomplished past.*

The results of the data analysis also made clear that although the availability of resources is very important at the adoption stage, resources are even more important at the implementation stage. Organizations may be able to go through the process of developing the performance measures, but if they do not have adequate resources, the performance measurement system cannot be sustained. This point can be illustrated by a comment made by a respondent from a county government:

> *Once again, fiscal constraints [hinder the ability to adopt and implement performance measures]. We were doing a lot on this subject [performance measures], sent four managers to a special symposium, obtained lots of literature, [and] brought in specialists to give hours of training. Then fiscal constraints stopped progress. I am the one who is primarily leading the effort and it is my work plan to move ahead next year.*

In addition to the centrality of monetary resources, this comment by the respondent brings up another important rational/technocratic factor that is related to the organization's technical capacity: the need for having access to pertinent performance measurement information through training or other means. Having this access is important for both stages of the process of Utilization. However, this is particularly important for implementation. Although it is possible for organizations to develop performance measures by relying solely on external consultants, the findings presented here indicate that learning how to use the information, refining it, and adapting it to needs, requires more permanent skilled personnel.

This is further highlighted by comments made by respondents regarding the need for more training on how to use performance measures, indicating that such knowledge could lead to greater use of performance measures. For example, a respondent stated that the lack of understanding of how performance measures can be used contributes to her municipality's inability to adopt and implement performance measures. That is, because they did not know what and how performance measurement could contribute to management of their programs, the municipality had not tried to develop and implement a performance measurement system. A recent experience with a state employee can further illustrate this point. Although his office was created with the goal of diminishing health disparities among minorities, he did not realize that the programs under his jurisdiction did not have a direct impact on the expected outcome until we drew an outcome line representing the logic model for his program and its place in the health department. The logic model, a tool often used by program evaluators, showed him that his program contributed some valuable outputs and outcomes that, assuming the program theory was correct, could contribute indirectly to diminishing disparities. It was evident that not having a clear understanding of what the program could or could not do was leading to unrealistic expectations. Further, he did not have a valid monitoring and assessment system that could help to determine program effectiveness and inform decisions.

Beyond this understanding of the possible contributions of performance measures in terms of how they could be used, practitioners need training on how to develop and implement a meaningful system with appropriate indicators of performance. They need to know: What data need to be collected and how to make sure the data are valid and reliable. Moreover, to make the most out of performance measurement information, they need to know: how to analyze the data; how to interpret the information; what information would be useful for what purposes; and how to best report the information.

Unfortunately, for a number of reasons, access to this type of training is not as prevalent as it should be. As mentioned above, one of the reasons is lack of resources to pay for it. Another reason is the sheer lack of availability and difficulty in getting it. For example, the following comment from one survey respondent from a municipality showed his frustration with trying to get the required training:

> *TQM [Total Quality Management] was taught at the local community college about 3+ years ago. All supervisors were required to attend. The emphasis was on manufacturing. All supervisors resented this as a waste of time. We planned to attend the performance management seminar offered by the University of Vermont and ICMA. They were charging $55 for a 1.5 hour seminar that would take 2 hours + travel time. We tried to get details on advertised web site and Netscape, but could not locate the web site advertised in literature. It was disappointing all the way around.*

That goal orientation, the third rational/technocratic factor examined, was found to be significant for the process of performance measurement is not surprising. The cases reviewed prior to conducting the survey revealed that development (adoption) and implementation of performance measures should be linked and guided by the mission, goals, and objectives of the organization (Bryant, 1996; Blanche-Kapplen and Lissman, 1996; Tracy, 1996). Furthermore, legislation such as GPRA and the "managing for results" movement explicitly call for this linkage. The centrality of goals is exemplified in the case of Prince William County, Virginia, where

> *management and staff reviewed and refined program proposed statements and the various program activities were identified, costed, and then rated on their relative quality and importance to achieving the program's purpose and goals. Development of measures was greatly facilitated by this level of clarity on program purpose and activity. (Marshall, 1996, p. 6)*

Moreover, presumably organizations that are driven by goals are likely to want to have a system that allows them to determine whether or not they are achieving those goals. In the event organizations find that they are not moving in the desired direction, they would attempt to make the necessary adjustments to get back on track. Thus, the development of the measures depends on management's ability to articulate and communicate the mission and goals of the organization, as well as the strategies for achieving them. Resistance to this approach, or inability to do so, contributes to organizations' lack of drive for adopting and implementing a good performance measurement system. And if they do adopt performance measures, they are likely to do so half-heartedly and would be less likely to implement the information. This is illustrated by a comment made by a respondent from a municipality, who said that in his organization, departments want to stay with workload indicators, and politicians do not want a clear goal. Such lack of clarity of goals and refinement of measures is not conducive to performance-based management. PBM requires the coordination of goals with objectives and indicators. It requires a comprehensive system looking at many aspects of the operation in an organization. Although useful for some purposes, workload measures can contribute only to a limited degree to the understanding of organizational performance. They are not, by any means, substitutes for outcomes, efficiency, and process measures. Output measures complement them.

Politics and Culture in the Realm of Rational/Technocratic Factors

The discussion above, which is based in part on the empirical findings of the survey data, established the important role that resources, access to information, and goal orientation play in the process of performance measurement utilization. However, as suggested by the quantitative results presented earlier, in spite of any claims to the contrary, the presence of formal politics and the rational/technocratic factors is not sufficient to guarantee the success of performance-based management. Furthermore, certain organizational factors actually help explain the presence of resources, access to information, and a goal orientation. At the same time, these rational/technocratic factors help to create conditions that may change the behavior of other organizational factors with regard to the process of utilization. Therefore, from the perspective of model building, consideration of goal orientation, resources, and access to information is critical.

Influence of Formal Politics (Internal and External Requirements)

After including the rational/technocratic factors goal orientation, resources, and access to information in the model, the findings, summarized in Figure 7.1, continued to show that external and internal requirements exert a more significant and important impact on adoption than on implementation. Regardless of the presence of these three rational/technocratic factors, the effect of external requirements on implementation will always be significantly smaller than that of internal requirements. Furthermore, the effect of internal requirements on both stages of utilization of performance measurement information will be greater than that of external requirements. This pattern not only is consistent with the earlier discussion, but also confirms the argument that when organizations that do not have the necessary resources are mandated to have performance measures, adoption occurs at a slower pace. In contrast, when the organizations have the necessary technocentric conditions, it occurs at a faster rate. Some government agencies have recognized the limited effectiveness that a policy mandating performance measurement could have if no additional resources to follow through are provided. For example, according to some of the survey respondents, the State of Minnesota helped local governments overcome this barrier by providing aid to those governments that were working on implementing performance measurements, thus avoiding the usual response to unfunded mandates—inaction.

One of the patterns that the mediated analysis allowed to emerge was that in contrast to external requirements, part of the effects of internal requirements on the dependent factors *adoption* and *implementation* of performance measures occur through the rational/technocratic factor resources. This may suggest that when internal policies are enacted, there is a tendency to create the mechanisms necessary to carry out the intended purposes of the policy. Alternatively, the mechanisms that facilitate carrying out the policy are put into place at a faster rate than when the organization is mandated to carry out an external policy. In this case, one of the mechanisms necessary to carry out a policy for performance measurement is having adequate resources. There is no question about it, as echoed by one of the respondents: effective implementation of a policy necessitates resources. Otherwise, the policy would have no teeth, like so many other unfunded mandates.

Furthermore, an internal requirement without real commitment can be damaging to employee morale, and therefore hinder the implementation efforts. A respondent from a county government indicated that in her organization the internal policy is just that performance measures are desirable. This leads to the perception that the direction to use performance measures is not strong, and therefore, said the respondent, "the incentive to do the 'heavy-lifting' of performance measurement is daunting." The result of this practice has been that performance measures continue to be viewed as "time consuming, more bean-counting which takes away from 'real' work."

Threaded here is evidence for the argument that by themselves, requirements, internal or external, tend to be more formalistic in nature. Even though requirements may facilitate implementation, this step does not automatically follow or is expected to follow, and thus, in most cases, adoption will be the first and last stage. Organizations will call attention to a collection of measures that, when looked at closely, will be revealed to be just that, a collection of measures, and not a system intended for managing performance.

Influence of Organizational Politics (Internal and External Interest Groups)

One can argue that internal political activities such as the formation of coalitions, measured here as internal interest groups working in support of performance measurement, are a reflection of the commitment and leadership of management and nonmanagement employees to the performance measurement effort. This commitment leads to the mobilization of resources within the organization to help support the effort. The experience of Prince William County, Virginia, supports this assertion.

Like any new initiatives, the fact that managing for results requires resources, time, and effort puts it in competition with other efforts and, as a result, turns it into a political initiative. Thus, in order for managing for results to succeed, it needs to be of strategic importance to the organization (Marshall, 1996); and through the commitment to this strategic value, the appropriate technical capacity can be developed.

Conversely, the lack of commitment could hinder the efforts, as suggested by one of the respondents to the survey. The respondent said that there is a "desire by the city manager to develop and maintain meaningful performance measures; but there has not been a willingness to provide the resources necessary to accomplish this." Without this willingness, it is unlikely that in this case the process will proceed beyond adoption.

Furthermore, as suggested in Figure 7.1, the empirical findings support the notion that continued success of a performance measurement system depends on the continued support of elected officials and the public. This support may be shown in two ways. One is by allowing the organization to devote resources to the performance measurement effort. The other is by using the information even when the results contravene the political agenda. These two points are often made evident in practice as stated by comments made by several of the survey respondents. In particular, this can be captured in the following comment made by a respondent from a municipal government regarding the lack of success of their performance measurement effort: "Budget constraints and indifference from elected officials [contribute to the lack of use].... The community must be willing to accept change and pay for it."

The results of including rational/technocratic factors not only confirmed the differential effect of interest groups, but also provided further evidence for another argument. Specifically, it was suggested earlier that internal interest groups represent an internal abstract or symbolic influence. This argument is supported by the finding that these groups are effective in explaining adoption, but not so much in explaining implementation. Organizations appear to be more compelled to implement performance measures by the pressure or involvement of external interest groups. To some extent, the reason these groups are more compelling is the influence they could exert on the availability of resources.

Influence of Culture (Attitude and Rewards)

Having a culture that embraces change and that rewards risk taking contributes significantly to developing an organization's technical capacity for performance measurement. Such a culture is more conducive to organizations developing a goal orientation, which in turns helps to inform performance measurement and thus PBM. In addition, the findings presented here show that organizations with a culture of change will be more likely to make available the resources that are necessary for the performance measurement effort. A culture that embraces change is particularly important for the implementation stage, which, as discussed earlier, poses the greatest challenges and risks in the process of utilization of performance measurement information.

These findings have a particular theoretical and methodological repercussion. Schein (1992) has argued that all the dimensions of culture are not equally relevant to a given group's functioning. Thus, he deems surveys inappropriate to gain knowledge about organizational culture. In contrast, Reichers and Schneider (1990) have argued that a questionnaire can get to the issue of culture if it is developed for the particular organization or subgroup. The findings here suggest that although it may be difficult to assess the impact of culture, as argued by Schein (1992), given the specific dimensions of the interest here and the topic and groups involved, we were able to capture some of the nuances of this concept. The questionnaire was certainly useful, but it was also the case that the data analysis approach used here, which included several forms of elaboration, allowed for a better assessment of some of the dimensions of culture. Again, it may be interesting to assess the effect of culture; however, even more interesting is to know how culture works, as was demonstrated here.

Will Organizations That Adopt Implement?

As the reader will guess, the answer to this question is not necessarily. The elaborated analysis presented in Chapter 6 of this book clearly showed that adoption is certainly a direct precursor for implementation, obviously a necessary step in the process. However, adoption is not sufficient to guarantee implementation. In fact, the evidence suggests that adoption can be considered a symbolic gesture unless other mechanisms are in place that make the organization move forward in the process and actually use the performance measurement information.

As Figure 7.1 suggests, moving to the stage of implementation will require the continued support and involvement of citizens and elected officials. This is not to say that internal interest groups are not important, but as an internal influence they represent an abstract force, and thus are better predictors of symbolic actions such as adoption. This is well supported in the path model that was developed in Chapter 6. In the final analysis, elected officials and citizens hold the purse strings. In fact, as suggested by former Utah Speaker of the House Nolan Karras during a meeting of the Utah Tomorrow Strategic Planning Committee, citizens' involvement might be the key to implementation. Expressing his frustration with legislators not using readily available performance measures to inform their decision, Speaker Karras said that he believed that the only way legislators would do so was if citizens got involved and put pressure on them.

Requirements may help set in motion the mechanisms that lead to implementation, but they are more effective in promoting adoption. Indeed, one of those mechanisms is adoption of performance measures. But their lack of direct impact on implementation when the entire utilization model is examined suggests that they have a limited effect on implementation and speak of the abstract (or symbolic) notion that they embody. To be sure, internal requirements may reflect a genuine commitment by management, shown by an inclination to make resources available and to voluntarily commit to use performance measures. In this case, implementation will be easier because necessary infrastructure or process mechanisms are created. But unless this becomes part of what the organization does, the more concrete factors, those that may put the organization in a vulnerable position, opening it to public scrutiny, affect implementation.

Now, some may observe that organizations still comply with external requirements. The findings presented here do not deny this reality. However, as was pointed out to me a couple of years ago by a former legislative assistant, and just recently by an employee of a nonprofit agency, organizations that do not want to change and do not believe in the philosophy embodied in those requirements, more often than not, tend to do the bare minimum required to comply with mandates. In the context of performance measurement, this means that it is very unlikely that they will make effective use of the information as expected in an organization that truly believes and wants performance-based management.

The utilization model also suggests that although the effect of unionization might not be as overtly pressing as some would expect at the beginning of the utilization process, unions need to be carefully considered at every stage of the process, but particularly at the implementation level. Unionization will have a moderating effect on whatever impact the internal interest groups have, and once the organization moves to implementing the information, they will become more active in their direct actions. As has been argued here, the adoption of performance measures creates uncertainty; however, it is the implementation of the measures that could lead to real consequences that have an undesirable impact on employees and the organization. Though the purpose is not to demonize unions, the evidence appears to support the theoretical arguments and the comments made by some of the respondents to the survey that unions do tend to act as deterrents to activities that can be threatening to their members. Thus, performance measurement and PBM may be perceived as potential threats. Given this, unless the appropriate measures have been taken with regard to unionized employees, it is not a given that when there is passive reaction to adoption, the same reaction should be expected for implementation, and thus the organization will sail into and through the implementation stage.

Another factor to consider when predicting the chances of adoption leading to implementation is the type of governmental organization being discussed. The evidence presented here shows that once the resource barrier is overcome, municipalities and counties implement at a faster rate than states. Given the access to resources that state agencies have and the fact that they tend to be focused on one specific policy area, one might expect that it would be easier for them to implement. This was not the case here. There are several plausible explanations for this outcome. Some of these were alluded to at a question and answer session during a recent performance measurement summit I attended. One staff member from the governor's office indicated that inflexible personnel rules, the size of agencies, entrenched attitudes, difficulty of monitoring, and lack of interest of long-time personnel made it difficult to implement performance measurement at the state level. On the other hand, de Lancer Julnes and Mixcoatl (2006) concluded that the ability to implement and sustain performance measurement at the state level may be dependent on the leadership of governors, and on governors' length of stay in power. The longer the governor stays in power, the greater the opportunity for continuity and institutionalization of any reforms or changes.

Summary

This chapter provided a discussion of the implications of the findings of the mail survey. The discussion focused on the differential effect that various organizational factors, both internal and external, have on the process of utilization of performance measurement. This process, as discussed here, appears to have at least two stages, adoption and implementation. The implications of this discussion make it very clear that performance measurement is of strategic importance to PBM.

Furthermore, it was shown that the assumption that adopting performance measurement will lead to the implementation of information, and thus to the fulfillment of PBM purposes, is not well founded. The confluence of different actors and influences on the process points to the need for different strategies at the different stages of performance measurement utilization if the promises of PBM are to come to fruition.

Chapter 8

Contextualizing the Quantitative Model

The empirical findings described in the previous chapter of this book were an important step toward achieving an understanding of the utilization of performance measurement information. The different methodological approaches and analytical techniques allowed for the development of an empirical model that can help explain what organizational conditions are more likely to lead to adoption and implementation of performance measures.

Although the empirical model is valuable in providing insights, it needed to be taken a step further. For this purpose, elaboration took a different form. In this chapter, I discuss the results of the follow-up telephone interviews that sought to provide greater depth and contextualization of the dynamics involved in the process of utilization of performance measurement information. In addition to helping verify the linkages of the empirical model, the results of the interview provide further insight into what practitioners mean when they say that performance measures are used, what kinds of actions and characteristics of organizations encourage or discourage utilization of performance measures, and the challenges that must be overcome in order for these efforts to succeed.

Performance Measures Being Adopted

To assess the organization's capacity for action, one of the first questions asked of interview participants was the types of measures that their organization had adopted. In addition to the three types of measures that were included in the mail

Table 8.1 Performance Measures Developed

	Types of Measures	Number and Percent Responding
Measures included in the survey	Output	15 (83%)
	Outcomes	12 (67%)
	Efficiency	11 (61%)
Additional measures included in the follow-up interviews	Inputs	15 (83%)
	Effectiveness	5 (28%)
	Other (workload, quality, explanation)	4 (22%)

survey (outputs, outcomes, efficiency measures), respondents were asked if they had adopted input and effectiveness measures. The findings shown in Table 8.1 are consistent with the pattern found in the answers to the mail survey.

As can be observed in the table, interview participants tended to say that they had developed output measures (83 percent) more than outcome and efficiency measures. A significantly smaller number of respondents said that they had developed effectiveness measures (28 percent), and an even smaller percentage mentioned that they had developed other types of measures. On the other hand, input measures were mentioned as often as output measures.

Some interview participants indicated that although they have been developing output measures for a long time, they did not have a very comprehensive performance measurement system. This appears to validate what some have feared—that to a large extent, even when they have a rudimentary performance measurement system, organizations tend to overstate its importance when asked if they have performance measures. It also helps explain in part the gap between the apparent disproportionately large number of organizations claiming to have a performance measurement system, and the smaller number saying that they actually use the information. Another interesting twist, which may also help explain the gap, emerged in comments from two interview participants. They said that in their organization they were no longer calling their efforts to quantify program activity or explain program performance "performance measurement." Apparently this was a conscious effort because the term had a negative connotation for many employees.

A related comment was made by another participant who stated that there is a need to get away from the performance measurement lingo because it makes interpretation too complicated. Moreover, another stated that in her organization they did not use traditional labels such as outcome, output, or efficiency measures because many people were not able to differentiate between output and outcomes, for example; so "they send tons of measures and we go through them and see if they make sense."

These poignant comments also offer a glimpse into specific difficulties that some organizations may face when trying to create a PBM culture. For example, these comments, which relate to the rational/technocratic factor access to information, highlight the need that organizations may have for training to help employees and others understand what the measures are, how to develop them, and what they mean. Another pragmatic difficulty that organizations may face is learning how to develop more sophisticated and meaningful measures of performance, such as outcome measures, given that others tend to have little control over long-term results. This is of particular concern for many, and is highlighted by a comment made by a participant, who pointed out that for the most part, outcome measures are difficult because clients go away after they receive the service. This makes it very difficult for service providers to follow up and find out what the results of their intervention were. It was also noted that because the clients may receive services from multiple sources, it is difficult to isolate the effect of a particular program. As succinctly put by a participant: "We are all in a learning curve at different levels. It's hard to understand how it all works together; what's a goal; what's an objective."

Thus, as suggested by Table 8.1, organizations seem to have an easier time sticking to output measures than moving toward adopting outcome and effectiveness measures. Unfortunately, output measures are very limited in terms of the depth and breadth of the information they provide. As a result, they present limitations regarding how to use them and for what purposes. This latter point will be expanded upon in the next chapter of this book, which discusses purposes and uses of performance measures.

What It Means to Implement Performance Measures

Taking a deeper look into implementation or actual use of information was next in order. To do this, I read to interview participants a list of uses of performance measurement information. This list was the same as that used in the mail survey. Participants were asked whether performance measures were being used in these ways. The responses to this question are summarized in Table 8.2. Then, to understand what participants meant when they said that they had implemented performance measures, they were asked an open-ended question.

The distribution of the different ways of implementing performance measures shown in Table 8.2 closely resembles the distribution found in the responses to the mail survey reported in Chapter 5. It also looks very much like the findings of a recent study on strategic planning and use of performance measures among U.S. municipalities conducted by Poister and Streib (2005).

Table 8.2   Implementation of Performance Measures: Discrete Choices

Implementation	Number and Percent Responding
Resource allocation	11 (61%)
Program monitoring	11 (61%)
Strategic planning	9 (50%)
Reporting to elected officials	9 (50%)
Reporting to internal management	8 (44%)
Reporting to citizens or media	6 (33%)

Adapted from de Lancer Julnes (2006).

As shown in the table, monitoring programs and resource allocation were the most often mentioned implementations of performance measurement information (61 percent, or 11 responses). Strategic planning and reporting to elected officials were the second most often-cited forms of implementation (50 percent, or 9 respondents). A total of 44 percent said that performance measures were used to report to internal managers and only 33 percent said that they were used to report to the citizens and the media.

The percentage of participants in the telephone interview who said that they used performance measures for resource allocation was larger than that of the participants in Poister and Streib's (2005) study. In their study, of the 255 who responded, 48 percent said that performance data played an important role in resource allocation. The authors also reported that 56 percent of their 225 respondents stated that performance measures were used to track the implementation of projects or initiatives called for by the strategic plan. However, in a pattern of use similar to that found here, Poister and Streib found that only 48 percent of those who answered reported performance measures associated with the strategic plans to the city council. Similarly, only 35 percent report to the public on a regular basis.

The open-ended question that my interview participants were asked regarding how performance measures were used revealed an even more interesting reality about the place of performance measurement in decision making. In general, the initial response of those interviewed was that performance measures influenced action but did not drive decisions. The examination of 23 comments made by the participants indicated that when they spoke of using performance measures for strategic planning, they meant that the measures were included in the strategic planning document. There was no evidence that performance measures were considered an integral part of strategic planning.

Likewise, the comments of those who spoke of using performance measures for resource allocation showed that although the information may be part of the budget process, it was usually included only as a reference point. That is, the measures were included as part of a budget request, not as the main reason for the amounts requested. They also served the purpose of explaining to executives and legislators why a particular target was or was not achieved. Furthermore, the responses indicate that performance measurement information is rarely used to cut budgets due to poor performance. Other matters seem to drive such decisions.

For example, a participant from a county government stated that when making resource allocation decisions, the board and county administrator focused not on the efficiency of programs, but more on whether the programs were experiencing increased demand for services or, as put by one participant, "how they [citizens] view their government. If they think the borough is not providing services, they voice their concerns and those weigh on administrative issues." Such realization beckons Martha Wellman and Gary Van Landingham's (2008) conclusion that performance-based budgeting in Florida will never have a significant impact on political policy making, but has had an impact on how managers "spend the resources they receive." Thus, it seems that there is more of a passive approach to the use of performance measures than performance-based management proponents would have hoped for. In fact, a recurrent theme in the answers of participants was that performance measures do not drive decisions, but make you think about your programs in a more systematic way.

In terms of what it meant when they said that performance measures were used to report to elected officials, participants stated that this was mostly done through the budget document. In that performance measures are part of the budget request, the reporting occurs during the budget process. No other systematic way of reporting was indicated. As far as reporting to citizens and media, the response was similar. According to interview participants, this was usually done by making the budget document available at the local libraries or on the Web. No special reports were prepared, nor were other forms of dissemination to citizens mentioned. This is intriguing given that several interview participants said that they needed to have performance measures to respond to transparency requirements. It appears that citizens are not the ones asking for more transparency. Otherwise, more participants would have reported that their organizations systematically communicate performance measurement information to citizens.

A Political Perspective on Use of Performance Measures

The responses given by the interview participants clearly underscore the notion that performance measures alone do not drive decisions. A number of other issues, some with more saliency than others, are taken into consideration when making decisions. As was revealed by the survey reported in previous chapters, these issues include politics and its variants. Indeed, in the context of budgeting, Wildavsky (1988) argued that decision making is political, particularly if the program in question serves a strong group. According to Wildavsky, the agency "may not only fail in this purpose [using performance information that deems a program inefficient or ineffective] but may actually see the appropriations increased as this threat mobilizes the affected interests."

Therefore, budgets are one of the main political struggles in organizations because they deal with limited resources. As such, stated Wildavski "the problem is not only 'how shall budgetary benefits be maximized'"…but also "who shall receive budgetary benefits and how much?" By the end of the budget process inevitably some actors will be perceived as winners while other will be perceived as losers (Meld, 1974). This too makes the budget process a political endeavor and makes it consistent with Pettigrew's (1973) definition of political behavior. He stated that this was "behavior by individuals, or in collective terms, by sub-units, within the organization that makes a claim against the resource-sharing system of the organization." The resources could be salaries, promotion opportunities, capital expenditure, new equipment, or control over people, information or new areas of a business.

Therefore, given these observations, most of the responses provided by interview participants with regard to how performance measures were used can be categorized as politically rational. Of 23 comments made by the participants, political use emerged 50% of the time. Political use means using performance measures for budget related purposes, including providing justification for the amounts requested, and for transparency purposes. Although budgeting is often viewed as a neutral and technical exercise, as suggested by Wildavsky (1988) and the responses of interview participants, in reality budgeting is a political activity. As a result, there is a desire to influence it. Performance measurement information appears to be a tool that can be used for this purpose.

Approximately 38% of the comments made by informants regarding use referred to using performance measures for monitoring and evaluating. Although at face value monitoring and evaluating may seem to be rational/technocratic activities, Pettigrew's (1973) definition of political behavior, gives a different perspective. In that monitoring and evaluating can and are used for controlling and influencing people, they fall under the realm of politics. However, no evidence was found from the interviews that the performance measurement information drove any kind of personnel decision or other resource allocation decisions.

Although, the overarching sentiment among interview informants appeared to be that performance measures did not drive decisions, performance measurement information seemed to be used to somehow influence decisions. While some may dismay about the apparent lack of direct linkage between performance measures and allocation decisions, the fact that they are included and thought of during the budget process, and that they are used for transparency purposes can be claimed to be a form of use and thus an accomplishment and a step forward toward PBM.

Reasons for Adopting and Implementing Performance Measures

Participants in the follow-up interviews were asked what has encouraged or would encourage the adoption and implementation of performance measures in their organizations. The most prevalent answer given by participants was a need to respond to calls for accountability, with 11 (61 percent) of the participants mentioning it. Paradoxically, far from seeing accountability as an important motivator, a good number of the participants saw accountability as a deterrent to adopting and implementing performance measures.

The main reason for viewing performance measurement for accountability as a deterrent was a fear of retribution. This fear is reflected in this comment made by a participant: "Management team is not receptive to performance measurement. There are concerns as to what the numbers say; how they present the issues … they are worried about accountability issues." A related comment pointed at outcome-based accountability as a source of concern. The informant said that people were afraid of being held accountable for outcomes. Apparently managers were particularly worried about the need to set "lofty program goals" in response to political pressures, only to find that they are not able to achieve them.

There were also fears that elected officials would use accountability as a reason to micromanage and "to set performance measurement standards arbitrarily." For performance measurement efforts to be successful, suggested one participant, there has to be agreement that performance measurement is a management tool "to help us change the way we do business; to do our job better rather than a method meant to be an accountability hammer or to significantly change budget allocation."

Verification of Model Linkages

Overall, the responses presented below verify the accuracy of the hypotheses tested and the models developed using data from the mail survey. The responses are also consistent with many of the lessons learned from the case studies summarized in Chapter 2 of this book. The findings of the interviews are discussed here in terms of the linkages of the empirically derived path model.

Factors That Predict Adoption

Internal Interest Groups

To assess the accuracy of the predictive power of internal interest groups, interview participants were asked whether there were individuals, groups, or circumstances that were particularly influential in promoting development of performance measures. Of the 19 comments received, 67 percent of the time (12 times) participants mentioned management, including department/agency heads and city or county manager, and nonmanagement employees as being influential. According to the responses, these actors tended to work together in informal teams that supported the development of performance measures.

A related question asked interview participants to identify the groups or individuals and circumstances that had complicated development of performance measures. Participants were very candid in describing their circumstances. Many of the comments made by the participants blamed the complications they faced on negative attitudes toward performance measurement. One participant in particular described a pervasive negative attitude among employees, especially among those who had been in the organization for a long time. According to the respondent, usually they oppose the effort because they often think of performance measurement as "not my job." As a result, there had been no buy-in from management and staff. When there is no buy-in, suggested the informant, chances are that if the effort is undertaken, it will be half-hearted, resulting in performance measures that are not useful to anyone.

In 22 percent of the comments (five comments), management and legislators attitudes and lack of support were mentioned as complicating the adoption of performance measures. One participant illustrated this by lamenting that in his department, the department head was not particularly excited about performance measures. As a result, this did not conduce to adopting performance measurement.

Requirements

External groups and actors such as elected officials, including the governor, legislators, county boards, and city councils, were mentioned seven times (or 33 percent of the comments) as being influential. The reason informants suggested that these groups were influential is because they could use the mechanism of requirements to compel organizations to develop performance measures. That is, they can enact external requirements. Specifically, when participants were asked about circumstances that have been influential, seven comments (or 58 percent) attributed development to legislation, laws, or simple expectation and requests that performance measures be included in the budget process.

Other circumstances related to requirements that had an influence on adoption included having an internal requirement coming from the top, budget pressures in the form of revenue shortfall, and membership in a professional organization such as Governmental Accounting Standards Board (GASB), which encourages organizations to experiment with service efforts and accomplishments (SEA).

Rational/Technocratic Factors

Five of the comments (22 percent) indicated that lack of expertise, time, data, and other resources made development of performance measures difficult. According to one respondent, "Department heads feel strapped for resources; thus, they do the minimum required." Other comments attributed the difficulty to the belief that developing a good performance measurement system takes a lot of effort, and the need for training on how to develop performance measures was cited three times as a circumstance that makes it difficult.

Other Factors

Misperceptions about performance measures, fears on the part of managers of getting their budgets cut, being told what to do, or being punished if their programs are found not working also seemed to have a negative impact on adoption of performance measures. Legislators were also cited as fearing losing control of their decision-making power because they are used to making decisions based on line items instead of program appropriations. This last point is often found in the literature regarding legislators' (lack of) use of performance measures (see, for example, de Lancer Julnes and Mixcoatl, 2006).

Factors That Predict Implementation

External Interest Groups

In line with the findings of the mail survey, informants were also asked what individuals or groups were most influential in the implementation of performance measures. Of the 15 comments, eight (53 percent) pointed at elected officials, including governors, legislators, county boards, city councils, and mayors, as being very influential in the implementation of performance measures. Some of the other comments attributed influence to city managers, department heads, and county administrators.

Overall, participants felt that the success of performance measurement efforts depended on whether the top leadership used the information. Thus, when asked which individuals or groups have complicated implementation of performance measures, participants said that one major problem was that elected officials did not use performance measures. More specifically, participants said that the lack of use and active participation of legislators and county board members are factors that complicate implementing performance measurement information. In one instance, a participant from a state agency indicated that because they have a part-time legislature, members "don't have time to digest the [performance information]." As a result, they do not use the information and, in some cases, have mandated the agencies to drop the performance measurement efforts all together.

Culture

As far as circumstances positively influencing implementation, 43 percent of the participants highlighted the importance of organizational culture. For instance, one participant said that a culture with an atmosphere that accepted change is necessary in order for implementation of performance measures to occur. This is not an easy task; as one participant said, "Change is scary to a lot of people." As a result, it leads to struggles and puts people on the defensive, as was illustrated by a comment made by another participant, who said that turf issues had complicated the process in his organization.

But in the opinion of one of the informants, because "performance measurement is not going away," organizations will have no other choice but to develop a culture that embraces performance measurement. Yet, as was suggested in two other comments, such a culture will require that there be incentives to encourage and nurture the use of performance measures. Without this, it is unlikely that implementation will take place.

Internal Interest Groups

When asked which individuals or groups have complicated implementation, six comments were related to management. Specifically, resistance or just mild support from department heads and agency heads was reported as complicating actual use of performance measures. Also, circumstances cited as complicating implementation included fear of being held accountable, particularly for outcomes.

Rational/Technocratic

Some of the comments identified the difficulty in understanding performance measurement systems as contributing to the lack of use. Related to this, an interview participant talked about the existence of a performance measurement learning curve. Getting past this was difficult without the appropriate training, especially on how to use performance measures. Interview participants also mentioned the perception of performance measurement being a waste of time, lack of data, and lack of resources as factors that complicate the implementation of performance measures. Nonetheless, as suggested by one of the informants, training and resources might not be enough given that "what to do with the information is a political decision."

Perceptions of Effectiveness of Performance Measurement

Interview participants were asked to provide an overall assessment of the effect of performance measurement in their organization. They were asked to assess whether performance measurement had worked, had helped to improve performance, had made things better, or had made things worse. Most of the responses were positive (83 percent of comments, out of 18), with two specifically making the point that performance measurement had made things better. Some of the comments reflected the feeling that those who had actually used performance measures were very satisfied, with one saying that her organization "would not have it any other way" (that is, it could not function without performance measurement information). Another said that "when performance measures are used the way they are supposed to be used, performance measures are useful."

Performance measures were described as helping to provide awareness and allowing for reflection about programs. The responses indicated that in the view of the interview participants, performance measures allowed managers and elected officials to think carefully about programs and helped to "open people's eyes as to where you are and where you would like to be." In the field of program evaluation, when information contributes to this kind of reflection and awareness, it is said to be used for enlightenment (Weiss, 1998a).

Also, informants said that performance measures were particularly useful because they allowed for better monitoring of program activity and results. To this effect, one of the participants said that performance measures gave his organization the ability to monitor their goal attainment. In the parlance of program evaluation, this type of knowledge use is called instrumental (Weiss, 1988a).

Three other comments portrayed performance measurement as a useful tool. One of the participants said that performance measures were a useful instrument for obtaining more resources. They can be used to make a case for increased resources during the budget process because they help to explain why more money is needed, or to show what has been done with the money. Another participant said that performance measures are an effective tool for helping to change organizational culture and to be transparent by showing to the public the overall performance of the services they receive.

On the other hand, three of the interview participants exercised caution and were skeptical of the usefulness of performance measures. One participant said that he was not sure about the contributions of performance measurement, stating, "I don't know I can attribute changes to performance measures." Another participant, mentioning that he had experienced other management improvement efforts, such as Planning Programming Budgeting System (PPBS) and Zero-Based Budgeting (ZBB), questioned the contributions that performance measurement can make. He stated, "I don't know what they [performance measures] do for anybody," indicating that he expected performance measurement to suffer the same fate of previous efforts that he had seen "come and go."

Finally, in the view of another participant, performance measurement efforts are counterproductive. The participant said that performance measurement made things worse "because there are many things you can't quantify and [decisions] should not be driven by measurement systems that simply count things."

Challenges of Performance Measurement

Participants were asked to identify challenges that are likely to face performance measurement efforts. In total, there were 36 comments to this question. In analyzing the comments, four main challenges emerged: the need for buy-in, developing a meaningful performance measurement system, the actual implementation of performance measures, and the need for continuity.

When explaining what they meant by buy-in being one of the major challenges, respondents referred to the need to change their organization's culture to gain support for performance measurement efforts. Specifically, two comments highlighted the fear that performance measurement brings up in people. One participant said that "people are afraid when they can't explain in quantifiable terms the services and actions they are performing." Another said that people are afraid to be held accountable for outcomes of services that are difficult to measure. Therefore, creating an environment of trust is essential for overcoming these challenges.

Participants' comments suggest that unless there is a culture that accepts, understands, and embraces performance measurement, the critical buy-in that the effort requires would be difficult to obtain. Otherwise, even if the organizations succeed in developing performance measurement systems, the likelihood is that the system will not be allowed to evolve and mature with the changing needs of the organization, and thus will remain underutilized. Interview participants also said that the necessary culture change not only must occur within the organizations, but also must include a change of attitude among elected officials.

In some ways another major challenge identified by participants relates to the change in culture cited above, but also highlights the pragmatic aspects of performance measurement. Participants said that being able to develop a meaningful performance measurement system was problematic because developing a useful system required that there be agreement on what measures need to be developed and their purpose. Wholey (1996) has long advocated the inclusion of those directly affected by performance measurement. Meaningful participation in the process by those who are going to be held accountable for the performance of the programs being measured, can help facilitate obtaining the needed agreement.

Some of the interview participants also said that performance measurement systems need to be easily understood and must link systematically to what is being done. These particular insights call attention to an increasingly growing concern about the need for organizations to have appropriate training not only on performance measurement, but also on how to better integrate this tool with the overall management of the organization. Again, this integration will also require that there be agreement as to the purpose of such integration.

The third major challenge identified by the interview participants was a related concern about how to use performance measurement information. More specifically, the participants found particularly challenging the task of properly interpreting information that showed successes and failures. They also believed that making the necessary adjustments (i.e., translating the performance measurement information into action) is a challenge for organizations.

Additionally, as part of the challenges in implementing performance measures, informants identified the need for organizations to learn how to report performance measurement information. This is indeed a challenge that until recently has been overlooked. Although calls for accountability emphasize the need for organizations to report on their performance, little attention has been given to developing ways for organizations to appropriately and effectively report this information to their stakeholders and other interested parties.

Another important challenge that emerged from the comments was that for performance measurement efforts to be successful, there needs to be continuity. The difficulty, as identified in the comments, is that performance measurement must be part of the culture of the organization so that it will continue to be an important part of the organization's life even after the administration that supported the process goes out of power. As simply put by a participant, "We must develop the system and stick to it." Political time horizons make this difficult. This is a process that requires time, and making it part of the culture takes even longer than any politician would be willing to wait.

On the other hand, a related challenge is making sure that the system adjusts according to the changing conditions of the environment in which the organization operates. So, it must be kept alive, refining measures as needed and making sure that it responds to current demands for information and action.

The availability of resources was only mentioned twice. This by no means suggests that resources are not important. As demonstrated by the discussion in the previous section and suggested by some of the challenges discussed here, this is hardly the case. However, it reinforces the notion that resources are part of the mechanisms that help organizations develop a capacity to adopt and implement

Table 8.3   Major Strategies for Addressing Challenges

Strategy
1. Performance measures must be used by top leadership.
2. Provide training on performance measurement.
3. Take small steps.
4. Create expectation for use.
5. Show examples that it can be done.
6. Include stakeholders.
7. Provide incentives for use of the information.

performance measures. As indicated by two comments made by participants, performance measurement can be very challenging when organizations are required to take on the task but are not given extra time, money, or people to do it. As a result, performance measurement becomes an additional burden in an environment of already increasing demands and therefore must compete for resources.

Strategies for Addressing Challenges

In addition to sharing the challenges that they have confronted and that other organizations should be aware of, interview participants were asked what strategies might help to address those challenges and help to increase the chances of success of performance measurement efforts. Participants provided many insightful suggestions, which can be grouped into seven broad categories, shown in Table 8.3. The first three of the strategies were the most often mentioned by participants.

Interview participants suggested that if their governing body uses the information "so that people see it," then it will become part of what people do. A respondent from a state noted that "the legislature must start using it for its funding decisions. That will make agency heads use it." Conversely, one respondent thought that one strategy should be involving customers "so that department heads see that it is them who want it and not the administration telling them what to do." Another indicated that use has to be a directive from the (county) board and not from the county administrator. That will give performance measurement more power. You need to "push from the top, if not there will always be resistance," said another interview participant. A key part of this strategy is the need for leaders to model the behavior that they want those at lower levels to embrace. Thus a related strategy, suggested other participants, is to create an expectation for use of performance measures by management. Some of the interview participants said that this could be accomplished if the governing body emphasized performance measurement and used the information for decision making.

Consistent with the findings of the mail survey regarding the need for training, participants identified providing training on adoption and implementation of performance measures as a key strategy for having a successful performance measurement system that is actually used. Participants suggested that organizations need to have personnel with the skills to develop appropriate measures of performance, analyze performance data, and know which measures can be used in which ways and for what circumstances. Although some participants suggested bringing in consultants, others suggested that having an in-house person with whom others could consult would be ideal. The need for training has long been advocated by Wholey (1999), who concluded that as public agencies move toward heavier involvement in performance-based management, the need for training will increase, but also, there will be *a premium on managers and staff with the knowledge, skills, and abilities to develop a reasonable level of agreement on goals and strategies for achieving the goals; develop performance measurement systems of sufficient quality …; ensure that performance information is used in management systems, in providing accountability to stakeholders and the public, to demonstrate effective or improved performance and to support resource allocation and other policy decision making. (p. 302)*

The tendency for government agencies to start "big" with new efforts like PBM was touted by some of the participants as the wrong approach. They pointed out that performance measurement efforts would be more successful if they started with small, baby steps to build the effort into the day-to-day operations of the organization. One participant pointed out that utilization of performance measurement means that you have to change the way you do business, but change takes time. Therefore, for performance measurement to be successful, you have to "grow it, and don't expect results right away."

Another strategy suggested by respondents is to show evidence to those involved in performance measurement efforts that performance measurement works and "can be done." In particular, participants indicated that showing examples of how performance measurement information has been used to improve operations to those who resist performance measurement and think that it is a wasted effort could help overcome the resistance. Documenting successful and even unsuccessful applications of performance measurement was also one of the calls made by Wholey (1992) and Greiner (1996) regarding the research that is needed to support performance-based management.

Finally, interview participants alluded to culture when they suggested that people should be rewarded for using performance measures. In particular, one respondent said that agencies should reward when goals are attained. However, comparing this suggestion with some of the lessons learned reported in Chapter 2 of this book indicates that there is mixed support for the strategy. While there is agreement for providing incentives for using performance measurement, how to do so remains an issue open to debate.

Summary

I discussed here the follow-up telephone interviews, which allowed for further inquiry into what practitioners mean when they say that they have adopted and implemented performance measures, why their organizations engaged in performance measurement, what their perceptions are of the effectiveness of their performance measurement efforts, and what challenges they face. The goal of this inquiry was to gain more insights into the context of the mechanisms highlighted by the quantitative model, thus verifying its accuracy in portraying utilization.

The more we understand the context, the more likely we will be able to shed light on the challenges that lie ahead of performance management efforts and can come up with better strategies for overcoming these challenges. Indeed, another contribution of this attempt to understand context and validate empirical findings was getting interview participants to share the ways in which they thought some of the challenges of adopting and implementing a performance measurement system could be overcome. Three of the top suggestions included getting top leadership including elected officials to use performance measurement information, providing training, and taking small steps.

The results discussed here not only support the claim that performance measurement is composed of at least two stages, but also give more insights into how each of the factors that were found to have an influence in the process actually behave. They also helped illuminate the manner in which organizations really implement performance measures, suggesting that in many cases it is not as direct as one might hope. This also suggests that when judging the level of usage of performance measures, and their success for that matter, critics must look deeper to see the subtle ways in which this tool contributes to performance improvement as well as other purposes and uses in support of performance-based management.

Chapter 9

Two Overarching Themes

As we reflect on the findings of the mail survey and the follow-up telephone interviews, two important themes, with implications for theory and practice, emerge: (1) performance measurement utilization is a complex process, and (2) use of performance measures is a multidimensional concept. These two themes are explored here.

The first major discussion in this chapter deals with the conceptualization of performance measurement as a complex process. Five state and local government examples of experiences with performance measurement are discussed to illustrate this. Building on these case examples, three subthemes that provide suggestions for practice are identified.

The second major discussion, which focuses on use, draws from the comments made by the telephone interview participants and the extant literature. A main argument is that implementation, or actually using performance measurement information, takes many forms. Although this is something often discussed in evaluation, not enough attention has been paid to the different types of use in the context of performance measurement. As a result, there is not a clear understanding of what it means for performance measurement information to be used and its implications for performance-based management (PBM).

Performance Measurement Utilization: A Complex Process That Requires Skills, Strategy, and Resources to Manage

The first step toward promoting performance-based management or any management system based on performance measurement is to recognize that Utilization is a process much like the processes of innovation and policy change. As with any policy for change, however, when performance measurement moves from adoption to implementation, the effort faces challenges that were either not present or not as predominant at the adoption stage (Cibulka and Derlin, 1998; Cronbach, 1980).

The evidence gathered through the studies presented here, and the experiences of public entities experimenting with performance measures, confirm that the utilization of performance measurement is a complex process, not a monolithic phenomenon that can be easily manipulated. This process is differentially affected by contextual factors, and it is composed of at least two stages: adoption and implementation. Because utilization is a process, characterized by some practitioners as requiring small, slow, and iterative steps, it needs time and effort to succeed. Furthermore, given the many factors that become relevant along the way, sometimes disrupting the process and other times enhancing it, the process needs to be managed strategically.

The process of Utilization can be best understood by looking at the implications of having two stages in the process. First is the stage of adoption or development of performance measures. There has to be agreement in the organization that performance measurement is desirable. This may come about because: (1) a government or funding agency's requirement; (2) there is a change in administration, which brought in reform-minded people; (3) there was an audit or an evaluation, and one of the recommendations was that there was a need to improve program management; or (4) simply stated, the organization is learning. Then there needs to be a way for deciding what measures are to be developed, for what purposes, and who will be involved in developing these measures. In addition, current organizational practices will need to adjust, but at the same time, there needs to be some continuity so that the process of utilization can be institutionalized, not a small feat for public organizations.

By *institutionalization* I mean that performance measurement becomes something that the organization does; it is part of the organizational culture. Institutionalization means that even when actors change, the process lives on. Again, this should not be construed as meaning that the system is static. On the contrary, as a manager in a federal agency told me, and as mentioned by participants in the follow-up interviews, performance measurement systems need to be constantly revised. You need to make sure that the measures are relevant—that the data continues to be valid. Performance measurement has to be a living thing!

But institutionalization also implies that there is implementation of performance measurement information. This second stage of utilization refers to the information actually being used. One of the causes of the downfall of performance measurement is the perception that decision makers do not pay attention to the information and do not use it in some fashion. At that point, performance measurement becomes a fruitless exercise of paper shoving, busywork. The individuals involved in the production of the information get demoralized and have no incentive to continue the effort. Nevertheless, as the findings presented here suggest, implementation of performance measures is easier said than done.

In what follows I present excerpts of the experiences of state and local governments that exemplify the nature of the process of utilization and the amount of time, effort, and negotiation that is required to develop a system that is credible and acceptable to those affected by the information. By no means are these examples exhaustive. They are a sample of the cases that I am familiar with because of professional experience and are representative of the theme discussed here.

Dakota County, Minnesota

For a long time, Dakota County has been considered one of the most efficient and innovative local governments in the nation. In recognition for its efforts, in 2006 it became the first county to receive the Minnesota Quality Award. The journey to getting this recognition has been the product of arduous and strategic performance measurement efforts.

When Dakota County started its performance measurement program, the departments that were participating worked with other counties and the state government to develop statewide indicators to be tracked at the county level. Departments were given time and technical assistance to develop mission statements and goals that had buy-in from employees, department managers, and department stakeholders. In addition, an on-line discussion during the Ninth Public Sector Productivity Conference (1998), Meg Hargrave, now former county evaluator, said that departments selected theory-based indicators that related directly to their mission and goals. Furthermore, the board of commissioners developed a countywide mission and vision, and began to track its performance by conducting an expanded citizen survey and developing an expanded community indicator report.

One of the main approaches used by the departments in Dakota County was to critically review their programs to identify all the challenges that affected the performance of their programs and services. Then the budget documents and discussions were refocused around the challenges the departments faced and the strategies to be used to address these challenges. One of the greatest challenges at the time was that countywide evaluation staff consisted of only one in-house evaluator. This complicated collecting and analyzing the data they were interested in.

These efforts do not occur overnight and are not inexpensive. Dakota County undertook a systematic and comprehensive effort that has now flourished. Developing mission statements attempting to link multiple goals and objectives to these mission statements, and adopting the appropriate measures of performance required a tremendous amount of investment of time and effort from multiple stakeholders. Coordinating with different agencies and people, developing and conducting surveys, putting together reports, getting agreements on measures, goals, and objectives—all required time and resources.

State of South Carolina, Department of Health and Environmental Control

The formal impetus for performance measurement in the Department of Health and Environmental Control (DHEC) of South Carolina began with the creation of the Office of Performance Management (OPM) in early 2004. The creation of this office was part of the implementation plan of comprehensive, systemwide performance management for health services. This project was developed by a team that included the deputy commissioner and the assistant deputy commissioner, who attended a yearlong public health leadership academy. At that time the team also decided to use the Turning Point Performance Management National Excellence Collaborative's model, which was specifically developed as a means to improve the outcome of health agencies by integrating performance standards, performance measurement, a quality improvement process, and the reporting of progress (for more information on this collaborative effort, see http://www.turningpointprogram.org/Pages/perfmgt.html). Since then, senior leadership started working closely with the director of OPM, Joe Kyle, and with other leaders in the central office and the regions to develop and implement the systemwide performance management system.

Beginning in 2005 the director of OPM met will all program areas (38 different organizational units), where program staff identified key performance standards and their performance measures. In addition, they discussed the frequency of data collection and how these data were to be collected and entered into the performance management database.

In the fall of 2006 and through mid-January 2007, DHEC started an implementation pilot project of the 286 performance measures that were identified. After the pilot, the director and staff of OPM met with all 38 units to review the results of the pilot and identify areas that needed improvement, as well as with regional leadership to obtain feedback on the impact of the performance management system on their staff. The pilot project revealed that there was a need for more information on each performance measure. They found that the performance measures were lacking information on their rationale, the performance standard they were associated with, as well as their data sources and collection procedures. The meeting with the regional leaders allowed for determination of the appropriate number of measures on which data should be collected and analyzed for inclusion in the performance management system. The results of the pilot project led to a decrease in the number of the initial measures from 286 to 206. Meetings with senior leadership regarding the prioritizing of the measures resulted in a final list of 34 priority measures.

In all, the process of coming up with the final list of performance measures for inclusion in the performance management system took about 100 meetings and numerous e-mail correspondence to keep people informed. In addition, the director and staff of the OPM conducted multiple meetings that brought together central office and regional leadership to clarify the performance management process, expectations, and revision of measures, and to share concerns about the system.

It should be noted that although DHEC had a Health Services Continuous Quality Improvement (CQI) committee since 1996, it was not until the impetus for performance management began that this team was more fully included in the overall planning for the health services area. This team, which includes representatives from each of DHEC's eight health regions, five major health bureaus, the agency's Office of Quality Management, as well as other health-related workers, educators, and volunteers, was created to assess and streamline quality assurance across all programmatic areas. Today the CQI team provides leadership and guidance on the implementation of the performance management system, developing materials and providing consultation as the system is implemented.

King County, Washington

In King County, Washington, receiving a low "managing for results" mark from *Governing* magazine in 2002 solidified a traditionally intermittent and weak interest in performance management and managing for results. Since the early 1990s there had been on and off attempts to conduct performance measurement; there was a rudimentary and rather unpopular system in place, mostly consisting of workload measures. In part, the lack of success of such efforts was because the council and executive's efforts were not integrated, and they were not sufficiently related to the business of county government. For example, performance measures were not clearly driven by county goals and objectives.

But it was not until the county received its grade of C that council members sought advice from experts in the field and agreed on the need to develop an effective performance measurement and management system. To that end, the council passed resolutions in 2002 and 2003 that refocused the efforts, charging the King County Auditor's Office with facilitating the development of such a system.

Thus ensued an effort in 2003, led by the auditor's office, that involved representatives from executive offices and departments, and the council. This became an advisory work group that developed a set of guidelines for performance measurement that were used to evaluate departments' annual business plans and measures. The work group accomplished its assignments in phases. For the initial phase, an outside consultant provided training, facilitated the activities of the working group, and assisted in the development of the guidelines—a strategic planning template to guide agencies' preparation of their strategic plans.

By 2005, armed with the work group's early successes in defining its mission and performance measurement guidelines, and in critiquing departmental business plans, the council created additional legislation to expand the work group to include other county units not under the control of the council. The expanded group included representatives from the two court systems and other countywide elected officials, such as the prosecutor, the assessor, and the sheriff. This new group developed a work plan for establishing a countywide system of performance measurement, management, and reporting. The plan proposed four phases for further development and implementation of the countywide system.

Recently the work group proposed a set of recommendations to the county council that include establishing provisions in county code for a system that incorporates strategic planning, performance measurement, public reporting, and citizen engagement. In addition, the group will prepare work products to assist departments and agencies in developing plans and measures and in implementing other aspects of the performance measurement work plan. King County Auditor Cheryle Broom, a national and international expert on performance measurement, has played a key role in this performance management effort. In the words of one executive branch employee, the county auditor and her work group have been instrumental in moving the county forward.

While working on countywide performance management efforts, the executive branch has continued to work toward improving its own performance measurement and management system. In 2006 King County's executive's office hired a performance management director to coordinate the implementation of a performance management system across the executive branch. The executive branch's effort has been dubbed KingStat. Since then, the county has published its performance report, "King County AIMs High: Annual Indicators and Measures" (see http://www.metrokc.gov/aimshigh/index.asp). According to a county employee, the performance management director has been instrumental in the development and maturation of departments' use of performance measures and planning tools.

To top off the complete turnaround of the county's efforts, King County recently received the prestigious national Association of Government Accountants' Certificate of Excellence in Service Efforts and Accomplishments Award for two accountability reports. Also, in 2007 King County received a Trailblazer grant award from the Center on Municipal Government Performance of the National Center for Civic Innovation. The award recognizes the county as one of the leading-edge governments that are advancing innovations in citizen-informed performance measurement and reporting. A more in-depth analysis of King County's performance measurement efforts can be found in Broom and Jennings (2008).

State of Utah

In the state of Utah, the impetus for strategic planning and performance measurement started with strong advocacy from members of the House of Representatives and the Senate in the late 1980s. Several senators and house representatives attended national meetings to learn from the experiences of other states that had been experimenting with strategic planning and performance measurement. This was followed by town meetings to determine the level of support for strategic planning and performance measurement among citizens and representatives of state agencies.

As a result of these endeavors, in 1990 the legislature authorized the creation of the Utah Tomorrow Strategic Planning Committee (UT), with the responsibility of recommending an ongoing and comprehensive strategic planning process for the state. The legislators called for the inclusion of all segments of Utah society in the process. The 12 original members of the committee worked to develop a vision for the future of the state, which went through several iterations. Subsequently, the committee created task force groups to develop goals, objectives, and performance measures for 10 key areas of government. The groups included interested citizens, representatives from state agencies, and legislators from the appropriations and interim committees in these key areas (UT, 2000).

The work of the task force was then refined by the UT committee. The committee produced a draft strategic plan that was followed by a series of town meetings and teleconferences throughout the state to seek citizens' input. After these meetings, the committee began working more closely with state agencies and local governments in an effort to further refine the goals, objectives, and performance measures that had been identified in the draft and then reviewed based on citizens' input. The first report of the committee, which included all the selected measures, was published in 1993. Also, since 1993 the Governor's Office of Planning and Budget has been providing free training upon request on performance measurement. In looking back, one legislator agreed that although it was important to have such an inclusive and iterative process, the process was lengthy and required more time than legislators really had (see de Lancer and Mixcoatl, 2006, for more details).

Utah Tomorrow was discontinued in 2004 by the state legislature. Shortly thereafter, newly elected governor Jon Huntsman introduced his own initiative, Utah Performance Elevated, an initiative that seeks to improve government performance and efficiency. At the core of this new initiative are performance management, strategic planning, collaboration and training, and enterprise innovation. Utah Performance Elevated is touted as an effort that goes beyond the Utah Tomorrow efforts. It is an attempt to focus on strategic planning and performance measurement, developing a more integrated and comprehensive management approach that can serve as an internal management tool. The balanced scorecard is viewed as a small, but critical aspect of this performance and efficiency improvement effort in Utah.

Teen REACH Program, Illinois

In 1998 the Illinois Department of Human Services (IDHS) began an effort to develop a performance management system for its newly created Teen REACH (Responsibility, Education, Achievement, Caring, and Hope) program. In June of that year the department had awarded contracts to 30 nonprofit and public agencies to directly or indirectly, through subcontractors, develop or expand community-based programs that help youth develop positive expectations for their future success through nonschool, structured activities. There were four core areas that IDHS wanted the program to focus on: (1) academic enrichment; (2) recreation, sports, and activities; (3) positive adult mentors; and (4) life skills education. At the time there were 70 providers. To help providers develop the performance management system, IDHS contracted with the University of Illinois–Springfield evaluation team. At the time, I was part of this team (see de Lancer, 2001, for more details).

To begin the work of developing the performance management system, we divided the provider agencies (contractors and subcontractors) into five geographic regions. Then the team conducted two rounds of facilitated meetings/workshops with agency representatives in each region. In attendance were representatives of provider agencies, including staff, executive directors, and program managers. The IDHS coordinator for the Teen REACH program also attended all workshops. In addition to the workshops, there were several planning and reporting meetings between the evaluation team and IDHS officials during and after the period of the workshops.

The outcome of the workshops was the development of an overall mission for the program, goals for the four core areas of the program, objectives for each goal, and indicators for each objective. By the end of the first round of workshops (five, one in each region), over 125 objectives were generated. During the second round (another five workshops), these were prioritized and the most relevant selected.

The third round was a workshop that brought together in a statewide meeting all the representatives of provider agencies. During this meeting, individuals were again assigned to working groups by core area and asked to prioritize each of the goals and objectives previously identified, and to vote on the objectives that they felt should be reported on to the IDHS. Their decision took into consideration the feasibility of achieving the objective and appropriateness of the indicator(s). They debated on issues such as data collection strategies, data availability, and the extent to which they felt their program could have an impact on the particular behavior. Once these smaller groups completed their task, they were brought back as a large group and a spokesperson from each of the four smaller groups reported the results of their discussions. All attendees then voted on adopting the four goals, one or two objectives per goal, and the indicators that were identified by the smaller groups. These were to become the goals, objectives, and indicators Teen REACH service providers would report on, and IDHS's funding and management decisions would be based, in part, on this information.

What These Cases Tell Us

Someone Has to Be in Charge

As indicated in the examples above, the process of developing and implementing a quality performance measurement system is lengthy and complex. The process cannot be done in haste and requires that someone be in charge. It is imperative that organizations designate a group or unit to manage the efforts. There need to be people in charge of coordinating the various activities; facilitating interaction among the various stakeholders; recording, summarizing, and organizing the outcomes of group activities; and reporting these outcomes. In addition, once there is agreement on the measures, individuals or units must be given the responsibility for collecting, organizing, and, in some cases, analyzing data and reporting the information.

The reason the last statement must be qualified with the words "in some cases" is that there are several options for analysis. One of these options is that each agency or unit not only collects its own data, but also analyzes it and prepares its own report. Because those in charge of doing this are part of the organizational structure, they may be perceived as being more trustworthy and knowledgeable of organizational needs. But in such a scenario, where, for example, each department in the city government has a performance measurement unit, the city government might not be taking advantage of economy of scales. Furthermore, for these individuals, performance measurement may be more work on top of their usual job responsibilities; they might not be properly trained, lacking the skills necessary to assist in developing, implementing, and maintaining a quality performance measurement system.

Another option, as shown in the cases of the South Carolina Department of Environment and Health and King County Auditor's Office, is a performance measurement unit that works with all agencies across the county and is in charge of coordinating and analyzing the data collected from the different agencies. There are advantages to this model. One of the advantages of having a central unit whose primary responsibility is performance measurement for an entire organization is that lines of responsibilities are clear, and the central unit can ensure that the appropriate measures are reported for the specific purpose. The individuals in the performance measurement unit would be experts with up-to-date knowledge on methods and techniques for performance measurement and performance-based management. This performance measurement unit would not only analyze the data, but also compile reports and provide training and guidance.

Furthermore, they would work with agencies to facilitate the identification of measures and refine the measures to fit the organizational purpose at hand. So, for example, if the purpose is accountability to citizens, then the central unit would help the agencies identify the data that can show the results that matter to most citizens. If the purpose is program improvement, the centralized unit would suggest the kinds of process measures that management could use to determine where changes are needed.

You Have to Be Strategic

At the beginning of this chapter I mentioned that the process needs to be managed strategically. To begin with, the process requires the involvement of many; it also requires sustained leadership. There is a need to obtain consensus and buy-in and to develop an organizational culture that is supportive of the effort. Evidently, a top-down approach would not help the process. But neither would a bottom-up approach. A successful process needs to have top-down, bottom-up, and sideways involvement. Managing such a diverse group of interest requires skills and an understanding of the motivations of these actors and the types of influences each actor could exert on the process.

What are some of those motivations and influences? One particular argument that is made throughout this book is that although there is some risk in adopting performance measures, the real risk is implementing this knowledge because of the consequences that it may bring. For example, if performance information is reported out of context or without sufficient information explaining why such performance is less than expected, it may lead to negative reactions against the organization.

This possibility may cause some decision-makers to adopt performance measurement to satisfy requirements or to appear to be modern and responsive—at the cutting edge of management practice. Or they may have originally intended to go through the whole process, but did not prepare themselves for using the acquired knowledge in the manner suggested by the measures.

Therefore, for those wishing to embark in the performance-based management adventure, recognizing these dynamics and developing the appropriate strategies can make a world of difference. One of those strategies is having an appropriate balance between rewards and sanctions. For Osborne and Plastrik (2000), if organizations do not have both rewards and sanctions, the performance measurement system will lack the necessary creditability with elected officials and will not motivate performance. But again, rewards and sanctions must be done with caution.

Another strategy is to be as inclusive as possible. In particular, those who will be affected by performance measurement information or will be held responsible for what the performance measures say must be part of the process from the very beginning. The earlier they are included, the better the chances of avoiding backlash.

It Is Expensive, but the Cost Will Decrease over Time

The message should have reached home by now. Performance-based management will be expensive. There is no question about it. Organizations have to invest in people, information, and infrastructure. To develop and implement a quality performance measurement system, employees will require training. They will also require time to dedicate to the effort. In addition, new personnel may need to be hired, and other participants may need to be compensated.

Also, implementing quality performance measures will not be possible unless the system is built with quality data. Having data that are reliable and valid is not necessarily cheap. And although some data may be readily available, organizations may need to collect their own. For example, although census data on the health status of residents may exist that can be used as benchmarks, to assess outcomes of health interventions, organizations may need to conduct a survey of service recipients. In addition, the organizations may need to invest in an information infrastructure (hardware and software) to house the performance measurement data.

Once the appropriate human and information infrastructure is established, there will be a need for maintaining, refining, and improving as necessary. The cost, however, will decrease over time because the appropriate infrastructure would be in place and the start-up cost already absorbed. This should be the case if performance measurement becomes the norm rather than the exception.

Use of Performance Measures Is More than Meets the Eye

The examination of the comments made by the telephone interview participants made evident that in addition to the web of organizational factors that impact the utilization of performance measurement, making it a rather complex process, the concept of use of performance measures is multifaceted and complex as well. Although empirical observations appear to show that actual use of performance measures is not common, part of our inability to see actual use is due to our insistence in narrowly defining use and, as argued by Hatry (2008), what appears to be an almost exclusive use of performance measurement information for accountability purposes. As a result, current definitions of use of performance measures fail to capture the nuances of the concept, leading us to look for evidence of use defined from an instrumental perspective.

The comments made by interview participants revealed what Weiss (1998a) has observed in the area of program evaluation: that there is more than just instrumental use of knowledge. By *instrumental* she means that the information has a direct and visible impact on decisions, such as budget and other resource allocation decisions; or causes the organizations to make visible changes; or, even more, leads to judgments with concrete repercussions for the organization and the program. Weiss has argued that there are other uses that can be just as significant but less evident. Specifically, in addition to instrumental use, she cites three other noninstrumental uses: conceptual, persuasion, and enlightenment. By *conceptual use* Weiss means that the evaluation findings help change the understanding of what the program is and does. *Persuasion* is when the information is used to mobilize support for an already held position. And *enlightenment* is when the evaluation findings add to knowledge accumulated, leading to changes in thinking and actions. Evidently, these different conceptions of evaluation knowledge use can be readily applied to further our understanding of performance measures use.

The running theme in the interview responses was that although performance measurement information does not directly cause people to make particular decisions, the information, nonetheless, has some influence. This theme evokes Weiss's

(1998a) classification of knowledge use as noninstrumental. On the other hand, as discussed in Chapter 8, many of the interview participants talked about using the information for accountability. Accountability is a purpose of performance measurement; that is, it represents a reason or goal for conducting performance measurement. It is an example of instrumental use, a visible and concrete purpose. For the most part, when discussing the many possibilities of use of performance measures, scholars focus on specific purposes. As a result, when these purposes are not observed, the conclusion is that performance measures are not used.

In what follows, I present a typology that differentiates performance measures use from purpose. Though this typology builds on Weiss's classification of knowledge, it goes a step further. It puts various purposes in the context of the uses and also provides specific examples of the measures that are useful for particular purposes. By the end of this chapter, the reader should take away the idea that even if performance measurement information only serves to enlighten discussions, that too can be considered use and is nonetheless a contribution to decision making. Therefore, this chapter should provide hope for scholars frustrated with the apparent lack of use of performance measures. Managers will take heart that their efforts are recognized and that measurement is not necessarily a waste.

The Purpose in Using Performance Information

Using as a foundation Weiss's basic classification of knowledge use, as instrumental and noninstrumental, the framework I present here teases out the differences between the concept of use and the concept of purpose. Consequently, this adds an extra dimension that helps to clarify a key concept we have been discussing throughout this book: knowledge implementation. The argument advanced here is that when executed, purposes represent knowledge converted into action, and hence knowledge implementation. As an example, when organizations conduct performance measures for the purpose of accountability, and this purpose is executed by reporting to the public and other stakeholders, this can be considered knowledge implementation. In addition, this can be thought of as an example of an instrumental use of information.

Another factor that helps to further clarify purposes and uses is the locus of the intended primary audience of this information. This is because the information needs of audiences located inside the organization will be different from those located outside of the organization. Furthermore, the intentions of those providing the information vary according to the intended audience. These different ideas are depicted in Figure 9.1.

The margins of the 2 × 2 table in Figure 9.1 show that the way performance measurement information is used (nature of knowledge use) and the audience for which it is intended (primary audience) frame the purpose of the information found inside the table.

Nature of Knowledge Use	Primary Audience	
	Internal	*External*
Instrumental	Improvement	Accountability
Non-Instrumental	Understanding	Mobilization

Figure 9.1 Purposes, uses, and audiences of performance measurement information. (Adapted from de Lancer Julnes 2008; reproduced with permission of Palgrave McMillan).

As shown in the first quadrant (upper-left-hand corner), for internal audiences an instrumental purpose of performance measurement information is program improvement. These stakeholders are interested in performance indicators that will allow them to answer the question of what adjustments or changes, including real-location of resources, would be needed to improve the performance of the program in question. Note also that the termination of a program may contribute to the overall improvement of an agency's performance. And if performance measurement information is used for that purpose (not just to justify an already made decision), this can be considered an instrumental or concrete use of the performance knowledge. Most likely, when the focus is on improvement, the audience will be interested in having available information on program outcomes, processes, and efficiency.

It is important to remember that audiences should be provided with a set of measures. This does not mean that they are to be provided with 5 or 10 of the same types of measures. Certainly, different audiences will be interested in different kinds of measures, but the different types (outcomes, inputs, processes, etc.) complement each other. No matter how many of one type of measures are provided, by itself each type provides only a glimpse of one aspect of performance (e.g., the direct result or product of activities—outputs; the resources used—inputs; and so forth).

What is the level of this instrumental use of performance measurement information? According to Dulhy (2006), studies conducted in the 1990s on the use of performance measures by city governments reported that approximately 37 percent of them used performance measures for performance evaluation, strategic planning, and in the budget process. However, later studies have shown a decrease in this percent (down to 28 percent). While Dulhy attributes part of the decrease to the way the questions were worded, with new studies attempting to determine the extent to which performance measurement is integrated into the performance management system, the reality is that instrumental use remains low. Accordingly, in their study at the municipal and county levels, Melkers and Willoughby (2005) found that between two-thirds and three-quarters of respondents stated that performance measurement information was not important or only mildly important in the budget process.

At the federal level, the findings are similar when it comes to these forms of instrumental use. According to the results of six separate surveys, conducted beginning in 1996 and ending in 2003, only a small percentage of U.S. government agencies actually make funding and other resource allocation decisions based on performance measurement information (Newcomer, 2007). Although Newcomer (2007) suggests that there is a growing trend in these types of use, the findings showed that on average, only 23.5 percent make use of performance measures in this instrumental manner. Though the reasons for this level of use are not specifically stated, the different factors that were found to influence the process in the Utilization model offer a plausible explanation for the tendency to use the information in a less than instrumental fashion.

As we move on to the second quadrant of the table in Figure 9.1, accountability is categorized as representing an instrumental use. The audience in this instance tends to be external. For this audience, inputs and outcomes, and to some extent efficiency, would be the preferred performance measurement information. Still, when it comes to accountability to citizens, the bottom line is outcomes or results. Jonathan Koppell's (2005) typology of accountability offers a very useful way to think about how performance measures can contribute to the purpose of accountability, and also suggests the audiences that would be interested in this type of information. Although the typology identifies five dimensions of accountability and five key questions attached to these dimensions, three of Koppell's dimensions can be specifically addressed with performance measurement information (Koppell, 2005, p. 96):

1. Transparency: Did the organization reveal the facts of its performance?
2. Controllability: Did the organization do what the principal (e.g., congress, president) desired?
3. Responsiveness: Did the organization fulfill the substantive expectation (demand/need)?

The first of these three dimensions, transparency, can be satisfied by conspicuously reporting performance information. The second and third, controllability and responsiveness, can be satisfied by reporting to interested parties the accomplishments of the agency or program. For these dimensions, the agency would be wise to reveal the number of clients served, the population that was served, the resources that were used, and the activities that took place. The results of program activities will be of particular importance to citizens and decision makers interested in making a valuative assessment regarding the organization and its programs meeting stated goals. One additional consideration here is that to properly satisfy these dimensions of performance and accountability, the performance measurement system must be of quality. That is, goals and objectives as well as measures of performance must be linked, and the performance data must be valid.

Of the two instrumental purposes shown in Figure 9.1, accountability, mostly observed in the form of reporting to external audiences such as elected officials and citizens, is one of the most often observed purposes of performance measurement. For example, in their study of U.S. municipalities cited earlier, Poister and

Streib (2005) reported that 35 percent of the respondents stated that performance measurement information was communicated to the public on a regular basis. In the telephone interviews reported in Chapter 8, approximately 50 percent of the interview participants said they used performance measurement to report to elected officials, and 50 percent specifically mentioned accountability as the reason for having a performance measurement system. In the 2003 Government Accountability Office's survey on the use of performance data at the federal level (one of the six surveys discussed in Newcomer [2007]), a large percentage, (63 percent) of respondents stated that they have performance data that could demonstrate to external audiences whether they are addressing their intended result—a dimension of accountability. At the same time, 57 percent felt that performance measurement information was being used for the purpose of holding managers accountable for the accomplishment of agency strategic goals.

Nevertheless recent research supports the notion that noninstrumental use of knowledge occurs more often than instrumental use. In particular, Amara et al. (2004) argue that non-instrumental use of knowledge is important for day-to-day managerial and other professional activity. Noninstrumental use of performance measures is depicted in the two bottom quadrants of Figure 9.1. In the third quadrant (continuing clockwise), mobilization is presented as a noninstrumental purpose for performance measurement. In this instance, the performance information is intended for external audiences. In her discussion of use of program evaluation, Weiss (1998a) argued that it is not unusual for managers to have a preconception of what it is that needs to get done to improve or change a program. In this case, the evaluation information is not necessarily used to effect change, but rather to mobilize support for the positions that managers already hold. In the case of PBM, by publicly promoting the findings of performance measurement, managers may try to obtain support for an agency's program. Such an approach is an example of performance measures used for promoting, one of the purposes discussed in Chapter 1 of this book. When it comes to mobilization, outcome measures, which would call attention to achievement, can be especially useful.

But managers are not the only ones who may want to support a decision that they want to make. Elected officials also may use performance information to justify their decision to kill a particular program. There are plenty of examples of elected officials requesting program performance assessment to take away the funding of a program that they do not like, and therefore would like to make disappear.

Lastly, shown in the fourth quadrant, for internal audiences, a key purpose of performance measures is to understand the programs, a noninstrumental use. The performance information may give them ideas for future course of action. The information may suggest possible changes and different directions they may want a program to take when the time is right. Although program understanding is a perfectly legitimate reason for conducting performance measurement, in most instances the stated purpose is likely to be program improvement or accountability. Such purposes sound better in justifying performance measurement efforts. Yet, consciously or unconsciously, managers may know that there is little chance of making major changes at the time the information becomes available. Likewise, it is possible that those asking for performance measurement information originally had in mind program improvement as a purpose. However, for one reason or another, the purpose may have changed during the process. As a result, performance measurement does not get used in an instrumental manner; it may be used by the internal audiences to understand how their program works and what it does.

Advocates of instrumental uses of performance measurement become optimistic when they see reports like those presented by Newcomer (2007). According to Newcomer, approximately 54 percent of the federal managers responding to one of the surveys she analyzed said that they use performance data to understand and improve. Although there may be good reasons to be optimistic, this number may be misleading. It is not possible to determine what proportion of the 54 percent actually used performance measurement for the purpose of improving programs and what proportion used it for the purpose of understanding. Further research would be necessary to get an accurate representation of when performance measurement leads to immediate decisions for improvement, and when it leads to further dialogue but not immediate change. Certainly, there are instances when it is necessary to make changes, or if changes are made, they are not too disruptive. However, argues Weiss (1998a), unless there is a perception that the program in question is in a state of disarray, it is likely that the decision will be to maintain the status quo. Even with the status quo, however, process and outcome measures would be very useful in helping to understand how a program works and what it does.

Linking Purpose and Use

Building on the purposes shown in Figure 9.1, what follows is a more in-depth exploration of the differences and linkages between purposes and uses of performance measurement information. In Figure 9.2 the four purposes discussed above are linked to five additional elements that represent distinct categories of knowledge use. Each of the types of knowledge can contribute to one or more purposes of performance measurement. Furthermore, Figure 9.2 depicts a bar that is meant to represent a continuum. Rather than classifying the nature of the five different types of uses of performance measurement information as instrumental and noninstrumental, the bar shows the nature of knowledge use as being three distinct but complementary forms.

More specifically, the continuum shown in Figure 9.2 follows Beyer's (1997) conceptualization of three types of use of research findings (p. 17):

> *Instrumental use involves applying research results in specific, direct ways.*
> *Conceptual use involves using research results for general enlightenment:*
> *results influence actions but more indirectly and less specifically than in*

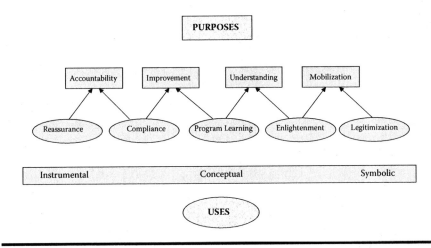

Figure 9.2 Nature and type of knowledge use in relation to purposes in the context of performance measurement. (Adapted from de Lancer Julnes 2008; reproduced with permission of Palgrave McMillan.)

> *instrumental use. Symbolic use involves using research results to legitimate and sustain predetermined positions.*

Indeed, Amara et al. (2004) concluded that one type of knowledge use does not preclude the other; thus, managers and other professionals mostly see these different types as complementary rather than conflicting in their daily pursuits.

Focusing on the bottom part, in the left-hand corner of the figure, the first concept is reassurance as a type of knowledge use. For this use the performance measurement information is mostly produced and used to make sure that everything is going well and under control. This information can be used to convey to external audiences that government is doing what it is supposed to be doing with taxpayers' money. Thus, for example, performance measures can be used to reassure citizens that the tap water is safe to drink; that local schools are meeting performance standards; and that the streets are safe at night. The information can be used to ensure citizens that the state is fiscally responsible but innovative and, as a result, the quality of life remains high even though costs are being kept down. This type of use is instrumental. It goes beyond conceptual use and allows the audience to make judgments that could have consequences for the program in question. Notice also that this type of instrumental use is linked to accountability.

The next type of use depicted in the figure is compliance. Because of laws and administrative regulations that call for performance measurement, government agencies will feel compelled to have performance measurement to comply with these requirements. For example, the federal No Child Left Behind Act requires schools to measure student achievements and report the results to receive federal funding. For many reasons, including shortcomings of assessment systems and the fact that reported information is being used to punish schools, this law has been widely criticized. However, one of the things that it has done is force schools to be more transparent in terms of the accomplishments of *all* students. Schools are required to disaggregate test results by race and ethnicity, forcing administrators to acknowledge achievement gaps among minorities. It is possible that unless required to do so, schools or other agencies would not analyze the performance of programs at such a level of detail, or would measure performance but would not report findings that might bring about controversy and criticism.

Another example of the need for information for compliance can be found in the grants-making world. More and more foundations and federal agencies are requiring grant recipients to monitor and evaluate the performance of the projects they fund. They are interested in seeing evidence of the performance of those projects. For nonprofit service agencies, which tend to rely on the resources provided by grant-making foundations, this is a relatively new development. Traditionally utilization of performance measurement has been rather scant. But these increasingly common requests for evidence have started to focus nonprofit agencies' attention on performance measurement in order to be responsive to these requirements.

As shown in Figure 9.2, both reassurance and compliance are expected to contribute to accountability. Nonetheless, as was suggested earlier, accountability, even when it is used for reassurance, can be a double-edged sword. For some the information poses a threat because, by its own nature, it opens the door for judgment and criticism. This fear may cause them to become defensive (Solberg et al., 1997). During a recent meeting on a benchmarking project, a city manager illustrated these points when discussing a newspaper article about the performance of certain cities. He said that once the media gets hold of this performance information, there is no telling how they are going to use it. "The city loses control of how it is represented and how it [the information] gets interpreted." Because of these fears, the tendency of some public officials is to want to maintain the status quo rather than allow comparison between the performance of their organization and that of others (Ammons, 2001).

On the other hand, the information used for the purpose of accountability also presents an opportunity to benchmark, praise, and reflect. Even if the unit or the program in question is not performing at the expected level, it is important to know where it stands. As stated by Ammons (2001), it is not possible for everyone to be above average. Thus, knowing where one stands should be not so much about wanting publicity and praise, but about a desire to improve.

Compliance is followed by program learning, a third type of knowledge use that can be instrumental or noninstrumental, depending on organizational politics and capacity. As argued by Stewart and Walsh (1994), because of the political nature of performance measurement, the information should be a means to the end of helping to understand accomplishments of programs, how they work, and what might be done to improve them. Thus, one should not expect performance information to automatically and directly cause decision makers to make changes to a particular program or the entire agency. The argument above is at the core of Weiss's (1998a) contention that in the case of the use of evaluation results there is a tendency to refer to users of information as individuals. Weiss's argument is that programs and projects are part of organizations, and it is the organization and its interaction with the environment that provide the context for knowledge use. That is, the manner and purpose in which the information is used will depend on a variety of environmental and organizational factors. This argument is in line with the explanations provided by the performance measurement Utilization model developed in this book. In the model, an organization's characteristics, including the political and cultural context, as well as capacity for performance measurement are influential in explaining the adoption and implementation of performance measurement information.

Thus, given Weiss's (1998a) and Stewart and Walsh's (1994) arguments, it is apparent that when it comes to the utilization of performance measures, the concept of the learning organization becomes very relevant. The theory of the learning organization is grounded on private firms, and to some extent it is about the survival of the fittest. This paradigm expects that organizations that do not change (learn) in response to changes in their environment will disappear. The theory of the learning organization also rests on the existence of (partial) rational behavior in decision making (Cyert and March, 1963). According to proponents of the learning organization, some of the characteristics of such organizations include: having people who continually expand their capacity to create desired results, and where innovation is nurtured and people learn how to learn together (Senge, 1990); being skilled at creating, acquiring, and transferring knowledge and modifying behavior to reflect the new knowledge (Garvin, 1993); having employee involvement in and accountability for change that is directed toward shared values or principles (Watkins and Marsick, 1992); and being a place that facilitates learning for all its members and that is continually transforming itself (Pedler et al., 1991).

As can be inferred from the characteristics listed above, a key assumption in organizational learning is that learning always leads to a transformation or change. However, in reality, as suggested by Weiss (1998a) and by the Utilization model, in order for changes to occur, organizational conditions may have to be changed. This is easier said than done, given that organizations and the programs that operate within them "function within rigid limits imposed by law, tradition, procedures, regulations, accustomed habits of doing things, and restraints from other organizations in the interorganizational field" (Weiss, 1998a). This suggests that even if the organization learned from the performance measurement information, program learning may not lead to program improvement or any kind of visible change. What it might lead to, however, is a better understanding of what the program does and how it works. This may in turn lead to a more informed dialogue, and thus can be considered a valuable noninstrumental contribution to PBM.

As we move along the spectrum of the nature of knowledge use in Figure 9.2, we find enlightenment. Even though much of the research conducted on the use of performance information focuses on seeking evidence of instrumental uses, the evidence appears to indicate that enlightenment is one of the most prevalent uses of performance measurement in the public sector. Although research findings often indicate that public officials believe that performance measurement information is valuable in the budget process because it informs debate, and somehow influences action, they also suggest that the information does not replace traditional considerations when it comes to resource allocation decisions (Melkers and Willoughby, 2005). Internally, enlightenment can lead to more informed decisions. Because stakeholders are more educated about the program and processes in question, the content of their discussions is enhanced with new insights and ideas about how to improve the way they do business. Furthermore, enlightenment can help to change assumptions and perceptions, which, when the conditions are right, may lead to organizational transformation. The value of enlightenment, with its contribution to understanding, has been recognized by those promoting the use of the balanced scorecard. For example, Niven (2003) argues that employees understanding the organization's strategy can lead to greater organizational capacity "as employees, perhaps for the first time, know where the organization is headed and how they can contribute during the journey." Likewise, in participatory program evaluation, Patton (1978, 2001) has long argued that the process of evaluation itself, not so much its outcome, is an important mechanism to promote understanding. He argues that being involved in an evaluative process may lead individuals to change their thinking and even their behavior due to what is learned through the process. This includes being able to think and act evaluatively, which can have a lasting impact well beyond that of the evaluation findings.

Externally, enlightenment can lead to mobilization of support for a program or a particular course of action. For example, performance measurement information may show that because the motor vehicle office is understaffed, customers have to endure long lines, and thus have to waste a lot of time as they wait to be served. For many reasons, decision makers may not act on the information and fail to allocate the required resources to improve customer service. However, they may be influenced to do so if there is a public outcry about the situation. Thus, as stated by Moynihan (2008), agencies may use the information as an advocacy tool for mobilizing external support and to "win legitimacy and funding." On the other hand, organizations can also get support by publicizing their accomplishments and educating the public about their programs and the benefits that they bring to the community. At the macro level, the accumulation of program evaluation knowledge can lead to paradigm shifts, influencing thinking at a broader level, and in time leading to shifts in action (Weiss, 1998a).

The last category of knowledge use, legitimization, is suggested by Ansari and Euske's (1987) discussion of performance measurement information being used to rationalize, justify, or validate current, past, and future courses of actions or decisions. This contribution of performance measurement was illustrated by comments made by the informants of the follow-up telephone interviews described in the previous chapter of this book. Some of the informants made it clear that in their organizations performance measurement information did not play a central role in the budget process. Performance measurement information played a supporting role, as it was used to justify budget requests, and not to drive decisions.

Similar findings are reported by Modell and Wiesel (2007). The authors compared the use of performance information by three state agencies in Sweden. They found that there was a tendency for agencies to use performance measurement to legitimize current practices. In one of the cases discussed by the authors, the agency used customer satisfaction indexes to defend itself from criticisms raised by the National Audit Office. Sharing the performance data also allowed the agency to mobilize support for what it was already doing. Thus, as suggested by Figure 9.2, when performance measurement information is used externally for legitimization, one of the purposes it can contribute to is mobilization of support for what the organization is already doing or wants to do.

The understanding of the differences between use and purposes of performance measurement leads to a reconceptualization of the PBM figure presented in Chapter 1. The new rendition is shown in Figure 9.3. The figure is meant to convey that PBM requires performance measurement and strategic planning; that different

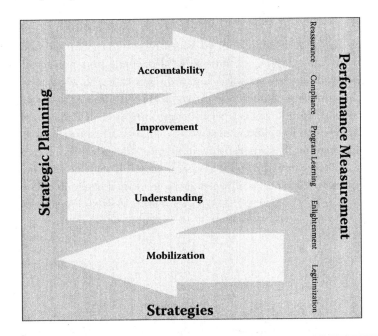

Figure 9.3 Performance-based management: the complete approach.

uses contribute to different purposes; and that together these four elements inform organizational strategies.

Summary

The purpose of this chapter was to explore and discuss two overarching themes that emerged from the survey results and the follow-up telephone interviews: that performance measurement is a complex process and that use of information is more than what most people think it is. Although in general these two themes may be considered by some to be common sense, the reality is that this same way of thinking has precluded their proper treatment in theory and in practice.

One of the consequences of this is that we have not developed a sound theory of performance measurement utilization. Without such theory on which to couch recommendations for practice, it is not possible to move practice forward. Another consequence is a certain amount of frustration on the part of practitioners and researchers. For practitioners, not enough credit is given to their performance measurement efforts. Accustomed to needing observable action, researchers, and even practitioners, fail to see that there is value in those actions that cannot be directly observed.

One of the first things that need to be clearly understood is the complexity of the performance measurement utilization process. The discussion here contributes to this understanding. Based on empirical evidence, the discussion highlighted two major overarching themes that run through the gamut of experiences organizations typically have with performance management and performance measurement. In discussing the complexity of performance measurement utilization, three related subthemes emerged that provide suggestions for practice: the need to have someone in charge; the need to manage the process strategically, and the need to realize that there are costs involved, but these will diminish over time.

With the second theme, the use of performance measures, the discussion focused on differentiating the types of use of performance measures from purposes. In differentiating use, five types were identified that fall on a continuum ranging from instrumental to conceptual to symbolic.

It was argued that given the complexity of organizational life, the noninstrumental use of performance measures should also be considered a success rather than a failure. The risks of using performance measurement in an instrumental manner are real and have been discussed in previous chapters. This is not to say that instrumental use should not be the goal. Rather, the conditions in the organizations have to be "right" for this to occur. When the right conditions aren't there, organizations find it difficult not only to convert their capacity for action into action, but also to use what has been learned about a program, for example, and move from a noninstrumental purpose, such as program understanding, to an instrumental purpose, such as program improvement, and ultimately change.

Part IV

SUMMING UP AND MOVING FORWARD

Chapter 10

Summary and Final Recommendations for Theory and Practice

Like Shadish, Cook, and Leviton (1991) I'm going to risk repetition for the benefit of those wanting a quick synopsis of the work presented in this book. As such, this final chapter provides a summary of the methods and findings discussed in the previous chapters. But it also provides concluding thoughts about the theoretical and practical implications of this work for performance-based management (PBM). This is done in two ways. First, focusing on the theoretical aspect, the chapter summarizes the procedures involved in developing the Performance Measurement Utilization Model, which provides the grounding for this book. The underlying argument in this summary is that for research to aid in developing more sound practice-friendly theory on PBM, researchers need to look beyond traditional models and approaches to inquiry. Particular emphasis is placed here on the usefulness of pattern-matching and elaboration as an important tool for theory development.

Second, based on the findings and discussions presented previously, the chapter provides some practical suggestions for building and sustaining a successful PBM and for moving practice forward. A critical recognition here is that the one-size-fits-all approach is not adequate, even in the face of evidence that suggests general patterns. Although this evidence must serve as the foundation for supporting practice, any proposed course of action must be context sensitive. As such, the main recommendation here focuses on assessing organizational readiness for PBM. The chapter concludes with a brief discussion of opportunities available for supporting practice.

Theoretical Implications for Building Practice-Friendly Theory in Performance-Based Management

Because performance management is about constructing and using knowledge, it was natural to look in the field of knowledge utilization for some guidance in determining the reasons for a lack of utilization of performance measures. Yet, previous studies conducted under the banner of the knowledge utilization framework did not provide the guidance necessary for a meaningful understanding of utilization of performance measures. Some may argue that the reason for this is that those studies were not explicitly trying to develop such an understanding. That is, they were not looking for evidence of the use of performance measures.

However, the more compelling explanation for the field's failure to provide such guidance is that the field of knowledge utilization did not provide a sufficiently sophisticated approach for inquiry (Wingens, 1990). In spite of decades of research, the field is still in its infancy, lacking a unified utilization framework that can help explain the conditions that lead to knowledge utilization (Landry et al., 2001). The explanation of the weaknesses of the field can be attributed to at least three factors.

First, the field of knowledge utilization has been too restrictive in its inquiry. Studies in the field have not particularly paid attention to contextual aspects of knowledge utilization. This can be attributed in part to the two-communities metaphor, which at the beginning of the field provided valuable ways to gain insights, and continues to be the dominant model of inquiry. The problem with the "two communities" metaphor is that it explains utilization (and lack thereof) by focusing on the cultural differences between the social scientists (producers of knowledge) and the decision makers (end users of knowledge). This focus has not allowed for the inclusion of contextual organizational factors. One of those factors is organizational politics, which was shown here to be an important determinant of the utilization of performance measurement information. Even though some scholars in the field have lamented that politics has not received adequate attention, for a long time, little, if any, research explored the impact of this factor. As a result, the two-communities metaphor's emphasis on cultural differences ceased to provide satisfactory explanations of utilization, and the continued reliance on this approach has led to the stagnation of the field.

Second, studies in the field have often been too narrow in their definition of knowledge utilization; and so their measurement of knowledge use has focused on finding evidence of instrumental use of the knowledge. With regards to the former, utilization has often been seen as a monolithic concept. Only recently have there been attempts to define utilization as a process comprising many stages (see, for example, Landry et al., 2001). But even when scales of knowledge use were developed, they were used in the aggregate to represent a single dependent variable that could then be explained (Landry et al., 2001). Regarding the latter, the traditional approach has been to look for evidence of particular research studies leading to specific decisions that would not have been made without the knowledge provided in the study (instrumental use). Recognizing the limitations of such a view, scholars in the policy sciences, such as Beyer and Trice (1982) and before them Pelz (1978), and in program evaluation (Weiss, 1988, 1998a) have introduced other types of use that are also important but often neglected. Specifically, they introduced the notions of conceptual and symbolic use.

A third reason, made evident by the call of many knowledge utilization scholars for an integrated model of inquiry that takes into consideration all the different factors that are believed to influence knowledge utilization, is that the field has remained fragmented. But even beyond this call for integrating theories, what the field requires is more elaboration. That is, it is not enough to add variables to an analysis and claim that the resulting model is integrated. Instead, there is a need to develop data-guided models of the mechanisms that explain utilization and to contextualize these models so that they can more closely resemble reality.

The triangulated model for knowledge utilization in performance-based management developed here responds to these limitations. Unlike previous knowledge utilization models, the one developed here was not restricted to one theory or mode of inquiry. It was developed borrowing insights from various fields of study, tested using data from a mail survey, analyzed and elaborated using a pattern-matching approach to inquiry, and further elaborated by conducting follow-up interviews of a sample of respondents to the mail survey.

By using a mixed methods approach, it was possible to isolate the effect of several political and rational factors on the process of performance measurement utilization, and to determine the reasons for the observed changes in the parameter estimates found in the various regression models used here. Furthermore, elaboration made it possible to identify the mechanisms through which the factors included in the models worked.

The resulting understanding provided by the approach used here emphasizes the need for having more empirically based studies that go beyond the traditional conception of knowledge and organizational behavior. As was shown here, what happens in organizations is not just a matter of economic or technical rationality. In fact, the theoretical framework provided by theories of organizational politics and culture is central to the search for answers to questions of performance in public organizations, providing the context in which traditional rational factors work. Building on work in these different areas, the following briefly describes the steps used to develop the performance measurement utilization model with its two stages and provides suggestions for future research.

Steps toward a Refined Model of Utilization of Performance Measures

Pattern Matching

Central to the refinement of the knowledge utilization theory, and of the utilization of performance measures in particular, is the distinction of adoption from implementation. This distinction follows from Stehr's (1992) analysis of social science knowledge as being comprised of practical knowledge and action knowledge. These two components of knowledge utilization represent capacity for action and knowledge converted into action. Similarly, in the realm of performance measures utilization, I have made a parallel distinction between adoption as the capacity for action and implementation as the knowledge converted into action.

In order for this distinction to be capable of providing an understanding of the lack of utilization of performance measures, it was necessary to elaborate it. This was first accomplished by means of analyzing survey data. Using pattern matching with respect to the outcome, predictions of how different factors would help to explain two dependent variables, adoption and implementation of performance measures, were tested. The findings were compared to those of a third model that had a dependent variable that conceptualized knowledge use as a single entity. Together these procedures helped confirm that indeed there are at least two different stages of performance measurement utilization.

Then, this was followed by the purification approach, or pattern matching with respect to the cause to tease out the factors that were responsible for the observed outcomes. More specifically, this helped to establish the predictive power of several factors with and without the rational/technocratic factors. I was able to conclude that, even though organizations need to have the technical capacity to adopt and implement performance measures, this is not a sufficient condition for implementation to occur.

The findings and subsequent discussion presented here, together with the extant literature and the experience of public organizations experimenting with performance measures, confirmed that utilization of performance measures is a complex process, and that the two stages, adoption and implementation, are differentially affected by several contextual factors. Furthermore, the findings provided support to the assumption that while there is some risk in adopting performance measures and, thus, developing a capacity for action, the real risk is implementing this knowledge because of the actions that it may suggest. Therefore if implementation is indeed riskier than adoption, it will succeed only if there are influences that counter this risk. And the more "concrete" the consequences, the more potent they might be in supporting implementation.

Moderation

The models of adoption and implementation were further elaborated by testing moderated relationships (interaction effects). Moderation implies that the effect of an independent variable on the dependent variable is dependent on the level of another independent variable. Two interactions were examined to see if the lack of effect of internal politics and external requirements on implementation was due to contextual factors.

The first interaction examined was between change and external requirements. Although the expectation was that a culture that is open to change would enhance the effect of external requirements (a relationship that would yield a positive interaction term for the two variables), this interaction effect was not significant. That is, these two factors, culture—as measured by attitude toward performance measurement and external requirements—appear to behave independently of each other or substitute for each other. Therefore, the effect of external requirements on both adoption and implementation is the same regardless of whether or not the organization accepts change. Equivalently, the effect of this culture of change is the same whether or not the organization is required to accept performance measures.

The second interaction, between level of unionization and internal interest groups, showed that the lack of impact of internal interest groups on implementation is consistent with the notion of their secondary influence. The significance of this interaction term in the implementation model indicates that the internal interest groups have less effect in the presence of high levels of unionization. The absence of significance of this interaction term in the adoption model reinforces the idea that unionization does not counter the influence of internal interest groups on adoption. This is to be expected given than of the two components of utilization, implementation of performance measures could be the most disruptive since it may bring negative consequences for unionized employees. Thus, while internal interest groups may have a desire to support implementation of performance measures, their effect will be significantly diminished by the power of unions. This also confirms that internal interest groups can be seen as having a secondary power in organizations.

Mediation

Another elaboration of the models consisted of including adoption as a mediator (or precursor) for implementation and, in addition, rational/technocratic factors as mediators for adoption and implementation. Mediation implies that part or all of the effect of an independent variable is through its effect on another independent variable.

The point of adding adoption as a mediating variable is that, as the most direct precursor to implementation, its inclusion allows us to differentiate factors that influence implementation through adoption from those that have a direct effect.

As expected, adoption had the strongest effect on implementation, but the most interesting findings were that the influences of the more formalistic internal factors disappeared (indicating that they operate via adoption), while the external organizational factors continued to exert their influence on implementation.

This elaboration was further conducted by including rational/technocratic factors in the models for adoption and implementation. It was found that these factors have an important effect on adoption and a lesser effect on implementation. Despite the general belief that these rational/technocratic factors are of primary importance in driving utilization of performance measures, the results show that they were secondary to the factors described above.

A natural sequence in this process of elaboration involved developing an estimated causal model of utilization of performance measures. This model consisted of including both adoption and rational/technocratic factors in the implementation model. With this model, in combination with the model for adoption, a causal path model for adoption and implementation of performance measures was estimated. The path model showed specific chains of events leading to adoption and implementation that need to be examined in future research.

Model Verification and Contextualization

The follow-up interviews with a sample of participants in the mail survey provided additional richness to the quantitatively derived model that helped to further clarify the mechanism involved in the utilization process of performance measurement. In addition, the information highlighted the nuances of how performance measurement information is actually used or implemented.

Exploring these nuances proved to be particularly helpful in developing a deeper understanding of knowledge use. The comments of the interview participants resonated with arguments that have been made by scholars in evaluation and in policy analysis for the need to recognize that there is more than one kind of knowledge use. Not all valued knowledge use is instrumental. Thus, together with the responses from the interview participants, these arguments provided the foundation for developing a framework of knowledge use with three overarching forms along a continuum. These three forms—instrumental, conceptual, and symbolic—provided the framework for further differentiating five types of knowledge use: reassurance, compliance, program learning, enlightenment, and legitimization.

One important argument had been made before developing this framework of knowledge use. I had argued that in addition to the contextual issues that influence the adoption and implementation of performance measures, the reason for not finding more evidence of use may be that the focus of the research has often been on finding evidence of particular types of instrumental uses. These particular types are what I referred to here as purposes. Here, purposes are distinguished from use and encompass accountability, program improvement, program understanding, and mobilization. Each of these purposes is supported by different types of knowledge use. These different purposes and uses do not necessarily contradict each other, but rather are complementary, with each purpose requiring some performance measures and not others.

Significantly, these insights have implications for the model of utilization of performance measure that was developed here. They take the modeling of performance measurement utilization one step further. The model should help practitioners and scholars as they try to understand (1) why organizations are more likely to use the information in one way and not another and (2) what kinds of strategies organizations should develop in order to ensure that the performance information gets used in the desired manner. The classification of knowledge use is also important because of the purposes that each type of knowledge use supports. Thus, for example, if the purpose is accountability, then the type of knowledge use that needs to be promoted is not program learning, but reassurance or compliance. Also, this classification allows for the identification of various audiences and clarification in terms of the types of performance information that they may need.

Implications for Practice

We have empirical support that explains why performance measurement information appears to be not as widely used in the public sector as many would want. The findings have shown that there are factors and groups that differentially affect adoption and implementation. At the same time, the findings suggest that the intensity of the effects of these factors and groups is going to vary from organization to organization. This implies that efforts to improve utilization must first begin with an assessment of the particular circumstances of the organization and continue in a deliberate manner, following the recommendations provided here.

Look (and Assess) before You Leap

Box 10.1 presents a list of questions organizations wishing to adopt and implement a comprehensive performance measuring system should ask. Answers to these questions will provide clues regarding the level of readiness of the organization, and the strategies that can be used to address shortcomings and take advantage of areas of strengths. This exercise will also be useful for organizations that are already in the midst of the performance measurement utilization process, as it will help highlight areas where work is needed in order for the effort to be successful. Note that the questions also get to the issue of use and purpose. During times of scarce resources, or in instances of programs that are rather stable and simple, developing, collecting, and analyzing all types of performance measures may not be desirable or necessary. Thus, getting clarity on what uses and purposes the system will serve can help the organization decide which measures, and for what programs, are more critical given the specific situation.

BOX 10.1 ASSESSMENT OF READINESS FOR PERFORMANCE MEASUREMENT AND PBM

I. Questions Related to Technical Capacity

1. What kind of performance measures, if any, are we currently collecting?
2. If we are collecting performance measures, what are we doing with the information?
3. Do we know if our current performance levels are on par with the organization's goals and objectives?
4. Do we have clear goals and objectives?
5. Are our current performance measures linked to these goals and objectives?
6. Do we have adequate technology to support collecting, analyzing, disseminating, and storing performance measurement information?
7. Do we have adequate personnel to support data collection, analysis, and reporting?
8. Do we have knowledgeable personnel in the area of performance measurement?
9. Can we devote the necessary resources (time, money, personnel) to this effort?

II. Questions Related to Politics and Organizational Culture

10. What performance-related questions are elected officials and citizens asking?
11. If we develop a performance measurement system, what is its immediate purpose?
12. What is the level of awareness of performance measurement among management, non-management employees, and elected officials?
13. What is the level of satisfaction with our services among the various internal and external stakeholders?
14. Are top management and elected officials supportive of performance measurement efforts?
15. Are they interested in supporting a performance-based management system?
16. Is there a mandate for using performance measurement?
17. Who do we need to work with? Is this part of a larger effort?
18. Do we have a track record of working with unions or other representatives of employees?
19. Do we typically engage employees in dialogue about major organizational changes?
20. What is the average age of our personnel?
21. How has personnel reacted in the past to organizational changes?
22. Is our incentive system adequate?
23. Is our incentive system flexible?

Positive answers in Part I of the questions posed in Box 10.1 will be an important foundation in terms of having a technical capacity on which the organization can build its system. It is an opportunity for organizational learning. It gives a chance to find out what it is that the organization is doing, what it has, what is lacking, and what it can do to move forward. In the context of PBM, if the organization is already collecting information, after deciding on purpose, it is possible that all that it needs is to refine of the measures. On the other hand, if it is found that the organization is collecting measures that do not appear to be linked to any goals and objectives, a deeper look and rethinking of the measures would be necessary. Obviously, some of this assumes that there is a strategic plan that spells out the mission, goals, and objectives of the organization, department, or program. If that is not the case, then a strategic plan will need to be developed, given that such a plan is central to a PBM system (see Figure 1.1 and Figure 9.3).

If this assessment finds that the technology and personnel are adequate to handle performance measurement needs, only minor enhancements, and hence smaller up-front expenses, would be required. Yet, while it is important to have adequate resources, as the findings presented in this book showed there are other factors that are equally important at the beginning of the performance measurement process. Those include having the support of employees and having a clear commitment to support performance measurement. This support and commitment can later lead to the reallocation of resources to accommodate performance measurement. The data analyses performed here suggest that an organizational policy requiring that managers and others use performance measurement can have a constructive effect on adoption, more so than external policies. As shown in this book, although not sufficient to guarantee action by itself, an internal policy may indeed be a signal that the organization is serious about the effort, and that the required conditions for having a successful PBM system will follow.

Thus, the Utilization Model suggests that organizations at the adoption stage should focus on getting acceptance and commitment from management and non-management employees. How much work will be required to obtain this commitment will depend on the answers to some of the questions in Part II of Box 10.1. But the model developed and the experiences of various organizations discussed here suggest that involving and educating these different groups about the value and benefits of performance measurement and PBM will prove beneficial during the early stages of the process and as the organization moves toward implementation. It should be remembered that management and nonmanagement employees are important stakeholders who ultimately may be held responsible for the outcomes of the programs and units they work for. As a result, without their support and buy-in it would be impossible to sustain the effort.

Clearly practical considerations will dictate who to involve to gain acceptance and commitment, and how to involve them. But whether the organization decides to start big, developing their performance measurement systems for the entire organization, or small, developing performance measurement systems for a subset of programs or units, representatives of management and nonmanagement employees should be part of the team leading or advising the effort. And, to the extent possible, the input of all stakeholders, not just their representatives, should be sought.

Furthermore, the size of the organization, resources available, and type of services provided must also be considered when choosing strategies for involvement. But no matter the size or limits, the intentions to move toward a PBM system and the benefits of performance measurement should be communicated throughout the organization. This will help in dissipating doubts and make the process less of a surprise and less threatening.

The cost of training is another issue to take into account. The more people involved, the more training that may be required. But at the same time, as more people understand the process and methods, the less threatening the performance measurements become and the more committed people may feel.

Another consideration is that older employees and employees who have been with the organization for a long time may need strategies of engagement that are different from those used with other employees. For the most part, these individuals tend to be accustomed to doing things a certain way and might not be as open to change as newer and younger employees. This may translate into resistance to performance measurement and PBM.

Finally, as the assessment questions suggest and as illustrated by the short case narratives presented in the previous chapter of this book, sometimes the PBM effort of an organization may be part of a larger PBM initiative. If so, those in charge will also have to address the issues highlighted in Box 10.2. This groundwork is critical if there is hope to have a sustainable PBM system.

You Are in the Midst of the Process, Now What?

Even though getting performance measures implemented has proven to be difficult and disappointing at times, the results of the path model developed in this book indicate that working toward adoption will prove to be a valuable step toward implementation. The culture that working toward and achieving adoption may create will facilitate getting the kind of support structure that was shown to be critical for the implementation stage.

BOX 10.2: WHAT IF PBM IS PART OF A LARGER EFFORT?

1. Identify who will need to work together
2. Determine the kind of work group structure that will be needed
3. Identify responsibilities
4. Develop mechanisms for communicating with different actors
5. Set clear lines of communications (i.e. who reports to whom?)
6. Determine who will pay for what

Particularly important is the role that external stakeholders such as elected officials, citizens, and the employee unions have in compelling or inhibiting implementation. These stakeholders are important in facilitating the needed resources. Thus, drawing from the studies presented here, the general advice to sustain the PBM effort is to motivate, include, educate, and use!

Motivate

Critical to success of performance measurement and PBM is the organizational culture. As those responsible for making decisions look at the responses to the assessment questions above, strategies need to be devised to deal with attitudes, and to counter fears of risk that is inherent in anything that deals with accountability, measurement, and change. Although the organization may succeed in getting everyone on board during the adoption stage by involving employees in one form or another, the real test is during implementation—what is actually done with the information. As articulated by an executive director of a state agency, although the governor is asking state agencies to have performance measurement information, the fact that he has not said how the information is going to be used has many agency directors worried. The questions in their mind are: What will the governor do if agencies report that they have not met their target? Will the information be used to punish, or will it be used to encourage improvement in a more positive way? Agencies' directors are concerned about consequences. Thus, as agencies and departments start developing performance measurement systems, and using them to report out, individuals will be thinking: Is this worth the risk? How fast should I go? How much should I show?

Part of creating a culture that promotes taking such risk is having an appropriate incentive system. The incentive system can be monetary, nonmonetary, or a combination of both. One example of both monetary and nonmonetary rewards is found in the State of Florida. Employees and managers of units that achieve their performance goals receive bonuses, and agencies are allowed increased budget flexibility. Another example can be found in Italy. The government developed a program in the southern regions where regional administrations were monetarily rewarded on the basis of achieving certain performance benchmarks (Brezzi et al., 2008). Regardless of what is used, the incentive system should meaningfully and appropriately reward those who achieve their stated performance goals and encourage them to continuously focus on improvement, but also, it should be carefully crafted so that it does not become a deterrent for nonachievers or those who may perceive their situation to be very different or difficult and therefore see no point in striving for improvement or change. They may prefer, as a result, to hide under the veil of performance measurement efforts that are vague and for the most part incomplete and ineffective.

Include

It cannot be emphasized enough that one of the most effective ways to motivate individuals to support PBM is to include them in the process of performance measurement utilization. The adoption stage provides the opportunity to include internal and external stakeholders and others who may affect or be affected by the process. Their participation at this stage can greatly influence the future success of PBM.

Extant research shows that when people participate, they feel more committed to and more satisfied with the outcomes of the process (de Lancer Julnes, 2001). Such commitment and satisfaction are essential, for performance measurement, given that using the information may entail consequences for some that, as has been argued here, make performance measurement and PBM a risky enterprise. When people are part of the performance measurement process, they are better able to understand it. Also, if the participation is done right, individuals will be able to have a say in those things that will affect them, and thus provide them with a sense of control over their future.

Educate

Some may call education a form of proselytizing. But one must spread the word because the value of PBM and its core component performance measurement may not be obvious to everyone. Elected officials, citizens, and other stakeholders need to be convinced that this is a good thing and that PBM warrants the required investments. Although the need for accountability is often touted, and management for results and citizen-driven governance are believed to be the goals of modern public management, the reality is that the contributions of PBM to achieve these demands and goals are not truly understood.

In addition, organizations' internal stakeholders need to be convinced about how an approach such as PBM can actually make their jobs easier and effective in the long run. Having clear objectives helps in developing the activities that will lead to the achievement of those objectives, and to the development of indicators that can tell whether there is progress toward those objectives, or if a further look is needed into the processes that transform inputs into outputs and results.

Education also entails training in performance measurement. Training is not just important at the adoption stage. Performance measurement skills are needed to effectively implement the performance measurement system within the parameters of PBM.

Use

As discussed in Chapter 8, the comments made by participants during the phone interviews clearly pointed at the importance of decision makers using performance information. These comments echoed those made by survey respondents, as well as numerous accounts of experiences of public organizations. Decision makers and policy makers need to use performance measurement information in a way that shows that it is important enough to warrant all the investments (monetary and otherwise) that are necessary to develop and implement such a system. The real implication of all this is that without some visible use of the information, performance-based management is not possible.

What about Purposes, Audiences, and Number of Measures and Indicators?

"What for?" and "For whom?" are guiding questions in the design of a system, but also during the implementation. These are key questions that can help focus the effort; and are particularly useful when there is not enough capacity to embrace a comprehensive performance measurement system. Furthermore, even though there may be agreement that there is a need for a certain number of measures, the current capacity may limit the ability to start collecting, analyzing, and reporting all the information that is desired. The sensible way to proceed is to go with what is most needed at the time and build from there. This is one more reason to pursue smaller successes by taking baby steps. Everything else in building a PBM system takes time, and each step builds upon the previous one and represents an opportunity for taking more successful steps in the future.

Consider these possible scenarios, which deal with needing information for different purposes and different audiences. One organization may have some of the organization readiness elements, but other elements need to be acquired or developed. At the same time, there may be pressure for information and for the organization to become more results-oriented. The organization will need to start moving toward PBM, recognizing that implementation will take more than just adopting a few measures and responding to one set of audiences.

In another scenario, an executive director of a state agency may decide that having information on the results of a program can be useful to mobilize needed support for a particular program or new initiative. This may lead her to start small, but as she gets into the process, seeing the utility of the information and achieving the desired result by using it, she may be encouraged to continue to expand the effort and eventually develop a PBM culture throughout the organization. At the beginning she will be responding to an immediate need, but this can serve as the foundation for moving forward toward PBM.

In a final scenario, a newly elected mayor may feel that the city could be doing much better in terms of the services that it delivers, but the information that he currently has about the programs does not suggest strategies for improvement. This particular thinking could increase the mayor's desire for a more comprehensive system, motivating the city to refine its information system. It may also lead to paying more attention to what the information suggests and putting those suggestions into practice; thus, PBM is born.

Related, as the performance measurement system evolves and matures, and it becomes part of what the organization does, the questions "What for?" and "For whom?" remain relevant. However, as the system goes through implementation, organizations need to reframe these questions, asking: What information needs to be communicated to which audience? And what is the best way to do it? Again, the purpose will dictate the answer to the first. Different measures are needed to satisfy different purposes. But this also depends on the audience. Different audiences will have different purposes and, as such, different information needs. The answer to the second question must be dictated by the audience. Not all audiences respond to the same information in the same way. Also, the way in which the performance information is presented, even if it is what the audience is interested in, will have an impact on whether the audience even looks at the information.

Thus, it is not enough to know that legislators are interested in information that can help them assess agencies' accountability, or that citizens are interested in results. It is also important to consider which approach to communicating performance will most likely satisfy these audiences. For example, legislators often complain that the way information is presented precludes them from effectively making use of it (de Lancer Julnes and Mixcoatl, 2006). They are interested in key pieces of performance information that they can quickly process. Citizens may prefer an electronic presentation or a report with graphs and data that do not take more than a few pages to clearly convey the information.

A question that naturally flows from these issues is: How many measures does an organization need for its internal and external audiences? Unfortunately, like everything else we have discussed here, there is not a magic one-size-fits-all answer. It really depends on practical and even political considerations. However, what we do know with certainty is that organizations must have a balanced approach to data collection, analysis, and reporting. Otherwise, there is a risk of being overwhelmed by all the effort required to have a whole bunch of information, or being underwhelmed and missing valuable insights because there just is not enough information to support any kind of use.

A reasonable suggestion was made during a recent electronic exchange in the Public Performance Measurement and Reporting Network hosted by Rutgers University. Participants, representing both practitioners and scholars, seemed to agree with the suggestion that organizations should report a few key indicators, but have a structure in place that allows them to obtain more information, should it be needed. One way to develop this structure is to invest in appropriate data management technology. Today there is technology available that can greatly facilitate the collection, analysis, and reporting of a large number of measures on demand.

Opportunities for Moving Forward

One thing that must be reiterated is that performance measurement information can serve multiple purposes for multiple audiences. The fact that performance measurement is an integral part of PBM speaks to the potential of this tool. As has been argued in the previous chapters in this book, there is a need to move away from equating performance measurement with accountability because such narrow perspective leads to underutilization and fear of this tool. The potential contributions of performance measurement to management and decision making are far more than just accountability. The many uses were discussed in Chapter 9 and include reassurance (contributing to accountability), compliance (contributing to accountability and program improvement), program learning (contributing to program improvement and program understanding), enlightenment (contributing to understanding and mobilization), and legitimization (contributing to mobilization of support). Given these multiple uses, and the multifaceted characteristics of performance measures, serving different audiences at different times, as well as the different factors that come into play in the process of utilization, there is a whole world of opportunities for strengthening the use of this tool. I will close this book by briefly discussing three such opportunities.

The Need for More Quality Training That Includes Program Evaluation Methods and Techniques

The centrality of training on performance measurement has been highlighted throughout this book. And when asked, practitioners usually say that to be able to develop a meaningful system that can be useful, they need to learn more about:

- What strategies to use for developing appropriate indicators of performance;
- How to account for outcomes given an agency's limited control of what happens to clients after they receive the services. Of particular importance is the need to understand and account for the impact that other agencies' services have on the desired outcome.
- What can be effectively quantified;
- How to collect quality data;
- How to report results; and,
- What the most effective ways are for developing goals and objectives and for tying them to budget decisions in a meaningful way.

Currently there is more training available than there used to be 10 or 20 years ago. In fact, some master's programs in public administration, public management, and nonprofit management have added performance measurement to their curriculum. But more is needed.

In particular, the quality of training programs needs to be improved. One way to do this is by including some of the theories and tools that have long been used in the field of program evaluation. Given the limitations of performance measurement, which were discussed in Chapter 1 of this book, performance measurement has much to benefit from program evaluation. Performance measurement and program evaluation are complementary tools; one does not make the other obsolete. The knowledge and skills that have been developed in the field of program evaluation can help in teaching how to ensure more use of performance measurement information by the various stakeholders, and how to effectively integrate the information into what the organization does.

Furthermore, program evaluators have developed methods and techniques that can be useful in gaining an accurate understanding of how programs work, what activities lead to what results, as well as help clarify program goals and potential outcomes. Such understanding is instrumental to a successful PBM system. Therefore, training in performance measurement that builds on program evaluation knowledge is likely to be an area of growth and importance in years to come.

The Need for Broader Dissemination of Successes and Failures

The more experiences are disseminated broadly, the more we stand to gain. Having information about the successes of others, their failures, their challenges, their strategies for overcoming challenges, is key to building a body of knowledge that practitioners can learn from as they undertake PBM.

A number of professional organizations hold conferences that feature individuals discussing their organization's experiences with performance measurement and management. However, these conferences tend to be expensive and rather narrow in scope. Academic journals, practitioner-oriented publications, and broad-based professional associations' conferences and newsletters can make a significant contribution to building this needed body of knowledge, which would also benefit scholars.

There is, however, a current bias that must be corrected—for the most part, only successes tend to be reported. It is as if we have nothing to learn from the failures of others. Being able to examine failures is just as important as examining successes. Indeed, one of the most practice-oriented program evaluation texts teaches some key aspects of evaluation by showing students what not to do and asking them to come up with suggestions for improvement. This practice can be instrumental in avoiding pitfalls that others have encountered, and in promoting creativity when solving problems in practice and more critical thinking when building theory.

The Need for More Systematic Research

The need for broad dissemination discussed above should not be construed as a call for reliance on anecdotal evidence. That is not a viable approach for building sound

PBM theory. Systematic analysis whether in the form of case studies or data driven empirical research, need to continue if we are to move forward.

Although we have made some inroads, there still are questions whose answers have not been fully developed. Among those we can list: What is the role of accountability in the quest for improving performance? What is the appropriate role of incentives in the process of performance measurement utilization? Which incentives are more appropriate for whom, and under what circumstances? How can we motivate elected officials in Congress, state legislatures, and county and city governments to be full partners in the process of utilization of performance measurement information?

Finally, although this has not been addressed here at length, the question of what strategies are more appropriate and fruitful for engaging citizens with different backgrounds, interests, and talents in PBM still needs further exploration. The work of Epstein et al. (2006) is making an important contribution toward practice in this area. However, more systematic research is needed.

Appendix A

National Center for Public Productivity
Survey on the Utilization of Performance Measures

I. **Performance measurement:** Please tell us about performance measurement in your organization.

1. How often do employees of the organization receive or have access to publications (e.g., books, journals, magazines, newsletters) or online services that have information on performance measurement?

Always	Frequently	Sometimes	Never
☐	☐	☐	☐

Can you list (or attach) some of those publications or online services?_____

_____

2. How often do the following attend conferences or workshops related to performance measurement?

	Always	Frequently	Sometimes	Never
a. Management employees	☐	☐	☐	☐
b. Nonmanagement employees	☐	☐	☐	☐

3. How extensively have the following performance measures been developed for **programs** in your organization?

	For All	For Many	For Some	For None
a. Efficiency measures (cost per unit)	☐	☐	☐	☐

239

b. Outcome measures (results of services)	☐	☐	☐	☐
c. Output measures (quantity of services)	☐	☐	☐	☐

4. How often are **efficiency** measures (cost per unit of output or outcome) used for each of the following?

	Always	Frequently	Sometimes	Never
a. Strategic planning	☐	☐	☐	☐
b. Resource allocation (budgeting)	☐	☐	☐	☐
c. Program management, monitoring, and evaluation	☐	☐	☐	☐
d. Reporting to internal management	☐	☐	☐	☐
e. Reporting to elected officials	☐	☐	☐	☐
f. Reporting to citizens or media	☐	☐	☐	☐

5. How often are **outcome** measures (results of services provided) used for each of the following?

	Always	Frequently	Sometimes	Never
a. Strategic planning	☐	☐	☐	☐
b. Resource allocation (budgeting)	☐	☐	☐	☐
c. Program management, monitoring, and evaluation	☐	☐	☐	☐
d. Reporting to internal management	☐	☐	☐	☐
e. Reporting to elected officials	☐	☐	☐	☐
f. Reporting to citizens or media	☐	☐	☐	☐

6. How often are **output** measures (quantity of services provided) used for each of the following?

	Always	Frequently	Sometimes	Never
a. Strategic planning	☐	☐	☐	☐
b. Resource allocation (budgeting)	☐	☐	☐	☐
c. Program management, monitoring, and evaluation	☐	☐	☐	☐
d. Reporting to internal management	☐	☐	☐	☐
e. Reporting to elected officials	☐	☐	☐	☐
f. Reporting to citizens or media	☐	☐	☐	☐

7. Is the organization required to use performance measures by (check all that apply)?:

a. Law_____   b. Administrative regulation_____   c. Internal policy_____

d. Other (please explain)_____

II. **Organizational orientation:** The following questions concern your organization's ability to conduct performance measurement. For each question, please answer with any of the following: to a: great extent, considerable extent, limited extent, not at all.

---

1. To what extent has the organization committed resources (e.g., time, people, money) to be used in measurement of program performance?

	Great	Considerable	Limited	Not at All
	☐	☐	☐	☐

2. To what extent does the organization assign staff to analyze and evaluate program performance?

	Great	Considerable	Limited	Not at All
	☐	☐	☐	☐

3. To what extent has the organization assigned the evaluation of program performance to a distinct department(s)?

	Great	Considerable	Limited	Not at All
	☐	☐	☐	☐

4. To what extent does the organization collect reliable and relevant data that can be used to assess program performance?

	Great	Considerable	Limited	Not at All
	☐	☐	☐	☐

5. To what extent are benchmarks used for evaluating program performance?

	Great	Considerable	Limited	Not at All
	☐	☐	☐	☐

6. To what extent is management trained in applications such as TQM, MBO, or computer-based decision-making techniques?

	Great	Considerable	Limited	Not at All
	☐	☐	☐	☐

7. To what extent are programs and departments guided by clear goals and objectives?

	Great	Considerable	Limited	Not at All
	☐	☐	☐	☐

8. To what extent do programs and departments clearly communicate strategies for achieving objectives?

Great	Considerable	Limited	Not at All
☐	☐	☐	☐

9. To what extent is your organization facing fiscal stress?

Great	Considerable	Limited	Not at All
☐	☐	☐	☐

Comments (or attach): _____

_____

III. **Organizational groups:** For the following questions, please rate **each** choice by marking any of the following: to a: great extent, considerable extent, limited extent, not at all.

1. To what extent have the services of private consultants been solicited to help develop and implement performance measures in your organization?

Great	Considerable	Limited	Not at All
☐	☐	☐	☐

2. To what extent have your organization's external constituents been involved in promoting accountability and efficiency?

Great	Considerable	Limited	Not at All
☐	☐	☐	☐

3. To what extent have each of the following individuals taken the initiative to promote the development and implementation of performance measures?

	Great	Considerable	Limited	Not at All
a. Management	☐	☐	☐	☐
b. Nonmanagement employees	☐	☐	☐	☐
c. Elected officials	☐	☐	☐	☐
d. Others (please describe)_____	☐	☐	☐	☐

Comments (or attach): _____

_____

4. To what extent did/have each of the following individuals formed working groups (formal or informal) to promote the development and implementation of performance measures?

	Great	Considerable	Limited	Not at All
a. Management	☐	☐	☐	☐

b. Nonmanagement employees	☐	☐	☐	☐
c. Elected officials	☐	☐	☐	☐
d. Others (please describe)_____	☐	☐	☐	☐

Comments (or attach): _____

_____

6. If performance measures have been/are being developed, to what extent have nonmanagement employees had an influence on the following? (If measures have not been developed, please go to question 7.)

	Great	Considerable	Limited	Not at All
a. The specific measures developed	☐	☐	☐	☐
b. The implementation of the measures	☐	☐	☐	☐

7. Whether or not you are facing the following influences, to what extent would they make your organization consider developing and implementing performance measures?

	Great	Considerable	Limited	Not at All
a. Pressures for privatization from elected officials	☐	☐	☐	☐
b. Legal requirements (laws, regulations, etc.)	☐	☐	☐	☐
c. Demands from citizens to be informed	☐	☐	☐	☐
d. Availability of measures developed by third parties (e.g., GASB, ASPA)	☐	☐	☐	☐

8. What other activity, group (e.g., union), or influence (e.g., legal or internal requirement) has affected your organization concerning the adoption and implementation of performance measures?_____

_____

_____

IV. **Organizational characteristics:** Please tell us to what extent you agree or disagree with each of the following statements concerning behavior in your organization. Please mark one of the following: strongly agree, agree, disagree, strongly disagree.

---

1. Management routinely solicits the input of nonmanagement employees in decision making.

Strongly Agree	Agree	Disagree	Strongly Disagree
☐	☐	☐	☐

2. The organization's mission, as practiced, promotes:

	Strongly Agree	Agree	Disagree	Strongly Disagree
a. Service/program quality	☐	☐	☐	☐
b. Service/program efficiency	☐	☐	☐	☐
c. Service/program effectiveness	☐	☐	☐	☐

3. Management is willing to implement appropriate organizational innovation and change.

Strongly Agree	Agree	Disagree	Strongly Disagree
☐	☐	☐	☐

4. Management views performance measurement as an important aspect of decision making (resource allocation, strategic planning, etc.).

Strongly Agree	Agree	Disagree	Strongly Disagree
☐	☐	☐	☐

5. Nonmanagement employees willingly accept organizational innovation and change.

Strongly Agree	Agree	Disagree	Strongly Disagree
☐	☐	☐	☐

6. Nonmanagement employees understand and view performance measurement as a vehicle for performance improvement.

Strongly Agree	Agree	Disagree	Strongly Disagree
☐	☐	☐	☐

7. There is a reward/incentive system in place in the organization that encourages:

	Strongly Agree	Agree	Disagree	Strongly Disagree
a. Improving performance	☐	☐	☐	☐
b. Risk taking (using innovative ideas with the goal of improving performance)	☐	☐	☐	☐

8. Elected officials support organizational innovation and change.

Strongly Agree	Agree	Disagree	Strongly Disagree
☐	☐	☐	☐

9. Managers are often forced to embrace external public policies they do not endorse (e.g., auditing or accounting policies).

Strongly Agree	Agree	Disagree	Strongly Disagree
☐	☐	☐	☐

10. There is a sense that external public policies distract the organization from its mission.

Strongly Agree	Agree	Disagree	Strongly Disagree
☐	☐	☐	☐

11. Once external public policies are mandated, they are implemented in a timely manner.

Strongly Agree	Agree	Disagree	Strongly Disagree
☐	☐	☐	☐

12. Do you have any additional comments regarding your organizational characteristics concerning performance measurement or innovation and change (or attach)? _____

_____

_____

V. Demographics: Please tell us about yourself and your organization.

Yourself

a. Do you work for? a) _____State agency b) _____Municipality c) _____County

b. What department or agency do you work for?_____

c. What is your official position/title?_____

d. For how long have you held this position? _____years

e. For how long have you worked in the public sector? _____years

f. What is the highest level of formal education that you have achieved to date?

a) _____High school graduate b) _____Bachelor degree c) _____Master degree

d) _____Other (please specify):_____

g. In what area of study is your highest degree?_____

Your Organization (entire governmental unit—state agency, municipality, or county government)

a. In what state is your organization located?_____

b. What is your entire governmental unit's total operating budget? $_____

c. About how many full-time-equivalent employees (FTEs) are there in your organization?

d. Approximately what percentage of all FTEs are unionized? _____

e. How would you characterize your organization's overall state of labor management relations?

_____Good: Management and labor work together in harmony with only a few minor problem areas.

_____Fair: Relations are good in some areas, but there are problems in others.

_____Poor: Relations are strained in many areas, creating a multitude of problems.

VI. Do you have any final comments regarding factors that may contribute to your organization's ability to adopt performance measures?

Appendix B

Protocol for Follow-up Telephone Interviews

1. I would like to begin by asking you: What are your experiences with performance measurement in your organization?

2. Ask about the level of development of performance measurement for programs in organization.
    a. How extensively developed ?– for all, many, some, none **(If they have not been developed, go to obstacles 4)**
    b. Which measures have been developed?
        1. Outputs _____
        2. Outcomes _____
        3. Efficiency _____
        4. Inputs _____

If they have been developed, ask about level of use.

3. How are performance measures used?
    a. Which ones are used for what?
    b. Do you use them for:
        1. Strategic planning _____
        2. Resource allocation _____
        3. Monitoring of programs _____
        4. Reporting to internal management _____
        5. Reporting to elected officials _____
        6. Reporting to citizens or media _____

Adoption

4. We want to understand some of the reasons why performance measures are or are not developed. (If they have not been developed go to 5)

   a. When you were developing the measures, were there individuals or groups that were particularly influential in promoting development? Which? (management, non-management, citizens, elected officials, unions)

   b. Were there any other circumstances that encouraged development? (policy?)

   c. Were there any circumstances that complicated development? (e.g., lack of individuals with expertise, lack of resources, culture, lack of information on how to do it)

   d. Were there any individuals or groups that did not support development? (management, non-management, citizens, elected officials, unions)

If developed, go to 6

5. What would you say are the reasons why they have not been developed? (e.g., groups, individuals, not useful, not necessary).

Implementation

6. We want to understand some of the factors that influence the actual use of the measures.

   a. Were there individuals or groups that were particularly influential in promoting the used of the measures developed? Which? (management, non-management, citizens, elected officials, unions)

   b. Were there any other circumstances that encouraged their use? (policies)

   c. Were there any circumstances that complicated their use? (e.g., lack of individuals with expertise, lack of resources, culture,)

   d. Were there any individuals or groups that did not support use? (management, non-management, citizens, elected officials, unions)

   e.

   f. Which of these uses seem to be particularly problematic?

   g. Which seem most useful or easy?

7. Find out when they were developed or for how long they've had their performance measurement system.

8. Let's step back and get your overall assessment of performance measures in your organization.

   a. Has performance measurement work? (e.g., Has it helped improved performance? Has it made certain things worse? Some things better?)

   b. What challenges do you think lie ahead?

   c. What strategies might be most useful in promoting performance measurement in your organization?

References

Achen, C. 1982. *Interpreting and using regression*. Beverly Hills: Sage Publications.

Amara, N., Ouimet, M., and Landry, R. 2004. New evidence on instrumental, conceptual, and symbolic utilization of university research in government agencies. *Science Communication* 26:75–106.

Ammons, D. 1992. Productivity Barriers in the Public Sector. In *Public Productivity Handbook*, ed. M. Holzer, 117–36. New York: Marcel Dekker.

Ammons, D. 1995. Overcoming the inadequacies of performance measurement in local government, the case of libraries and leisure services. *Public Administration Review* 55:37–47.

Ammons, D. 2001. *Municipal benchmarks. Assessing local performance and establishing community standards*. 2nd ed. Thousand Oaks, CA: Sage.

Ammons, D., and King, J. 1983. Productivity improvement in local government: Its place among competing priorities. *Public Administration Review* 43:113–20.

Attkisson, C., et al., eds. 1978. *Evaluation of human service programs*. New York: Academic Press.

Babbie, E. 1990. *Survey research methods*. 2nd ed. Belmont, CA: Wadsworth Publishing Company.

Barnett, C., and Atteberry, D. 2007. Your budget: From axe to aim. *Public Management* 89:6–12.

Barzelay, M. 1992. *Breaking through bureaucracy: A new vision for managing government*. Berkeley: University of California Press.

Behn, R. 2003. Why measure performance? Different purposes require different measures. *Public Administration Review* 63:586–606.

Berry, M., and Ikerd, J. 1996. *Outcome budgeting: Catawba County, NC*. Washington, DC: ASPA's Center for Accountability and Performance.

Beyer, J. M. 1997. Research utilization: Bridging the gap between communities. *Journal of Management Inquiry* 6:17–22.

Beyer, J., and Trice, H. 1982. The utilization process: A conceptual framework and synthesis of empirical findings. *Administrative Science Quarterly* 27:591–622.

Blanche-Kapplen, S., and Lissman, L. 1996. *Development and use of outcome information in government*. Washington, DC: Oregon Adult and Family Services, ASPA's Center for Accountability and Performance.

Bohte, J., and Meier, K. 2000. Goal displacement: Assessing the motivation for organizational cheating. *Public Administration Review* 60:173–82.

251

Bouckaert, G. 1992. Public productivity in retrospective. In *Public productivity handbook*, ed. M. Holzer, 5–46. New York: Marcel Dekker.

Bowden, M. 1996. *Development and use of outcome information in government: Oregon Department of Transportation*. Washington, DC: ASPA's Center for Accountability and Performance.

Brezzi, M., Raimondo, L., and Utili, F. 2008. Using performance measurement and competition to make administrations accountable: The Italian case. In *International Handbook of Practice-Based Performance Management*. ed. P. de Lancer Julnes, F. Berry, M. Aristigueta, and K. Yang. Thousand Oaks, CA: Sage Publications.

Broom, C., and Jennings, E. 2008. Advancing performance measurement and management for accountability. King County's collaborative incremental approach. In *International Handbook of Practice-Based Performance Management*. ed. P. de Lancer Julnes, F. Berry, M. Aristigueta, and K. Yang. Thousand Oaks, CA: Sage Publications.

Brown, R., and Pyers, J. 1988. Putting teeth into the efficiency and effectiveness of public services. *Public Administration Review* 48:735–42.

Bryant, S. 1996. *Development and use of outcome measures: Long Beach Police Department, Long Beach, CA*. Washington, DC: ASPA's Center for Accountability and Performance.

Caiden, G. E. 1991. *Administrative reform comes of age*. Studies of Organization 28. Berlin: de Gruyter.

Campbell, D. T. 1966. Pattern matching as an essential in distal knowing. In *The psychology of Egon Brunswick*, ed. K. R. Hammond. Holt, Rinehart & Winston.

Campbell, D. 1975. Assessing the impact of planned social change. In *Social research and public policies*, ed. G. M. Lyons, 3–45. Hanover, NH: Darmouth College, Public Affairs Center.

Cannon, J. 1996. *Utah tomorrow*. Washington, DC: ASPA's Center for Accountability and Performance.

Caplan, N. 1979. The two-communities theory and knowledge utilization. *American Behavioral Scientist* 22:459–70.

Carnall, C. A. 1995. *Managing change in organizations*. 2nd ed. London: Prentice Hall.

Cavalluzzo, K. S., and Ittner, C. D. 2004. Implementing performance measurement innovations: Evidence from government. *Accounting, Organizations and Society* 29:243–67.

Chebat, J. C., and Picard, J. 1991. Does prenotification increase response rates in mail survey? *Journal of Social Psychology* 131:477–81.

Christenson, L. 1996. *Integration of business plan, strategic plan, customer service plan, unit self assessment and employee performance appraisals. Washington State Department of Labor and Industry*. Washington, DC: ASPA's Center for Accountability and Performance.

Chronbach, L. J., et al. 1980. *Toward reform of program evaluation*. San Francisco: Jossey-Bass.

Cibulka, J. G. with Derlin, R. L. 1998. Authentic education accountability policies: Implementation of state initiatives in Colorado and Maryland. In *The politics of accountability: Educative and international perspectives*. ed. R. J. MacPherson, J. G. Cibulka, and K. K. Wong. Thousand Oaks, CA: Corwin Press.

Coe, C. 1999. Local government benchmarking: Lessons from two major multigovernment efforts. *Public Administration Review* 59:110–23.

Cohen, L. H. 1977. Factors affecting the utilization of mental health evaluation research findings. *Professional Psychology*, November: 526–34.

Colwell, W. L., and Koletar, J. W. 1984. Performance measurement for criminal justice: The Federal Bureau of Investigation (FBI) experience. *Public Productivity Review* VIII:207–24.

Critchlow, D. 1985. *The Brookings Institution, 1916–1952, expertise and the public interest in a democratic society.* DeKalb, IL: Northern Illinois University Press.

Croly, H. 1909. *The promise of American life.* New York: Macmillan.

Curcio, C. F. 1996. *Performance indicators: Phoenix Parks, Recreation and Library Department.* Washington, DC: ASPA's Center for Accountability and Performance.

Cyert, R., and March, J. 1963. *A behavioral theory of the firm.* Englewood Cliffs, NJ: Prentice Hall.

Dahl, R. A. 1957. The concept of power. *Behavioral Science* 2:201–15.

Dalziel, M. M., and Schoonover, S. C. 1988. *Changing ways. A practical tool for implementing change within organizations.* New York: AMACOM.

Davis, J. A. 1985. *The logic of causal order.* Beverly Hills: Sage Publications.

de Lancer Julnes, P. 2001. Does participation increase perceptions of usefulness? An evaluation of a participatory approach to the development of performance measures. *Public Productivity and Management Review* 24:403–18.

de Lancer Julnes, P. 2003. Performance Measurement. In *Encyclopedia of Public Administration and Public Policy,* ed. J. Rabin. 901-05. New York: Marcel Dekker.

de Lancer Julnes, P. 2004. The utilization of performance measurement information: adopting, implementing, sustaining. In *Handbook of Public Productivity,* 2nd edition. ed. M. Holzer and S-H. Lee. New York: Marcel Dekker.

de Lancer Julnes, P. 2006. Performance measurement: An effective tool for government accountability? The debate goes on. *Evaluation* 12:219–35.

de Lancer Julnes, P. 2008. Performance measurement beyond instrumental use. In *Performance information in the public sector: How it is used.* 58-71. ed. W. Van Dooren and S. Van de Walle. Houndmills, UK: Palgrave Macmillan.

de Lancer Julnes, P., and Mixcoatl, G. 2006. Governors as agents of change: A comparative study of performance measurement initiatives in Utah and Campeche. *Public Performance and Management Review* 29:405–32.

de Lancer Julnes, P., and Holzer, M.. 2008. *Performance measurement: Building theory, supporting practice,* ASPA Classics Series. Armonk, NY: M.E. Sharpe.

deLeon, P. 1988. *Advise and consent. The development of the policy sciences.* New York: Russell Sage Foundation.

Dluhy, M. 2006. Enhancing the utilization of performance measures in local government: Lessons from practice. In *Public financial management,* ed. H. Frank, 567–78. Boca Raton, FL: CRC Press.

Dunn, W. 1980. The two-communities metaphor and models of knowledge. *Knowledge* 1:515–36.

Dunn, W., and Holzner, B. 1988. Knowledge in society: Anatomy of an emerging field. *Knowledge in Society* 1:3–25.

Dusenbury, P., Blaine, L., Vinson, E. 2000. *States, citizens, and local performance management.* Washington, DC: Urban Institute.

Elliott, H., and Popay, J. 2000. How are policy makers using evidence? Models of research utilization and local NHS policy making. *Journal of Epidemiology and Community Health* 54 (June):461-68.

Epstein, P. D., Coates, P. M., Wray, L. D., and Swain, D. 2006. *Results that matter. Improving communities by engaging citizens, measuring performance and getting things done.* San Francisco: Jossey Bass.

Fischer, F. 1986. Reforming bureaucratic theory: Toward a political model. In *Bureaucratic and governmental reform*, ed. D. J. Calista and S. S. Nagel, 35-53. Greenwich CT: JAI Press.

Fischer, F. 1994. Organizational expertise and bureaucratic control: Behavioral science as managerial ideology. In *Critical studies in organization and bureaucracy*, ed. F. Fischer and C. Sirianni, 174–95. Philadelphia: Temple University Press.

Fischer, R. J. 1994. An overview of performance measurement. *Public Management* 76:S2–S8.

Flynn, N. 1986. Performance measurement in public sector services. *Policy and Politics* 14:389–404.

Fountain, J. 1997. Are state and local governments using performance measures? *PA Times*, No. 20, pp. PM2, PM8.

Fowler, F. J. 1990. *Survey research methods*. Rev. ed. Newbury Park, CA: Sage Publications.

Franklin, A. L. 2000. An examination of bureaucratic reactions to institutional controls. *Public Performance and Management Review* 24 (1):8-21.

Garvin, D. 1993. Building a learning organization. *Harvard Business Review* 71:78–91.

Goodnow, F. 1900. *Politics and administration*. New York: Macmillan.

Gouldner, A. W. 1959. Organizational analysis. In *Sociology today*, ed. R. K. Merton et al., 404–5. New York: Basic Books.

Government Performance and Results Act, GPRA. 1993. http://www.whitehouse.gov/omb/mgmt-gpra/gplaw2m.html#h2

Greene, J. 1999. The inequality of performance measurements. *Evaluation* 5:160–72.

Greiner, J. 1996. Positioning performance measurement for the 20th century. In *Organizational performance and measurement in the public sector. Toward service, effort, and accomplishment reporting*, ed. A. Halachmi and G. Bouckaert, 11–50. Westport, CT: Quorum Books.

Grifel, S. 1994. Organizational culture: Its importance in performance measure. *Public Management* 76:S19–20.

Grizzle, G. 1982. Measuring state and local government performance: Issues to resolve before implementing a performance measurement system. *State and Local Government Review* 14:123–36.

Guba, E. G., and Lincoln, Y. 1989. *Fourth generation evaluation*. Newbury Park, CA: Sage.

Halachmi, A. 2002. Performance measurement: A look at some possible dysfunctions. *Work Study*, 51 (5): 230–239.

Halachmi, A. 2002. Who gets what when and how: Performance measures for accountability? For improved performance? *International Review of Public Administration*, 7 (1):1-11.

Hanney, S. R., Gonzalez-Block, M., Buxton, M. and Kogan, M. 2003. The utilization of health research in policy-making: Concepts, examples and methods of assessment. *Health Research Policy Systems* 1(2), http://www.health-policy-systems.com/content /1/1/2 (accessed December 2007).

Harvey, E., and Mills, R. 1970. Patterns of organizational adaptation. In *Power in organizations*, ed. M. Zald. Nashville, TN: Vanderbilt University Press.

Hatcher, L. 1994. *A step by step approach to using the SAS system for factor analysis and structural equation modeling*. Cary, NC: SAS Institute.

Hatry, H. 1996. Foreword. In *Organizational Performance and Measurement in the Public Sector*, ed. A. Halachmi and G. Bouckaert, Quorum Books.

Hatry, H. 1997. Where the rubber meets the road: Performance measurement for state and local public agencies. *New Directions for Program Evaluation* 75:31–44.

Hatry, H. 1999. *Performance measurement. Getting results.* Washington, DC: The Urban Institute.

Hatry, H. 2008. Emerging developments in performance measurement: An international perspective. In *International handbook of practice-based performance management*, ed. P. de Lancer Julnes, F. Berry, M. Aristigueta, and K. Yang, 3–23. Thousand Oaks, CA: Sage.

Hatry, H. P., Fountain, J. R., Jr., Sullivan, J. M., and Kremer, L. 1990. *Service efforts and accomplishments reporting: Its time has come.* Norwalk, CT: Governmental Accounting Standards Board (GASB).

Heinrich, C. J. 2002. Outcomes-based performance management in the public sector: Implications for government accountability and effectiveness. *Public Administration Review* 62:712–25.

Henry, N. 1975. Paradigms of public administration. *Public Administration Review* 35:378–86.

Holzer, M. 1988. Productivity in/garbage out: The case of the New York City Department of Sanitation. *Public Productivity Review* 6(3): 37–50.

Holzer, M., and Halachmi, A. 1996. Measurement as a means of accountability. *International Journal of Public Administration* 19:1921–44.

Holzner, B., and Fisher, E. 1979. Knowledge use. Considerations in the sociology of knowledge application. *Knowledge: Creation, Diffusion, Utilization* 1:219–44.

Howard, R., and Schneider, L. 1994. Worker participation in technological change: Interests, influence, and scope. In *Critical studies in organization and bureaucracy*, ed. F. Fischer and C. Sirianni, 519–44. Rev. ed. Philadelphia: Temple University Press.

Huberman, M. 1987. Steps toward an integrated model of research utilization. *Knowledge: Creation, Diffusion, Utilization* 8:586–611.

Huberman, M. 1989. Predicting conceptual effects in research utilization: Looking with both eyes. *Knowledge in Society* 2:6–24.

Huberman, M. 1994. Research utilization: The state of the art. *Knowledge and Policy: The International Journal of Knowledge Transfer and Utilization* 7:13–33.

Jackson, M. 1996. *Lessons learned from Minnesota's government performance report.* Washington, DC: ASPA's Center for Accountability and Performance.

Jacobson, N. 2007. Social epistemology: Theory for the "fourth wave" of knowledge transfer and exchange research. *Science Communication* 29:116–27.

James, L. R., and Brett, J. M. 1984. Mediators, moderators, and tests for mediation. *Journal of Applied Psychology* 69:307–21.

Jones, L., and McCaffery, J. 1997. Implementing the Chief Financial Officers Act and the Government Performance and Results Act in the federal government. *Public Budgeting and Finance* 17:35–55.

Joyce, P. 1997. Using performance measures for budgeting: A new beat, or is it the same old tune? *New Directions for Evaluation* 75:45–61.

Judd, C., and Kenny, D. 1981. Process analysis: Estimating mediation in treatment evaluation. *Evaluation Review* 5:602–19.

Julnes, G. 2007. Identifying dimensions and types in public administration research: Introduction to principal components analysis, factor analysis, and cluster analysis. In *Handbook of research methods in public administration*, ed. G. Miller and K. Yang, 515–64. 2nd ed. New York: Auerbach.

Kamensky, J. M. 1995. Program performance measures: Designing a system to manage for results. In *Competent government: Theory and practice. The best of public productivity and management review, 1985–1993*, ed. A. Halachmi and M. Holzer, 239–46. Burke, VA: Chatelaine Press.

Kaplan, R. S., and Norton, D. P. 1992. The balanced scorecard—Measures that drive performance. *Harvard Business Review* 70:71–79.

Kim, J., and Mueller, C. W. 1978. *Factor analysis statistical methods and practical issues.* Beverly Hills: Sage.

King, G., Keohane, R., and Verba, S. 1994. *Designing social inquiry. Scientific inference in qualitative research.* Princeton, NJ: Princeton University Press.

Klein, K. K., and Sper Sorra, J. 1996. The challenge of innovation implementation. *Academy of Management Review* 21:1055–80.

Knight, K. E. 1967. A descriptive model of the intra-firm innovation process. *Journal of Business* 40:478–96.

Kopcynski, M., and Lombardo, M. 1999. Comparative performance measurement: Insights and lessons learned from a consortium effort. *Public Administration Review* 59:124–34.

Kopell, J. G. 2005. Pathologies of accountability: ICANN and the challenge of "multiple accountabilities disorder." *Public Administration Review* 65:94–108.

Korman, N. and Glennerster, H. 1985. *Closing a Hospital: The derenth park project. Occasional papers on social administration.* No 78. London: Bedford Square Press.

Kravchuk, R. S., and Schack, R. W. 1996. Designing effective performance measurement systems under the Government Performance and Results Act of 1993. *Public Administration Review* 56:348–58.

Landry, R., Amara, N., and Lamari, M. 2001. Climbing the ladder of research utilization. Evidence from social science research. *Science Communication* 22:396–422.

Lee, M. 2003. Is there anything new under the sun? *Public Voices* VI:72–83.

Lester, J., and Wilds, L. 1990. The utilization of public policy analysis: A conceptual framework. *Evaluation and Program Planning* 13: 313-19.

Lin, A. C. 1996. Bridging the gaps between research methods: Redesigning welfare research from different traditions. Paper prepared for the Annual Meeting of the American Political Science Association, San Francisco, August 29–September 1.

Lindblom, C., and Cohen, D. 1979. *Usable knowledge: Social science and social problem solving.* New Haven, CT: Yale University Press.

Long, E., and Franklin, A. L. 2004. The paradox of implementing the government performance and results act: Top-down direction for bottom-up implementation. *Public Administration Review* 64:309–19.

Lynham, S. 2002. The general method of theory-building research in applied disciplines. *Advances in Developing Human Resources* 4:221–41.

Mann, S. 1986. Politics of public productivity. In *Strategic issues in public productivity: The best of public productivity 1975–1985*, ed. M. Holzer and A. Halachmi, 33–45. Burke, VA: Chatelaine Press.

March, J. G., and Olsen, J. P. 1975. The uncertainty of the past: Organizational learning under ambiguity. *European Journal of Political Research* 3:147–71.

Mark, M. M. 1986. Validity typologies and the logic and practice of quasi-experimentation. In *Advances in quasi-experimental design and analysis*, ed. W. M. K. Trochin. San Francisco: Jossey-Bass.

Mark, M. M. 1990. From program theory to tests of program theory. *New Directions for Program Evaluation: Advances in Program Theory* 47:37–51.

Mark, M. M., Feller, I., and Button, S. 1997. Integrating qualitative methods in a predominantly quantitative evaluation: A case study and some reflections. *New Directions for Evaluation* 74:47–59.

Marquart, J. 1990. A pattern-matching approach to link program theory and evaluation data. *New Directions for Program Evaluation: Advances in Program Theory* 47:93–107.

Marshall, M. 1996. *Development and use of outcome information in government, Prince William County, Virginia.* Washington, DC: ASPA's Center for Accountability and Performance.

Martin, D. W. 1992. The management classics and public productivity. In *Public productivity handbook*, ed. M. Holzer, 47–62. New York: Marcel Dekker.

Mechanic, D. 1962. Sources of power of lower participants in complex organizations. *Administration Science Quarterly* 7:349–64.

Meld, M. 1974. The politics of evaluation of social programs. *Social Work* 448–45.

Melkers, J., and Willoughby, K. 2005. Models of performance-measurement use in local governments: Understanding budgeting, communication, and lasting effect. *Public Administration Review* 65(2):180–90.

Merjanian, A. 1996. *Strategic budgeting in Texas: A systems approach to planning, budgeting, and performance measurement.* Washington, DC: ASPA's Center for Accountability and Performance.

Modell, S., and Wiesel, F. 2007. Marketization and performance management in Swedish central government: A comparative institutionalist study. Presented at the European Accounting Association Annual Congress, Lisbon, Portugal, April 25–27, http://www.licom.pt/eaa2007/papers/EAA2007_0372_final.pdf (accessed February 2008).

Moynihan, D. 2008. Advocacy and learning: An interactive-dialogue approach to performance information use. In *Measurement beyond managerialism. Using public performance information in bureaucracy, politics and society*, ed. W. Van Dooren and S. Van de Walle, 35–59. London: Palgrave.

Mumford, E., and Ward, T. 1966. Computer technologists: Dilemmas of a new role. *Journal of Management Studies* 3:244–55.

Nelson, C. E., Roberts, J., Maederer, C., Wertheimer, B., and Johnson, B. 1987. The utilization of social science information by policy makers. *American Behavioral Scientist.* 30 (6): 569-577.

Neter, J., Kutner, M. H., Nachtsheim, C. J., and Wasserman, W. 1996. *Applied linear regression models.* 3rd ed. Chicago: Irwin.

Newcomer, K. 2007. How does program performance assessment affect program management in the federal government? *Public Performance and Management Review* 30:332–50.

Newcomer, K. 2008. Assessing performance in nonprofit service agencies. In *International handbook of practice-based performance management*, ed. P. de Lancer Julnes, F. Berry, M. Aristigueta, and K. Yang Sage, 25–44. Thousand Oaks, CA: Sage.

Newcomer, K. E., and Wright, R. F. 1997. Effective use of performance measurement at the federal level. *The PA Times*, No. 20, PM2, PM4.

Nicholls, J. G. 1984. Achievement motivation: Conceptions of ability, subjective experience, task choice, and performance. *Psychological Review* 91:328–46.

Ninth Public Sector Productivity Conference. 1998. Performance measurement, performance improvement, on-line, November 9-20. Sponsored by the National Center for Public Productivity, Rutgers University, Newark, NJ.

Niven, P. 2003. *Balanced scorecard step by step for government and nonprofit agencies*. Hoboken, NJ: John Wiley & Sons.

Nolen, S. 1988. Reasons for studying: Motivational orientations and study strategies. *Cognition and Instruction* 5:269–87.

Nyhan, R. C., and Marlowe, H. 1995. Performance measurement in the public sector. *Public Productivity and Management Review* 18:333–48.

Oh, C. H. and Rich, R. F. 1996. Explaining use of information in public policymaking *Knowledge and Policy: The International Journal of Knowledge Transfer and Utilization*. 9 (1): 3-35.

Olsen, R. T., and Epstein, J. 1997. Performance management: So what? *PA Times*, No. 20, pp. PM1–7.

Orlich, D. C. 1978. *Designing sensible surveys*. Pleasantville, NY: Redgrave Publishing Co.

Osborne, D., and Plastrik, P. 2000. *The reinventor's fieldbook. Tools for transforming your government*. San Francisco: Jossey Bass.

Pandey, S. K., and Garnett, J. L. 2006. Exploring public sector communication performance: Testing a model and drawing implications. *Public Administration Review* 66:37–51.

Patton, M. Q. 1978. *Utilization-focused evaluation*. Beverly Hills: Sage Publications.

Patton, M. Q. 2001. *Qualitative research and evaluation methods*. 3rd ed. Thousand Oaks, CA: Sage.

Pedler, M., Burgoyne, J., and Boydell, T. 1991. *The learning company. A strategy for sustainable development*. London: McGraw-Hill.

Pelz, D. 1978. Some expanded perspectives on use of social science in public policy. In *Major social issues: A multidisciplinary view*, ed. J. Yinger and S. J. Cutler, 346–57. New York: Free Press.

Perrin, B. 1998. Effective use and misuse of performance measurement. *American Journal of Evaluation* 19:367–80.

Pettigrew, A. 1973. *The politics of organizational decision-making*. London: Tavistock Publications.

Pettigrew, A., Ferlie, E., and McKee, L. 1992. *Shaping strategic change. The case of the national health system*. London: Sage Publications.

Pfeffer, J. 1981. *Power in organizations*. Cambridge, MA: Ballinger Publishing Company.

Pfeffer, J. 1983. Coalitions. In *Organizational influence processes*, ed. R. W. Allen and L. Porter, 312–20. Glenview, IL: Foresman and Co.

Pfeffer, J., and Salancik, G. R. 1978. *The external control of organizations*. New York: Harper Collins.

Piotroski, S., and Rosenbloom, D. 2002. Nonmission-based values in results-oriented public management: The case of the freedom of information. *Public Administration Review* 62:643–57.

Poister, T., and Streib, G. 2005. Elements of strategic planning and management in municipal government: Status after two decades. *Public Administration Review* 65:45–56.

Posner, P. L., and Fantone, D. M. 2007. Assessing federal program performance: Observations on the U.S. Office of Management and Budget's Program Assessment Rating Tool and its use in the budget process. *Public Performance and Management Review* 30:351–68.

Radin, B. A. 1998. The Government Performance And Results Act (GPRA): Hydra-headed monster or flexible management tool? *Public Administration Review* 58 (4): 307-316.

Radin, B. A. 2002. *The accountable juggler. The art of leadership in a federal agency*. Washington, DC: CQ Press.

Rainey, H. 1997. *Understanding and managing public organizations.* 2nd ed. San Francisco: Jossey-Bass.

Reichardt, C. S. 1988. Estimating effects. Unpublished manuscript, Department of Psychology, University of Denver.

Reichers, A. E., and Schneider, B. 1990. Climate and culture: An evolution of constructs. In *Organizational climate and culture,* ed. B. Schneider, 5–39. San Francisco: Jossey-Bass.

Rich, R. 1979. The pursuit of knowledge. *Knowledge* 1:6–30.

Rich, R. 1991. Knowledge creation, dissemination and utilization. *Knowledge* 12:319–37.

Rich, R., and Oh, C. H. 1994. The utilization of policy research. In *Encyclopedia of policy studies,* ed. S. Nagel, 69–92. 2nd ed. New York: Marcel Dekker.

Rich, W., and Winn, M. 1992. The politics of public productivity. In *Public productivity handbook,* ed. M. Holzer, 63–78. New York: Marcel Dekker.

Roberts, N. C. 2002. Keeping public officials accountable through dialogue: Resolving the accountability paradox. *Public Administration Review* 62:658–69.

Romzek, B. 1998. Where the buck stops: Accountability in reformed public organizations. In *Transforming government: Lessons from the reinvention laboratories,* ed. P. Ingraham, J. Thompson, and R. Sanders, 193–219. San Francisco: Jossey-Bass.

Rummel, R. J. 1970. *Applied factor analysis.* Evanston, IL: Northwestern University Press.

Ryan, K. 2002. Shaping educational accountability systems, *American Journal of Evaluation* 23 (4): 453-468.

Schein, E. H. 1992. *Organizational culture and leadership: A dynamic view.* 2nd ed. San Francisco: Jossey-Bass.

Schein, E. H. 1996. Culture: The missing concept in organization studies. *Administrative Science Quarterly* 41:229–40.

Scheirer, M. and Newcomer, K. 2001. Opportunities for program evaluators to facilitate performance-based management, *Evaluation and Program Planning* 24: 63-71.

Schwabe, C. 1996. *Development and use of performance indicators in the City of Coral Springs, Florida.* Washington, DC: ASPA's Center for Accountability and Performance.

Senge, P. 1990. *The fifth discipline.* New York: Doubleday.

Shadish, W., Cook, T., and Leviton, L. 1991. *Foundations of program evaluation.* ThousandsOaks, CA: Sage.

Simeone, R., Carnevale, J., and Millar, A. 2005. A systems approach to performance-based management: The national drug control strategy. *Public Administration Review* 65:191–202.

Skaff, L. F. 1996. *Ramsey County, Minnesota: Performance contracting at the county level.* Washington, DC: ASPA's Center for Accountability and Performance.

Snow, C.P. 1959. *The two cultures and the scientific revolution.* New York: Cambridge University Press.

Solberg, L. I., Mosser, G., and McDonald, S. 1997. The three faces of performance measurement: Improvement, accountability, and research. *Journal of Quality Improvement* 23:135–47.

Spector, P. E. 1992. *Summated rating scale construction: An introduction.* Newbury Park, CA: Sage.

Stehr, N. 1992. *Practical knowledge: Applying the social sciences.* Newbury Park, CA: Sage.

Stewart, J., and Walsh, K. 1994. Performance measurement: When performance can never be finally defined. *Public Money and Management,* April–June, pp. 45–49.

Sunesson, S., and Nilsson, K. 1988. Explaining research utilization. *Knowledge: Creation, Diffusion, Utilization.* 10:140–55.

Torres, R. and Preskill, H. 2001. Evaluation and organizational learning: Past, present, and future. *American Journal of Evaluation*, 22 (3) 387-395.

Tracy, R. 1996. *Development and use of outcome information: Portland, Oregon*. Washington, DC: ASPA's Center for Accountability and Performance.

Trochim, W. M. K. 1985. Pattern matching, validity, and conceptualization in program evaluation. *Evaluation Review* 9:575–604.

United States General Accounting Offfice. (2001). Results-oriented budget practices in federal agencies. Washington, D.C.: GAO

Utah Tomorrow 2000. *Strategic plan report*. Utah tomorrow strategic planning committee. Salt Lake City, Utah.

Wang, X. 2000. Performance measurement in budgeting: A study of county governments. *Public Budgeting and Finance* 20:102–18.

Watkins, J. 1994. A postmodern critical theory of research use. *Knowledge, Technology, and Policy*. 7 (4): 55-77.

Watkins, K., and Marsick, V. 1992. Building the learning organization: A new role for human resource developers. *Studies in Continuing Education* 14:115–29.

Weidner, M., and Noss-Reavely, M. 1996. *The Council on Human Investment: Performance governance in Iowa*. Washington, DC: ASPA's Center for Accountability and Performance.

Weiss, C. H. 1998a. Have we learned anything about the use of evaluation? *American Journal of Evaluation* 19:21–34.

Weiss, C. H. 1998b. *Evaluation*. 2nd ed. Upper Saddle River, NJ: Prentice Hall.

Weiss, C. H. 1988. Evaluation for decision: Is anybody there? Does anybody care? *Evaluation Practice* 9:5–20.

Welch, S., and Comer, J. 1988. *Quantitative methods for public administration*. Pacific Grove, CA: Brooks/Cole.

Wellman, M., and Van Landingham, G. 2008. Performance-based budgeting in Florida: Great expectations, more limited reality. In *International handbook of practice-based performance management*, ed. P. de Lancer Julnes, F. Berry, M. Aristigueta, and K. Yang Sage, 321–40. Thousand Oaks, CA: Sage.

Weyl, W. 1912. *The new democracy*. New York: Macmillan.

Wholey, J. 1996. Formative and summative evaluation: Related issues in performance measurement. *Evaluation Practice* 17:145–49.

Wholey, J. 1999. Performance-based management: Responding to the challenges. *Public Productivity and Management Review* 22:288–307.

Wholey, J. and Hatry, H. 1992. Commentary: The case for performance monitoring, *Public Administration Review* 52 (6): 604-610.

Wildavsky, A. 1961. Political implications of budgetary reform. *Public Administration Review*. 21: 183-190.

Wilkins, K. 1996. *Performance measurement; A work in progress*. Washington, DC: Minnesota's Department of Labor and Industry, ASPA's Center for Accountability and Performance.

Williams, D. 2003. Measuring government in the early twentieth century. *Public Administration Review* 63:643–59.

Wilson, W. 1968. Study of administration. In *The Papers of Woodrow Wilson 1885–1888*. Princeton, NJ: Princeton University Press.

Wingens, M. 1990. Toward a general utilization theory. *Knowledge Creation Diffusion, Utilization*. 12 (1): 27-42.

Yates, D., Jr. 1995. *The politics of management: Exploring the inner workings of public and private organizations.* San Francisco: Jossey-Bass.

Yin, R. K. 1989. *Case study research.* 2nd ed. Newbury Park, CA: Sage.

Index

A

Access to information. *See* Information access

Accomplishments, 12–13

Accountability, 217
  beyond, 15–17
  and citizens as actors in creating value, 14
  as deterrent to adoption and implementation, 187
  and disincentives for performance improvement, 113
  as double-edged sword, 214
  fear of, for outcomes, 192
  financial, 11
  as instrumental use of knowledge, 210
  as opportunity for benchmarking, praise, and reflection, 214
  performance-based, 10–14
  performance measures for purpose of, 208
  as purpose of performance measurement, 210, 226
  as reason to micromanage, 187
  response to calls for, 187
  for results, 14
  role in quest for performance improvement, 237
  as threat to elected officials, 41, 184

Achievement climate, 18

Action knowledge, *vs.* practical knowledge, 32

Adoption, 57, 71, 98, 100, 126, 162, 198
  acceptance and commitment for, 229
  average levels by government entity type, 106
  basic integrated model explaining, 127
  as capacity for action, 163, 224
  comparing with implementation, 136
  and compliance with regulations, 47, 164
  contextual factors, 224
  differentiation from implementation, 224
  direct effects, 151, 155
  effect of internal requirements on, 128
  effects of internal requirements on, 58
  effects of politics and culture on, 62
  estimated causal model of, 146–157
  factors predicting, 187–189
  failure to lead to implementation, 48
  and goal orientation, 59
  impact of rational factors on, 55
  influence from formal and internal forces, 158
  interaction of unionization and internal interest groups with, 133
  internal impact of, 47
  and internal interest groups, 165
  and internal requirements, 164
  as mediating variable, 225
  as mediator of implementation, 149–151
  pace of, and resources, 174
  path model explaining, 151–157
  of performance measurement system, 45, 103
  as precursor to implementation, 148–149, 177–179
  questions for follow-up interviews, 248
  with rational/technocratic factors, 141
  role of internal coalitions in, 65
  in state and local government organizations, 105–106
  and technical capacity, 61
  vs. implementation, 46

Adoption of knowledge